TURNING
around the
MAINLINE

TURNING
around the
MAINLINE

How Renewal Movements Are Changing the Church

Thomas C. Oden

BakerBooks

Grand Rapids, Michigan

Published by Baker Books
a division of Baker Publishing Group
P.O. Box 6287, Grand Rapids, MI 49516-6287
www.bakerbooks.com

Printed in the United States of America

Library of Congress Cataloging-in-Publication Data
Oden, Thomas C.
    Turning around the mainline : how renewal movements are changing the church / Thomas
C. Oden.
        p.   cm.
    Includes bibliographical references.
    ISBN 0-8010-6576-3 (pbk.)
    1. Evangelicalism—United States. 2. Protestant churches—United States—Doctrines.
3. Church controversies—United States. 4. Church property—United States.
5. Evangelicalism—Canada. 6. Protestant churches—Canada—Doctrines. 7. Church controversies—Canada. 8. Church property—Canada. I. Title.
BR1642.&5O34   2006
280'.40973—dc22   2005028265

To Howard F. Ahmanson Jr. and Roberta Green Ahmanson

Contents

Acknowledgments

There are times in the life of an author when he feels in his bones that decisive events are occurring and their accurate portrayal depends heavily upon his particular vantage point. He senses that what he is struggling to say is of wider import than many will at first see. This feeling is not that the author's views are important, but that the historical moment he is trying to describe is of great weight, portending potentially a decisive turn in history, or a turn already made in history but not adequately recognized. I have felt this sort of poignancy throughout the preparation of this book, which has been over five years in the making. This feeling has impelled me to state a reasonable argument passionately and to state it clearly to be heard, knowing that even when heard it is liable to be misunderstood in some quarters. This is why I pray that my reader will follow my reasoning step by step, with empathy and a critical mind.

I gratefully acknowledge my debt to colleagues of Religion and Public Life: A Research and Education Institute, World Evangelical Alliance, the Association for Church Renewal, and the Confessing Movement. Especially I express my gratitude for associates in the Institute on Religion and Democracy whose views have significantly shaped my thinking about the public duty of confessing Christians. Among those who have helped me see some of the many pitfalls in the description I am attempting are the late Diane Knippers, Judith Cox, Tal and Jane Oden, Bishop William B. Oden, Leceister Longden, William Abraham, Ira Gallaway, David Stanley, Senator Pat Miller, Bishop Fitzsimmons Allison, Bishop James Stanton, Parker Williamson, and James Heidinger, and all the members of the Confessing Theologians Commission. For their steady friendship and support I am deeply grateful to Howard and Roberta Ahmanson, to whom this book is affectionately dedicated.

Abbreviations

ABC	American Babtist Church USA
ABE	American Baptist Evangelicals
AMiA	Anglican Mission in America
CCDC	Christian Churches, Disciples of Christ
CH	Constitutional Hisotry of American Episcopal Methodism, John Tigert
Disc.	Book of Discipline
DSM	Doctrinal Standard of Methodism, Thomas Neely
ECUSA	Episcopal Church USA
ELCA	Evangelical Lutheran Church of America
EUB	Evangelical United Brethren
IRD	Institute of Religion and Democracy
JCD	Judicial Council Decisions
JGC	Journal of the General Conference, 1796–1836
MAC	Minutes of the Annual Conference of the Methodist Episcopal Church for the Years 1773–1828
M.E. Church	Methodist Episcopal Church
NCC	National Council of Churches
NOEL	National Organization of Episcopalians for Life
PCUSA	Presbyterian Church (USA)
SWN	Selections From John Wesley's Notes on the New Testament
UCC	United Church of Christ
UCCan or UCCanada	United Church of Canada
UM or UMC	United Methodist Church
WCC	World Council of Churches
WDS	Wesley's Doctrinal Standards, Nathaniel Burwash
WEA	World Evangelical Alliance

Introduction

The Confessing Churches—Who They Are,
What They Believe

This book for the first time brings together major themes and documents describing and interpreting *the renewing and confessing movements within the mainline*. It also presents a case study of the most pressing issue of these movements: property rights of local churches (in the last three chapters).

These movements are increasing in numbers, leadership, persuasiveness, courage, communication skills, and importance. The rapid momentum emerging around these movements—now in a phase of momentous ecumenical reconfiguration—may be an event of stunning potential significance in American church history. It represents the unexpected conjoining of the previously disparate renewal and confessing movements across the mainline, all aimed at transforming the mainline. All these renewing and confessing groups in different denominations had their first continent-wide meeting in 2002, having worked independently for several decades. Many within these historic Christian communions are convinced that *the era of denominational competitiveness is over*. But that does not solve the dilemma of how best to utilize the priceless resources accumulated in the historic Protestant communions.

A recent issue of *Christianity Today* featured a lead article on "Turning the Mainline Around," with a cover illustration portraying a huge ocean liner being slowly pushed into a new direction by a tiny tugboat.[1] This is a glimpse into the irony of believers within the mainline. What was previously regarded as a highly unlikely reversal is now in fact occurring: the turnaround of the mainline.

Who Is Listening?

The intended audience for this book is not only the faithful within the so-called *mainline* churches, but many orthodox and traditional and evangelical onlookers viewing the scene from afar. It will have special interest to Lutherans, Episcopalians, Presbyterians, Methodists, Disciples of Christ, and American Baptists, as well as United Church of Christ and United Church of Canada folk. But there is also a readiness among *evangelicals generally* (including Baptist, charismatic, and Pentecostal traditions) to find out what is happening among their distant relatives in these unexplored precincts, so long separated from each other.

This book is written primarily for a lay audience. Faithful churchgoers in all the mainline denominations are concerned about the strength and faithfulness and even the possible apostasy of their beloved churches. Laypersons are the key players in this drama. The turnaround is occurring largely by lay leadership, and often in the face of resistance coming from vocal clergy.

The numbers alone are impressive when one looks at evangelicals within the mainline. Once a scattered group of disparate and struggling movements, they are being recognized for their increasing impact. It is astonishing.

Now 643,223 individuals, 1,471 churches, and 4,377 clergy comprise one of these movements alone: the Confessing Movement Within the United Methodist Church, formed only in 1994. The Presbyterian Lay Committee, formed in 1965, now reaches a readership of about a half million. The Presbyterian churches that have signed on to the Confessing Church Movement since its inauguration in 2002 now number well over 1,500 local churches, constituting more than 15 percent of all PCUSA membership, and increasing steadily. The United Methodist *UM Action Briefing* now mails to over 350,000 supporters, with a plausible target of one million within two years. Four different but correlated renewing movements exist within the United Church of Canada alone, each with thoughtful newsletters, magazines, huge rallies, and church-law challenges on property-use issues, maladministration, and doctrinal integrity. They are united in seeking to restore biblical grounding, theological clarity, and moral accountability in their various historic Christian communions.

The polling data from Gallup, Pew, Barna, and others, and the available sociological studies are now yielding a new body of evidence that between 30 and 60 percent of the mainline laity view themselves as traditional Christians or orthodox or evangelical or born-again believers. They are already in the process of reversing the decline of the mainline in many local churches.

This reconfiguration is being recognized as a wake-up call for the institutional centrists of mainline Protestantism, and an unexpected and reassuring development for orthodox and evangelical believers everywhere. Yet very little is known about these movements outside of their own circles. Their newsletters and other communications are read largely by the faithful laity and by small donors. This argues, I think, for more deliberate ecumenical attention by culture watchers and reporters and church leaders.

A Prelude to Reading

Both liberal and conservative Protestants have good reason to reflect soberly upon these new developments. These have not been reported or articulately described or interpreted in the secular press. This neglect is even more pronounced in the religious media controlled by the denominations. Until recently the secular press has had only minimal interest in examining what any evangelical might think or believe. The power of the evangelical electorate, however, has awakened even the media titans to their presence and perseverance. The media elites who have dismissed evangelicals are now wondering what it is they have been missing and why they did not sooner pay any attention. Meanwhile many older liberal leaders are now worriedly scrambling to understand what is happening within their own under-funded and collapsing bureaucratic fortresses. This book is intended to illuminate their dilemma and offer constructive options. It is not for conservatives only.

Meanwhile many evangelicals within the mainline have not yet discovered that what they confess within their denominational domain has wide currency among evangelicals in other communions, and sweeping ecumenical implications. Evangelicals previously living within high denominational walls are now recognizing their deeper doctrinal affinity with classical Christian believers everywhere. They are learning that their confessional identity corresponds closely with that of diverse believers in distant confessional quarters. Many report that they feel deeper connections with orthodox Christians in other churches than with many of the most prominent voices within their own affiliation. This is one of the most common experiences attested in these movements.

Many bright young Christian believers in seminaries and colleges are becoming aware that they too are deeply attracted to traditional and orthodox belief. Even some of the liberal leaders in bureaucracies, mission agencies, and the meccas of social activism are quietly recognizing their own hidden affinities with the evangelicals that they had long ago dismissed. They are seeing that they are not up against some vast stereotyped right-wing conspiracy, but rather simply classic ecumenical Christianity coming again to new life. Meanwhile the mainline orthodox and evangelicals are learning that they do not have to apologize for their intellectual tradition or its basic forms of reasoning. They are realizing that they are not alone in their imagined isolation. These recognitions are moving toward greater understanding, richer civil discourse, charity in dialogue, and clarity in differences.

Archiving Texts

The texts of the confessing church movements upon which this study is focused have been silently collecting for over a quarter century or more. I have been avidly archiving them for years, well aware of their potential historical and ecumenical significance. Archival efforts in numerous locations (Princeton, Wheaton, Duke, Drew, Asbury, Tulsa, Fuller) are belatedly trying to catch up with these intense and rapid developments. Far more journalists, observers, pundits, and church leaders now are gradually waking up to this phenomenon.

I see my own task first as an archivist, and only secondarily as an interpreter. The trailblazers in Christian history that have given me inspiration for this study are the quiet, hidden scholars of ancient Christianity such as Jerome in his cave in Bethlehem, Vincent on the Isle of Lerins seeking to state accurately a consensus already well-formed, Cassiodorus in his isolated Calabrian scriptorium, and Alcuin of York with his library and students in the court of Charlemagne.

Jerome (fourth century) was cast out of Rome after having been secretary to the pope to go to Bethlehem to reflect, study, and critically comment on the struggle for apostolic Christianity. Vincent (fifth century) sought to grasp the center of the wholeness of classic Christianity for all times and places. Cassiodorus (sixth century) brought together a talented community of scholars who sought to bridge the Christianity of the East and the West. Alcuin (eighth century) preserved and transmitted the vast library of patristic wisdom at Tours as a resource for the future of medieval learning. Yet all of them, by archiving what was happening in their time, actively transmitted classic Christian culture to the emerging world. My decisive models for this task all lived in the first millennium. Trying to follow after them by archiving the texts of a vast contemporary movement has been humbling.

There is now more public interest in the rebirth of orthodoxy and evangelical teaching than ever before in the last hundred years. Now is the right moment to try to provide accurate reportage of these events. My role is to let these movements speak for themselves, rather than to filter their voices through some editorial censor.

Until recently these initiatives were taking place largely within the closed cells of denominational isolation. Now they are rapidly moving into a wide ecumenical configuration. Far more academic and journalistic observers (including historians, sociologists, and church leaders) are taking note of distinctly evangelical developments throughout the mainline. They are discovering a vast realignment that almost no one saw coming only ten years ago, yet now all can see before their eyes. This, of course, has gone on quite apart from (even distant from) typical forms of defensive liberal ecumenism huddling under the battered flag of the National Council of Churches, which itself now founders on the rocky reefs of endless financial crises and its ever-threatened denouement.

The church property issue is just now coming to a critical stage. The concluding pages of this book present a case study on local church property issues. The need is urgent for accurate historical information and legal counsel in reconceptualizing the current crisis in local church property ownership struggles.

The Road Ahead

The six parts of the story ahead are:

Coming Home in the Mainline
Inspecting Ground Zero
Trekking to the Other Side of the Stream
Relearning the ABCs
Coming to the Table
Paying the Mortgage

The trip through these pages will take us visiting the home place (the mainline); smelling the smoke of what remains standing (its implosion); exploratory trekking to the other side of the mainstream and back to elementary basics (the confessing movement); then attending the great feast (confession at the Lord's Table); and finally visiting the courtroom to deal with legal matters (who owns the property).

We must begin by returning home to inspect the damage. Then we will get reacquainted with how the families in the neighborhood have dealt with the crisis, which then compels us to go back to the primitive schoolhouse to rediscover the values that once made the neighborhood cohere. Only then are we prepared to come again to the great feast that unites the community and rehearses its history. At length we have unpleasant work to do: confer seriously about who owns the property now.

Why So Underreported?

All these North American mainline Christians quietly gathered for the first time in 2002 to explore their common commitments. In the wake of this first gathering of these renewing and confessing groups (in Indianapolis, October 24–26, 2002), an unexpected momentum has emerged that appears to signal a decisive stage of ecumenical reconfiguration. This has gravitas for the future shape of American Christianity. It represents the unexpected uniting (and embryonic ecumenism) of these heretofore disparate renewal and confessing movements.

It has taken over a quarter century for these evangelical movements to emerge with one voice. They have all faced dismissive resistance within their own mainline denominations. They are now flourishing with growing vitality in the length and breadth of the mainline—among Presbyterians, Lutherans, Episcopalians, Methodists, American Baptists, and Disciples of Christ, as well as United Church of Christ and United Church of Canada clergy and laity. They are already embodying what is now being called "the new ecumenism." This does not mean a new organization, but a new recovery of the unity of Christian believers, accompanied by a thoughtful critique of the older institutional and ideological forms of ecumenism.

These confessing movements have never been brought to light of day for several reasons: (1) They have been strictly marginalized by their own denominational publications, which are wholly owned subsidiaries of their central institutional bureaucracies. (2) They have been prejudicially ignored by a predominately liberal secular press as insignificant, backward, recalcitrant, and mean-spirited, despite their astonishing generosity in world food relief and medical ministries, and their incredible growth rate. (3) They have not until now had any viable ecumenical presence or expression, especially among those who define ecumenism only in terms of the languishing World Council of Churches. (4) They have not until recently been coordinated as a single movement that has potential import for the whole future of Protestantism. (5) They are entirely without the kind of institutional funding that is available within denominational coffers and ordinary fiscal channels. All their efforts have been based on voluntary initiatives with no bureaucratic support, and indeed much institutional resistance. Hence, despite their huge numbers and increasing presence, they have until now been virtually ignored by both the secular press and religious press.

SPINE

Those with *spine* have courage, perseverance, and determination. They are not easily discouraged or set back. The Latin root of spine is *spina*, meaning a backbone. It is based on the metaphor of a thorn. The issues ahead require spine even to examine. They are indeed thorny.

Core Phases of the Argument Ahead

We have identified key destinations of the six parts ahead, but it is now useful to give them a preliminary description, so their purpose, cohesion, and sequence can be grasped.

The purpose of Part 1 is to introduce the worldview of confessing Christians, surveying the confessing movements in the mainline, and ask if they are affecting the stability of the historic Protestant communions. In chapter 1 we will examine challenges, strengths, weaknesses, and limitations of confessing Christians. Chapter 2 examines the wrenching issue of whether they should stay within or leave their denominations, and shows why they believe that internal discipline is more urgently needed than physical separation.

Part 2 will measure, analyze, inspect, and inventory the smoky scene of the implosion of the mainline (chapter 3). Chapter 4 will describe how confessing Christians are changing their churches, engendering young leadership, and maturing in confidence and teaching. The heart of the book is in chapter 5, which shows how young confessing Christians today stand in continuity with the old, ecumenical, classic Christian tradition. It is the youthful voices in these historic communions who have taken the lead in speaking out on the crisis of the church, and in making practical steps to renew their theology, educational institutions, and discipline. Here in these pages, for the first time, these young leaders articulate their bold stand of faith (*status confessionis*) in the section called "Be Steadfast." At long last we can now hear the voices of major young theologians of confessing Christianity. They have joined together in issuing their first joint public statement on the decisive requirements for reform in the mainline. For confessing Christians in America this short statement has been regarded as analogous to the Barmen Declaration (of anti-Nazi Christians in the troubled Germany of 1934).

Part 3 will trek to the other side of the mainstream to visit this extended *family* of movements that constitute the renewing and confessing presence within the mainline. Chapter 6 shows how they are nurturing a new ecumenism, a basic realignment of Christian unity in our time. It also explores the challenges of confessing sin and grace within a democratic society, providing a nonpartisan rationale and validation for Christian social witness. Chapters 7 and 8 chronicle pivotal events of the history of these major families of confessional movements within the mainline—their struggle, their emergence, their recent accomplishments, and how these varied movements resonate together in a new ecumenism. We will take the pulse of the vital energies present in these movements as revealed in their understanding of their mission, vision, strategy, and priorities—who they are, and what they are doing. We will not only describe them at work in their separate organizations, but also report the deepening of the confessional tide among the wider laity in each communion. In chapter 9 we discuss the relation of truth and unity, and why truth-driven unity is the only unity worth celebrating.

Part 4 (chapters 10–13) sets forth key points of the beliefs and teachings of confessing Christians. Their voices are heard in their own teaching statements, as set forth in key orthodox and evangelical documents of movements that stand steadfastly *within* the mainline. In direct extracts these voices speak for themselves without editorial shading or comment. These statements are not an incongruent conglomeration of disparate historical memories and hopes. This core is ordered around classic triune teaching in accord with key topics of ancient Christian teaching, as found equally in the Reformation, evangelical revivalism, and modern evangelicalism. All the mainline confessing movements stand within this same apostolic tradition. These texts provide for the first time a documentary collection of primary sources for confessing Christians today. Carefully selected from a large mass of materials, these confessional statements have a history of inconspicuous publication in renewal newsletters and confessing movement ephemera. Never before collected as a unified teaching document, they deserve deliberate, substantial study. It is evident from this core that there is already a spirit of doctrinal unity among confessing evangelicals living within the diverse churches of the mainline.

Part 5 looks to Scripture to ground the basic teaching of confession, especially as it relates to baptism and coming in repentance and faith to the Lord's Table (chapter 14). This is an elementary lesson in biblical theology. Chapter 15 explores the history of the remnant who have survived the mainline implosion. The whole mainline dilemma is epitomized in the United Church of Canada, so we will tell the story of how it lost its ecumenical virginity (chapter 16).

Finally the issue comes home locally when we ask: Who owns contested church property? Part 6 asks the most urgent question being faced everywhere in these struggles: When a judicatory defies its own constitutional doctrine and discipline, and a local church scrupulously teaches the church's doctrine and discipline, what happens in a property dispute with those who defiantly reject their own received doctrinal standards? Can heterodox judicatory officials change the locks and bolt out faithful local believers? Chapter 17 analyzes the dilemma of property disposition in church conflicts within a highly connectional denominational system, in this case the United Methodist Church. Chapter 18 documents the historical record of the relation between property deeds and doctrinal standards in this tradition, showing constitutional restrictions on what the legislative bodies can do and cannot undo. The final chapter, 19, asks how civil law and church order correlate in this most vexing of issues: the disposition of church property, looking toward issues still pending, on which many eyes are now focused.

Thus from a bird's-eye view we have six important stops to make, six places to visit that represent the six urgent questions that beckon us in this book.

These are the steps required to describe the scope and breadth of the renewing and confessing movements within the North American mainline churches. It is first useful to clarify the ubiquitous presence of confessing Christians in member churches of the National Council of Churches. Each one of these denominations has spawned tenacious movements dedicated to the renewal of their theological integrity and social witness.

1

The Emergence
of Confessing Christians
in the Mainline

The Crisis of Theological Integrity

Mainline churches stand today not merely in a crisis of *numbers*, but in a deeper crisis of *faith*. Though often portrayed as a crisis of politics or demographics or moral values or sexuality, it is more profoundly a crisis of biblical authority and theological integrity. The confessing movement ventures into divisive political territory on the value of life and sexual ethics only because biblical faith requires it.

The decisive challenge for the mainline is not coming from some external quarter outside the church, but precisely from *within* the churches themselves. Powerful voices within the denominational leadership grossly diminish Christian teaching, refuse to follow reasonable discipline democratically arrived at, and discriminate unfairly against those who disagree with them. What happens when those who pretend to represent historic Christianity wander far from it, and even inveigh against it?

The most blatant challenges have to do with evasive or equivocal assertions about the very center of Christian teaching: Jesus Christ. These are not ancillary points. Some reject his atoning work as unique Savior of the world and deny his resurrection and his teaching on the sanctity of marriage. Crucial doctrines cannot be sidestepped. The biblical teaching of creation has direct consequences for deciding about the creation of man and woman in God's image, and the value of life. The biblical teaching of the oneness of God has direct bearing on the use of witchcraft motifs in worship or the veneration of the goddess Sophia. The biblical understanding of God the Father, Son, and Spirit is not to be used merely as a political ploy for leverage in disputes on language fairness.

The crisis lodges precisely within the worshiping community. The mainline churches are now unready to confess with one voice the orthodox Christian faith in God the Father, God the Son, and God the Holy Spirit. To confess Jesus Christ as the only Son of God, Savior of the world constitutes a particular stumbling block. Permissive leadership often looks the other way as opinions gain currency that are obviously contrary to ancient and historic ecumenical Christian teaching. No one calls them to task. Sometimes it appears that no one can. So worshipers have had to suffer through wild and idiosyncratic versions of the faith that they find nowhere in Scripture or classic Christian teaching.

When secularizing church leadership is distracted by false gospels, the outcomes are disastrous. Finances are misspent. Maladministration is allowed to grow. Valuable mission resources are channeled into experimental grant-making for social service projects—some of them weird and entirely lacking in any clear Christian identity or proclamation of the one on whose behalf they offer compassion. Much of the deep continuity with the historic consensus of faith is being forgotten or imperiled. Many theological seminaries, where it is assumed that ministers will be rightly prepared in Scripture and moral reasoning, have been inundated for three decades with such far-ranging diversions as highly speculative Scripture studies, neopaganism, channeling, voodoo, sexual permissiveness, absolute moral relativism, and gay-lesbian-bisexual-transgender activism.

When such straying occurs, the purpose of renewing and confessing Christians is gently to call the churches to confess classic Christian teaching in good conscience without evasion or dilution. Who has suffered the most from these diversions? The faithful worshipers in the pews who are forced to listen to thin sermons and are still expected to pay the bills.

The Mainline after the Moral Collapse of Modernity

It is now possible to speak confidently of the rebirth of orthodoxy in the mainline churches. To some modest extent it is also visible in their seminaries and legislative assemblies. Modernity is losing its power to intimidate. *Modernity* is the period and the ideology that prevailed in the time from 1789 to 1989, from the Bastille to the Berlin Wall. By *postmodern*, orthodox Christians refer to the course of actual history following the decline of modernity.

Youthful classic Christians are now well prepared by modernity to use the very methods of modern consciousness (that is: scientific, historical, hermeneutical, psychological, sociological, and behavioral change models) to *detoxify the illusions* of modernity that have eaten like acids into the bone of the faith, the family, the culture, and the mainline churches that have accommodated to the culture.

Confessing Christianity is not accurately defined as antimodern. It is not merely a censorious negative reaction against modernity—for there is no reason to be opposed to something that is virtually dead. A frustrated antimodern emotive reaction errs in overestimating the continuing resilience of modernity now in terminal crisis. Many in the renewing intellectual leadership of orthodoxy have already doubly paid their dues to modernity and now search for ancient wisdom long ruled out by the narrow dogmas of secular humanism. There is no way for us to reflect upon modernity except amid the collapse of modernity.

Confessing Christians do not despair over the plight of modernity. Rather, they celebrate the providence of God that works amid the wreckage of failed modern ideologies. They live amid withering forms of a tired Protestantism that has sold its soul to modernity. But *the end of the elite, modern old-line is the beginning of a new, ecumenical re-centering committed to orthodox Christian teaching.*

Even if the general condition of popular congregational health is in many places uncertain in the mainline, *there are in most every congregation lay believers resolved to renew the familiar, classic spiritual disciplines* that have characterized the apostolic faith in all ages. These disciplines require:

daily meditative study of the written Word under the guidance of the Spirit;

an earnest life of personal prayer—a daily order of praise, confession, pardon, and petition for grace in common worship;

mutual care of souls with intensive primary group accountability;

raising families honoring to God;

an ordering of daily vocational life in which persons seek faithfully to walk by grace in the way of holiness, regardless of how the environing world interprets it; and

a complete yielding of the mind, heart, and will to the glory of God.

These disciplines, never fully lost, are now returning with great energy within the mainline.

The Marxist-Leninism of the Soviet era is now gone. The Freudian idealization of sexual liberation has found it easier to make babies than parent them. The children of today's culture are at peril. The idealized modernity they expected has never arrived, and its fantasy has left a trail of devastation. *These once-assured ideologies are now unmasked as having a dated vision of the human possibility. None have succeeded in fashioning a transmissible intergenerational culture.*

Meanwhile amid the death cries of passing modernity, the receding culture imagines itself to be the unquestioned moral norm that presumes to judge all premodern texts and ideas. Under the tutelage of its ideologies, sex has been reduced to orgasm, persons to bodies, psychology to stimuli, economics to planning mechanisms, and politics to manipulation. These ideologies are today everywhere in crisis, even while still being fawned over by aging church leaders.

Providence Transcends the Death of Modernity

Biblically viewed, this dissolution is both a providential judgment of sin and a grace-laden opportunity. Those well instructed in classic Christianity are prepared to understand that amid any cultural death, gracious gifts of providential guidance are being offered to humanity, and above all to the faithful. Divine providence is forever hedging our choices in human history.

The grace-enabled community is celebrating its passage through and beyond modernity. The intricate providences of history are being recognized. Each dying historical formation is giving birth to new forms and refreshing occasions for living responsively in relation to grace.

The church that weds itself to modernity is already a widow within despairing ultramodernity. Confessing Christians have had enough of the sexual experimenters, the compulsive planners of others' lives, and the canonical text disfigurers who presume to lead the church they have denied. Confessing churchwomen are no longer intimidated by those who presume to speak for all women while acting in ways profoundly damaging to women. The great company of godly Christian women has been misrepresented and harmed.

The Seminaries

Most of the seminaries of the mainline have striven to adapt snugly to this vulnerable and passing modernity. The liberal old-line Protestant elites, gatekeepers, and bureaucrats have been slow to understand the moral language of the congregations they serve. Institutions long funded by evangelical donors and convictions have been taken captive. Dated modern habits of moral permissiveness, hyper-toleration, and secularism still have a stranglehold on many arteries of mainline church bureaucracies and their collusive academies.

But below the surface there is among these institutions an outlook of desperation and identity diffusion. The mainline seminaries, with few exceptions, are confused about who they are in relation to the church. They struggle also with their ambiguous relation to the university, but more desperately in their relation to basic Christianity as such. Their idealism itself has rendered them defensive and demoralized. The heart is gone from the idyllic nineteenth-century song of inevitable progress. It has become a twenty-first century dirge with a heavy, hard-metal beat.

These tired, fading modern illusions are woven together into an ideological temperament that still sentimentally shapes the knowledge elites of liberal Protestantism, especially its politicized bureaucracies and schools. They remain largely unprepared to grasp either their own weaknesses or their mission within this nexus of historical change.

Only a few denominational seminaries within the mainline have begun to reverse these trends and move toward classic biblical teaching: Among Presbyterian seminaries, Princeton, Dubuque, and Pittsburgh have taken the right turn. Among United Methodists, Duke has shown the most signs of regaining equilibrium, and among the Episcopal Seminaries, Trinity Episcopal School of Ministry is healthy, and Nashotah House is returning to the fold. For most, it will take a long time to turn around tenure overloads.

In the absence of mainline seminary reform, viable candidates for ministry are more frequently electing to go to places like Asbury, Fuller, Trinity Evangelical, and Gordon-Conwell, despite punitive resistance from their denominational officers jealous of their rising importance. More United Methodist ordinands go to Asbury (which gets no support from the United Methodist General Conference) than to the officially supported Iliff and Claremont and Ohio seminaries combined. Once a seminary faculty has been filled with permanently tenured radicals, its members easily fall into the temptation of cloning themselves with look-alike future colleagues. The ensconced bureaucracies of hyper-tenured faculties have learned well the fine art of Xeroxing themselves politically, repeating ever anew their own ideological biases, making sure that no one gets tenure who will challenge the prevailing ideological tilt. All this occurs under the surface, of course, and with a polite and tolerant smile.

The Collapse of the Armies of Liberation

The description I am making may tempt some to think that I am exaggerating. I am reporting only what I have seen. I have been teaching and lecturing in mainline seminaries from 1959 to 2004. This is not hearsay, but eyewitness reporting from the line of fire.

"Liberated" is not a term used lightly. It is not a term applied by detractors to these wayward ideologues, but a term they constantly insist on applying to themselves. The subtext of "liberated" is: doctrinally imaginative, liturgically experimental, disciplinarily nonjudgmental, politically correct, morally broad-minded, and above all, sexually lenient and permissive. As a former full-time card-carrying liberator, I know from experience how mesmerizing this enchantment can be.

When the liberated have virtually no immune system against heresy, no defense whatever against perfidious teaching, and no criteria for testing the legitimacy of counterfeit theological currency, it is time for the worshiping community to act to guarantee faithful Christian teaching. The ordinary worshipers in the pews are coming to understand that they have a decisive interest in the quality and apostolicity of the ministries they have been asked to trust and support. Trustees of church-related educational institutions are increasingly demanding the right to know why clergy leadership is so prone to political absurdities, moral permissiveness, and ideological binges.

Most worshipers have been spared from knowing the details of the arcane machinery of mainline liberal seminary education. They have no reason to doubt that their divinity schools are like any other institution—to some extent reformable. But those of us who have spent a lifetime in Scripture-deprived theological education are those most wary of the stubborn fact that the present system, short of some mighty act of Providence, is highly resistant to reform, and indeed seems practically irreformable. The irreversibly tenured faculty is so intractable that, lacking some special act of grace, its reform seems virtually unimaginable. *The tenure principle, which was designed to protect academic freedom, has become so exploited as now to protect academic license, neglect, incompetence, and at times moral turpitude, since once tenure is offered, it is virtually impossible to withdraw.*

The Trend toward Sanity

If the liberated have the freedom to teach apostasy, the believing church has the freedom to withhold its consent. If the liberated teach counter-canonical doctrines and conjectures inimical to the health of the church, then the church has no irreversible moral obligation to give them support or bless their follies.

The rhetoric of inclusivism has resulted in the fact of exclusion. This is especially seen in the *willful exclusion of orthodox and evangelical Christians* from leadership. Confessing Christians are at last learning how to communicate to absolute egalitarians how hollow the inclusion arguments sound to traditional believers who themselves have been so long marginalized.

What is happening amid this historical situation is a joyous return to the sacred texts of Christian Scripture and the classic guides of the ancient ecumenical faith. *Young confessing Christians are those who, having entered in good faith into the disciplines of modernity, and having become disillusioned with its illusions, are again studying the Word of God—that Word made known in history as attested by prophetic and apostolic witnesses whose testimonies have become perennial texts for this worldwide, multicultural, multigenerational remembering and celebrating community.*[1]

2

. . . .

Discipline, Not Separation

Separation Does Not Foster Discipline

The major issue before the mainline churches: Will they submit to their own discipline, or will the absence of discipline finally require division? Some leading commentators like Lyle Schaller have already predicted the necessity of division.

Countering this view, confessing Christians seek to maintain the unity of the church through discipline, not through division. The confessing movement is strongly committed to staying *within*. It is better for churches to learn to respect their own legislative processes and discipline themselves accordingly than to face the even greater problems of separation, division of property, and the anguish of divorce.

Confessing Christians seek to reform their churches, not leave them. Those who split off leave the patient in the hands of the euthanasia advocates, the Kevorkians of dying modernity. The Holy Spirit will not bless willful unnecessary divisiveness.

If classic Christians self-righteously leave, they abandon the legacy, the patrimony, the bequests, the institutions, and the resources that have been many generations in the making with much tears and sweat.

Walking away turns out to have weightier moral impediments than hanging in. *It seems unthinkable to abandon, without further prayers for special grace, those historic communions by which so many have been baptized.* The faithful have committed themselves for generations to the support of these communions, which their classic doctrines and evangelical revivals have engendered. To allow these resources to be permanently taken over by those inimical to the faith cannot be an act of responsibility.

These libraries, these alumnae/alumni, these endowments, and these mission boards will be abandoned only at great cost. A clean sweep seems both necessary and impossible. Hence there is a need for prayer for special grace, and for an army of prayer for the urgent reform of representational systems, wayward educational institutions, and world missions.

To flee the church is not to discipline it. No one corrects a family by leaving it. Separation does not foster discipline. Discipline is fostered by patient trust, corrective love, and willingness to live with incremental change if that is what the Spirit is allowing. Discipline seeks to mend the broken church by a change of heart.

The Premature Temptation to Split

The easier way is separation. The harder but more responsible way is discipline—patient, unwearied, and loving correction—loving enough to admonish and rectify unfruitful behavior.

This means that the emerging generation of confessing Christians in mainline denominations must learn to speak of accountability as clearly as freedom, of truth as persuasively as toleration. They must learn the language of heresy and know how to respond to it realistically. They must learn to speak of the church's holiness as the basis for the church's openness.

The emerging generation is more ready to tackle this task than the declining generation is ready to see the need for it. This is not a project for a year or a decade. It will take at least a generation, and probably more. It will require patience and endurance.

It is more true to the unity and apostolicity and catholicity of believers to seek discipline than separation in pursuit of an ephemeral and idealized holiness. Jesus calls the church to be one body, a participation in his incarnation in time. In faith the church is already one body. The temptation to split is calmed by trusting that the Spirit will find a way to reform the church in God's own time.

The ordained clergy are called to discipline the flock, not divide them. They must begin by disciplining themselves.

Discipline requires education, guidance, vigilance, and responsibility-taking. Like parenting, it may require going back again and again to corrective measures when challenged.

To divide the flock into those who follow discipline and teaching, versus those who do not follow discipline and teaching would be like dividing a single family into two families, one with the better children and one with the worse. That would be to miss the point of being a family. It is the very thought that the family is becoming divided that itself is disturbing, if the family is to be a family.

Despair over the Difficulties of Reform

Despairing voices often say: The establishment is entirely too far gone. It simply cannot ever be fully renewed. The bureaucracy is too deeply corrupted to be salvaged. If so, our best energies should be spent looking for a way out, so that a new denomination or at least new congregations might emerge in good conscience, consisting of those withdrawing from the mainline establishment, so as to form new denominations. Yet unrealistic fantasies about the absolute purity of the church in history dwell within this dream with its underlying despair.

Some friends and cohorts of the confessing movement have at times felt that they have already lived through too many decades of futile renewal efforts, and now are realizing that their hopes are not going to be fulfilled in their lifetime. So they have tried to persuade confessing Christians to be prepared with an exit strategy.

Most of those who have been persuaded of the church's absolute irreformability have left long ago. The evangelicals who have remained within the mainline are tenacious enough to still be there. They have a fierce reputation for tenacity and loyalty, far more than secular permissive advocates. This makes the moral dilemma of staying or leaving more acute for those most serious about the church.

Theological and Prudential Arguments against Leaving

Though respecting those who differ, the confessing movement has been, on the whole, steadily resistant to the schismatic view. Good conscience resists schism both on theological and prudential grounds.

First, theological: Believers cannot with an easy conscience be a part of the dividing of the body of Christ. Scripture warns against division. Paul warned the Roman Christians: "I urge you, brothers, to watch out for those who cause divisions, and put obstacles in your way that are contrary to the teaching you have learned. Keep away from them" (Rom. 16:17).

The key texts here are in Paul's first letter to Corinth: "But God has combined the members of the body and has given greater honor to the parts that lacked it, so that there should be no division [*schisma*] in the body, but that its parts should have equal concern for each other. If one part suffers, every part suffers with it; if one part is honored, every part rejoices with it" (1 Cor. 12:24–26). "I appeal to you, brothers, in the name of our Lord Jesus Christ, that all of you agree with one another so that there may be no divisions [*schismata*] among you and that you may be perfectly united in mind and thought" (1 Cor. 1:10). Divisions are proof of a worldly spirit (1 Cor. 3:3).

Under normal circumstances, schism is not even an option to be considered. Why? The body of Christ is already one in Christ. Christ desires and enables the unity of his body (John 17:21–23).

The Untimeliness of Leaving Now

The second argument is prudential: The timing is exactly wrong for pursuing an exit strategy. Just when the evangelical voices in the mainline are growing, when legislative victories are increasing, when repeated attacks of distracters have been soundly defeated, when articulate young orthodox leadership is emerging, that is precisely not the time to leave.

Why is this an ill-advised time to leave, and a propitious time for perseverance? (1) The confessing and renewing movements are gaining strength in every mainline denomination. (2) They are winning many legislative challenges and resisting most legislative defeats. (3) They are increasing in numbers and confidence. (4) They are just to the point of breaking the back of the ideology of liberation. Why leave now?

Part of the purpose of this report is to show that the results of decades of prayer and work to renew the church are just now beginning to bear real fruit. Change is in the air.

Why an Exit Strategy Is Self-Defeating

The abiding issue for many: Should confessing Christians be quick to look for an "exit strategy," or should they seek the transformation of the church that brought them to faith and baptized them, by reaffirming their steady, durable commitment to remaining in it and transforming it? The confessing movement was earlier somewhat ambivalent, but more and more the heart of the movement is saying: stay in. The timing to exit is poor. To leave the liberal bureaucracies just when they are collapsing is a singular misjudgment.

Within this frame of "discipline not separation," it is still permissible for confessing Christians to discuss scenarios by which those who want to leave the disciplined community can do so. But this view, which is sometimes called "amiable separation," must always be conceived as a gentle act of generosity to allow those whose conscience cannot abide discipline to go on their own without taking down the whole communion with them. It is not the faithful who want to exit. Nor is it the faithful who have a bad conscience about the polity and discipline and doctrines of the church. Those who cannot bear the thought of remaining in a church that they think is not free enough, not secular enough, not permissive enough, should not be restrained from leaving. There should be no barriers put in their way. They should not have to fight to recover their pensions and church properties. This is the notion of "gracious exit." This is not meant to malign or refuse to acknowledge the motivations of faithful Christians, who for reasons of conscience, choose to leave a mainline congregation, but to point to the alternative.

The idea of "gracious exit" should not ever mean that orthodox believers exit or split from their churches, but rather that they make it easier for those who repeatedly reject Christian doctrine and discipline to take their leave. What confessing Christians properly mean by "amiable separation" is not that the growing evangelical influence in the mainline might leave the endowments and institutions to the collapsing liberal wing, but that they are committed to reclaiming them, and providing a fair plan to permit voluntary, peaceful departure of those who refuse discipline, allowing them to take with them their local church property.

This is hard to explain to a biased press that often wants to portray evangelicals as schismatics. The concept is clear in the minds of confessing Christians, but almost always distorted when reported. *Amiable separation allows those whose conscience cannot abide discipline to go on their own way and retain their assets.* What part of that sentence is unclear? Its constant distortion is a willful act of misunderstanding. Believers who separate for reasons of conscience, when biblically informed, remain accountable to strong scriptural mandates against schism (1 Cor. 1:10).

The Holiness and Unity of the Church in Tension

Still these obstacles present many honest believers with the continuing moral dilemma: Should one remain in a local community of worship whose leadership has gone so far astray? Is the believer more right to stay or to leave?

The way each believer answers this pivotal question is closely related to the way each one views the very nature of the church as one, holy, catholic, and apostolic.

The major theological reason for *leaving* is the ideal of the holiness and apostolicity of the church. The major reason for *staying* the course is the hoped-for unity and catholicity of the church.

The argument for leaving: The holiness and apostolicity of the church calls the faithful to separate themselves from unbelievers. The argument for staying: The unity and catholicity of the church calls the faithful to unite with baptized believers despite differences, with all looking toward the forgiveness of God.

The argument is that an unholy church or a church that denies the apostolic witness must be abandoned. That is the argument of the Donatists, who chose what they regarded as holiness over catholicity. Augustine argued that the temporary disunity of the institutional church does not engender its holiness, provided it is seeking to correct its course.

The confessing movement argues that the apostolicity and catholicity of the church require it to seek holiness within the framework of its essential unity. The essence of the unity of the church is faith in the atoning work of the crucified Lord. This work engenders the unity of the body of believers who confess one faith, one baptism, one God and Father of us all.

Both those who stay and leave may confess with the Nicene Creed that the church is one, holy, catholic, and apostolic, but the weight may fall differently for some on the priority of these "marks of the church." Those who seek more to protect the holiness of the church than its unity may be more prone to consider leaving as a viable answer.

When these two options conflict, the whole church is called to humility, repentance, and prayer for wisdom and grace and charity. The church *is* one, holy, catholic, and apostolic, according to the New Testament. It cannot be either holy or apostolic without being united and *katholikos*—in communion with Christian believers of all times and places. And it cannot be united and *katholikos* without seeking and praying for holiness, and following the apostolic teaching.

The valid bearers of the ecumenical tradition are those who respect ancient ecumenical truth, not those who use the church for political purposes. The authentic advocates of the unity of the church are those who most care about its discipline and holiness, yet with humility and gentleness.

The Holy Spirit Has Time to Renew the Church

God's timing is not cramped in the same ways as human timing. It is not limited to some short-term perspective. God works through families, generations, nations, centuries, eras, and indeed the whole of history—creation to fall to redemption to consummation. Believers are not afraid of wheat and tares being for now mixed in the church, because they have been duly warned of this by Jesus himself, and know that God will find the fitting way of separating the wheat and tares on the last day.

In any case the time frame of change in the mainline is likely to be extended to decades, not years. It will require a great deal of patience. It will not depend upon a single legislative victory or judicial decision or a single generation of better or worse executive leadership.

The patient evangelical Anglicans of the last two centuries provide the best model for North American confessing Christians today. Those like John Stott and James I. Packer and Michael Green elected to stay through thick and thin within the Church of England. It took a hundred years of patient endurance to salvage the worldwide Anglican tradition. Only in the last half century have the global evangelical Anglicans proven their staying power and been successful in electing bishops, primates, and world leaders capable of defending classical Christian teaching, and even now these teachings remain much contested.

An increasing number of confessing Christians have decided that they are not bugging out. They are not going anywhere. They are there to stay. If others think they are going to be intimidated into dropping out, they are respected, but not followed. Many laypersons are answering firmly that until they know that their church is secure from constant and dangerous drifting, and until they can trust the faithfulness and integrity of church leadership, they will, like Athanasius, stand against the world, endure, remain, and seek discipline and transformation, not schism.

Consenting and Dissenting Traditions on the Holiness of the Church

In this debate there are two legitimate competing Protestant doctrines of the church: a *dissenting* tradition (traditionally related to the Novatians, Dissenters, and the Holiness "come-outers" and to many tendencies within the Reformed traditions), as distinguished from a *consenting* tradition (typified by Augustinians, Anglicans, and Wesleyans).

The *dissenting* tradition is epitomized by the Puritans, a great and fruitful tradition, but one that was so focused on creating a holy church that it drove away believing Christians who did not meet its standards. The *consenting* tradition is epitomized historically by the Anglicans who were so determined to sustain the unity of the church that they made the tent so large that it had no boundaries. They lapsed into a mentality of accommodation—to anything.

Admittedly the confessing movement has struggled with these two voices within, but the heart of the confessing movement has increasingly remained committed to staying in, transforming the church, and calling it to the disciplined and holy life. That is why it is called the Confessing Movement *within* one or another communion.

The Search for an Apt Analogy

Three analogies are often applied to this dilemma: the marriage or divorce analogy, the business partners analogy, or the holy communion analogy.

The marriage versus divorce analogy views the disciplined church and the permissive church as engaged in a conflict that could lead to divorce. Those who seek the continuity of marriage and family are trying to make the relationship more just. They are concerned about the children, even when the parents quarrel. To divorce is to give up on the promise of the family.

The business partners analogy views the question of remaining together more as a fiscal matter of whether property agreements can be made, or whether they must be divided up in a just way, if need be under a judge.

The communion analogy is entirely different: Its key metaphor is that of the penitent coming to the communion table. All are invited to the communion table, but only on the premise of repentance. Those who are penitent are the faithful who earnestly confess their sins and boldly confess the atoning Christ and receive forgiveness. Those who come to the communion table without repentance bring judgment on their own heads by their own choice.

The invitation to communion is open to all who repent and believe. Whether or not one is penitent is a matter of the heart. Only God knows the authenticity of repentance. Only God can judge the heart. The table is not barred, but the penitent church has a duty to warn rashly impenitent communicants about the consequences of their actions.

All three analogies are useful, but the most penetrating is the communion analogy, where the crucial matters are repentance and faith, not legal partnerships or separation of properties or the breakup of the family. This reframes the question to focus on where it ought to be: the grace of repentance at the communion table, and the willingness to seek the holiness of the church at that table.

PART 2

THE
MAINLINE
IMPLOSION

3

. . . .

The Internal Collapse

Defining "Implosion"

An implosion is an internal collapse. It is not an event that has some *external* cause, but a disintegration that occurs *from within*. It is not a cataclysm ignited by something apart, but one that crushes and dissipates toward the center, from within. It is not a bursting out from the circumference, but a reverse bursting toward the collapsing heart.

Implosion symbolizes a self-initiated, self-destructive collapse from within. The Soviet experiment did not explode, it imploded, fell of its own weight. The root word for implosion (substituting *im* for *ex* in explosion = Latin: "clap") implies a thunderclap in which the destructive force moves centripetally toward the center. What falls to pieces is not outside the detonated entity, but inside. It is the opposite of explosion.

It is not the mainline worshiping communities as such who are imploding, but their detached leadership is.

Defining "Mainline": Which Communions Are Involved?

The "mainline" refers to those Protestant ecclesiastical institutions that have for decades enjoyed an unofficial "establishment status" in American culture—churches long associated with the National Council of Churches, its leadership now in a state of financial distress, moral confusion, and doctrinal relativism. Related terms for the mainline are "oldline" and "sideline."

When we speak of the mainline, we are referring to some of the largest Protestant churches in North America with some of the most distinguished histories. Increasingly the mainline in North America is a defensive and morose church of diluted liberalism that has become wedded to a dysfunctional political and ecumenical agenda. The chief denominations that have been so wedded (but are now reversing course) are the familiar alphabet soup of American Protestantism:

ELCA (Evangelical Lutheran Church of America)
ECUSA (Episcopal Church USA)
UM or UMC (United Methodist Church)
PCUSA (Presbyterian Church USA)
UCC (United Church of Christ)
UCCan or UCCanada (United Church of Canada)
ABC (American Baptist Church USA)
CCDC (Christian Churches, Disciples of Christ)

Each of these has more than a million members. Over 20 million North Americans belong to churches served by these mainline denominations. All have lived through more than a half century of stressful alignment with the National Council of Churches and the World Council of Churches.

All bear the moral burden of being unable to account for the dismal failure of their institutions. All have been spiraling downward, out of control, for a quarter century. All have been until recently very proactively engaged and publicly identified in conspicuous political causes, some highly controversial, such as partial birth abortion, gay-lesbian-transgender rights to ordination, and far left-wing politics. The energy of this political activism is now far less vigorous than it was only a year or two ago, because these leadership nodes are now on the defensive and intensely fearful of losing their funding, prestige, and membership base.

Mark well that it is only for denominations threatening to apostatize that any talk of a renewing or confessing movement is even pertinent or thinkable. If there were no need to call the church to return to the apostolic tradition, then there would be no need for a confessing movement, and no urgent requirement to call the church back to its historic faith.

Some denominations have remained steadfastly faithful. Others have been tempted to apostasy, or have moved hazardously toward the slippery slope of apostasy. This study is focused exclusively upon those church bodies in which the historic faith is arguably in serious jeopardy, or indeed openly denied, with its seminaries mired in temptations to false teachings, and its history being reinvented. There is little need for or interest in a confessing movement within the Orthodox Church of America, for example, but there is within the United Methodist Church and the United Church of Canada, where the apostolic faith is at times ambiguously received at best and at worst demeaned and made laughable as an object of scorn.

Heartbreak and Hope

There are promising signs of hope in all of these faltering denominations. These hopes are emerging out of the ashes of the implosion of the vitality, confidence, and viability of the denominational institutions.

The old ethos that has ruled the roost in each of these denominations—once so self-confident—is now descending into a time of desperate confusion, imminent collapse, and loss of nerve, and it is defensive on almost every front. Some vital signs remain, but with diminishing strength and weakened cohesion.

The prominent church traditions that have dominated American religion in the last 200 years are all experiencing the same drastic slippage. They are following the dwindling path of the church in Europe, some arrogantly and intentionally, some faster, some slower.

It may be that some of these core leadership systems will survive the implosion. Some have enviable endowments that will fend off the implosive outcomes for some time. This is especially so in a few educational institutions and some wealthy local churches. But even if a few of their endowed bureaucracies and congregations survive, they appear to be losing their energy and vivre, and their ability to regenerate a new generation of committed followers. The communities of worship that have supplied them with moral vitality and spiritual wisdom and funding for two centuries are on a steep downward spiral in membership. Their currency is debased. Their moral high ground has been dissipated or lost.

It is the same story everywhere in the aging mainline leadership. In the Lutheran Church (ELCA) the Achilles' heel is an embittered conflict over proposed ecumenical realignments. In the Episcopal Church it has been the ordination of a homosexual bishop and the consequent response of a large majority of African and Asian Anglican traditionalists. In the Presbyterian Church USA it is the grassroots pocketbook revolution against an out-of-touch bureaucracy. The Achilles' heel of the imploding liberal leadership in the United Methodist Church is the local church property issue.

Different forms of soreness appear to be particularly tender in different traditions. Yet all these issues plague all mainline denominations in some form. The issues range far beyond the sexuality issues that are so prominent in news reports. These sometimes obscure the other more salient issues on biblical authority, baptism, ecumenism, financial accountability, and the fairness of representational systems vis-à-vis concentrated bureaucratic interests.

All of these motifs are brought together with special fury in the United Church of Canada. Yet there remain very determined forces within the United Church of Canada resolutely committed to stand firm and faithful to the Contract of Union and to the Confessional Standards of the Union of 1925 that brought the United Church of Canada into being, combining Reformed, Methodist, and Congregational church traditions. The United Church of Canada is in a more advanced state of implosion than any below the Canadian border.

Since the American Baptists, the United Church of Christ, and the Disciples of Christ have congregational polity, there is less intense conflict over church property issues than in those denominations with relatively more synodal or hierarchical government. But in all these denominations, regardless of polity, there are fiscal responsibility questions, sexuality conflicts, ecumenical follies, and bureaucratic misappropriations that have been devastating. They reflect the heartbreak felt within the weary trenches of the cultural wars that have split apart American society.

Signs of Renewal

Believers today are committing themselves anew to boldly confess the faith in the face of determined establishment resistance. They are reclaiming the historic Christian faith within their wayward denominations. The faith once for all delivered to the saints is being newly delivered within the mainline. The agents of change have sometimes been called the "young fogeys" who, having tasted the pretenses of modernity, are now turning in droves to the wisdom of classic Christianity. They are being called together to provide mutual encouragement, to listen to the Word of God, to pray for the empowerment of the Spirit. They are building rich relationships that have thus far had limited opportunities to grow during the years of fragmentation and rapid secularization. This is a time of desecularization, religious realignment, and the rebirth of orthodoxy.

The renewing movements are diverse initiatives in different church landscapes having the same goal, yet do not know each other well. They only now are being introduced to each other. They are recognizing themselves as a single family split apart in many distant regions and judicatories, yet all loyal to the same personal faith in the same Savior under the authority of the same Holy Writ and inheritors of the same family of God, and participants in the same great cloud of witnesses of all times and places. This is so, even while they have not been in touch with the details of each other's struggle.

They are rejoicing in the stirrings for renewal occurring in every nook and cranny of these mainline communions. Virtually every local church is affected by this reunion and rediscovery.

The waning waywardness of liberal Christianity has been engineered by those claiming to be "ecumenical," yet who have defied classical ecumenical teaching. While appearing to promote ecumenism, they have at the same time been trampling upon the ancient ecumenical truth that brings believers into unity in Christ. Believers are baptized into the one body of Christ, but find themselves now fallen into defensive denominational fortresses that neglect ancient ecumenical moral wisdom, and the unity to which the Holy Spirit calls all the faithful. Believers are now actively seeking to embody the unity of believing Christians within their own communions. They are coming together to celebrate their oneness in Jesus Christ, to learn from each other about how spectacularly the Spirit is working among them in their distant vineyards. They are asking the Spirit to guide them to grasp these new recognitions.

Renew and Confess as Complementary Movements

Two active verbs—to confess and to renew—point to two converging movements in mainline Protestantism.

There are several corollary terms for *confessing* Christians: the confessing church, the confessing movement, and confessing Christianity. All refer to a single diverse movement. Upon close examination it has a central core, a spine, which we will examine.

The terms *renewing* churches and the renewal movements, and their correlated expressions (the renewing church, renewing Christians, and renewing Christianity), all refer to a single movement that is full of vitality and touched with many features of spontaneity, charisma, and inspiration.

These two complementary terms (confess and renew) form an emergent and overlapping single movement. It is always in motion, which is the meaning of *movement*. So it does not yield easily to being described as a static object or an inert standing entity. A movement is a bird in flight, a wave breaking, a storm brewing. If it were not moving and changing, it would not be a movement. But it is moving—winging its way toward some as yet unknown historical destiny.

Renewal and Confession: Complementary Streams

These two terms best convey and name the two streams flowing into this one movement. The two streams might alternatively be visualized as:

Evangelical	Orthodox
Revivalist	Catholic
Modern Evangelical Teaching	Classic Ecumenical Teaching
Charismata	Liturgy
Renewal Movement	Confessing Movement

The renewing elements are more decisively influenced by the evangelical, renewalist, charismatic streams of pietistic revivalism. That would be true regardless of whether the denominational setting is Anglican, Presbyterian, Methodist, Baptist, or Congregational. The confessing elements are largely influenced by classical ecumenical teaching, the ancient church confessions, the confessional tradition of the Reformation, patristic teaching, and liturgical renewal.

These two streams have become firmly joined together as a single configuration that might be called the renewing and confessing movements. The confessing movement is the theological, historical, and exegetical face of the renewing movements that preceded it. The hyphenated term—renewing-confessing movements—points to an evolution in language that reveals this new configuration.

If for years these two streams had avoided each other, by the early 1990's there seemed to be good reasons to bring them together. Earlier the evangelical wing was much stronger, but in more recent times the classical ecumenical wing has become an equal partner.

The theological grandfather of this movement was the late Albert Cook Outler. One of the earliest evidences of the uniting of these two streams was the earlier-conflicted, then later-cooperative collaboration of Albert Outler and Edmund Robb in A Fund for Theological Education, which produced the John Wesley Scholars, out of which several deans of theological schools have come. Among other key leaders were Presbyterian John Leith and Episcopal Bishop FitzSimmons Allison.

These two streams have joined to bring about a decisive reconfiguration in the mainline. They have united into a single movement that is gathering cohesion, and promises to challenge young orthodox and evangelical leadership with boldness, courage, and solid biblical-traditional grounding. The hope is that all of these contemporary mainline denominations can be re-grounded and renewed in classic Christian and evangelical teaching.

Mere Christianity

To stop the further hemorrhaging of these churches, believers within the mainline have formed confessing and renewing movements composed of people and congregations who without apology have exalted the sole lordship of God the Son. They adhere simply to classical Christianity. This is what C. S. Lewis called "mere Christianity." They pray for the Spirit to strengthen the holy life. Many are young people. They embrace a great variety of believers. They are now calling upon their church leaders, trustees of institutions, board members of boards and agencies, and the seminaries to transmit the historic Christian faith without cowering. Seriousness about *donor intent* is now being recognized as a major responsibility of worshipers. They cannot yet see clearly where God will lead them. But they know they must once again contend mightily for the apostolic faith of the one, holy *katholikos*, and apostolic church. Under God's judgment and by God's grace they are standing together in small scale covenant accountability to participate in the Spirit's active reconstruction of the church. This renewing work, they know, is built only upon the foundation of their unity in the truth made known in Jesus Christ. This is a time for repentance, prayer, courage, and concerted action. The renewal, reform, and healing of these churches can come only through the life-giving power of the Holy Spirit.

These movements have arisen quickly like leaven in dough in all mainline denominations in North America. These church bodies have been linked for a half century with the National and World Councils of Churches, and are the main funders of modern ecumenism. The emerging faithful within the renewing and confessing movements of the mainline are doubling their efforts in their grassroots membership, their congregations, their giving, and in their legislative halls. They are determined to reclaim the errant mainline.

Is there, as some have grimly warned, only a brief window of opportunity to reclaim these rapidly failing denominations, seminaries, and institutions? Will they soon plunge into irreversible decline and terminal institutional illness? Or is there evidence that these valiant efforts are already beginning to turn the momentum around? Most confessing Christians believe the latter. At least it is clear that the Spirit seems to be giving these churches some time for repentance. These newly enlivened believers pray for the reclamation of their churches. They have laid aside other pressing duties to search for practical ways of accomplishing this. Their purpose is not merely to express outrage or self-pity, but to ask God for grace to show them how to renew their own church congregations in the faith once delivered to the saints. They seek to articulate an agenda for reversal in all of these historic communions. They seek a common vision sharable by moderates and traditionalists for the repossession of these once-faithful institutions, and ask what feasible goals might be set for the rehabilitation of their churches, hungry for a living relationship with the living Lord. They are praying for grace to avoid the temptations of resentment, reactionary defensiveness, despair, and lack of charity. They are seeking to understand how they can reclaim their historic mission, theological integrity, battered church identity, institutions, academies, governing boards, and their agencies and mission ministries.

A Broken Family

As traditional Christians, they are pouring out their hearts about a broken love affair, an endangered family. The confessing theologians have encouraged the faithful to speak from their hearts about both the dilemma and promise of the church.

As convener of the Confessing Theologians Commission, this writer has been charged with accurately presenting the view of these courageous young teachers. Extended conversations with them reveal their hope that their prayers and concerns can be heard accurately.

They understand themselves to be required by Scripture to warn the church about impending dangers. These admonitions best come with gentleness and empathy, and with deep love and compassion for all who work tirelessly in the grassroots struggle for the church. What follows attempts a composite view of confessing Christians within the mainline concerning the predicament and promise of North American Christianity.

4

How Confessing Christians Are Changing Their Churches

The Spirit Has Not Abandoned the Church

The Holy Spirit has not abandoned the church amid these ambiguous earthly struggles. God continues to offer the grace of perseverance by which the faithful are enabled to remain Christ's living body even while being challenged by infirmities, forgetfulness, heresy, apostasy, persecution, and schism. The church is being surely preserved to "proclaim the Lord's death until he comes" (1 Cor. 11:26).

The Lord has promised that against the church "the gates of hell shall not prevail" (Matt. 16:18 KJV; cf. Luke 1:33; 1 Tim. 3:15). This means that the church will never decline into total forgetfulness, since it is guided by the Spirit, who is promising always to remind and teach the church (John 14:26) even when the church seems not to listen. This is why the church, insofar as guided by the Spirit, does not ever fall entirely away from the fundamental truth of faith or into irretrievable error. She is preserved by grace, not by human craft or design (Gal. 2:5).

Confessing Christians attest to the biblical teaching that *the one, holy, catholic, apostolic church is promised imperishable continuance, even if particular churches or local bodies or denominations stumble and fall.* The church's future is finally left not to human willing or chance, but to grace. Many branches of the seasonally changing vine may drop off or become sick or withered, but the one whole church will be preserved till the end of time. Though individual believers or structures may come to shipwreck, and even whole communions lose their bearings during crises, the church is being preserved (John 16:7–13).

The Enduring Word

God will not be left without witnesses in the world (Acts 14:17). According to one traditional Order for Receiving Persons into the Church: "the Church is of God, and will be preserved to the end of time, for the promotion of his worship and the due administration of his Word and Sacraments, the maintenance of Christian fellowship and discipline, the edification of believers, and the conversion of the world. All, of every age and station, stand in need of the means of grace which it alone supplies."[1] This I learned by heart before my ordination. Although it no longer appears in books of worship, it still remains true.

Despite temporary apostasies and temptations, it is unthinkable that God would allow the church finally to become absolutely and continuously apostate or to lose all touch with the righteousness which Christ has once and for all bestowed upon her. "For you have been born again, not of perishable seed, but of imperishable, through the living and enduring word of God. For 'All men are like grass, . . . but the word of the Lord stands forever.' And this is the word that was preached to you" (1 Peter 1:23–25). The faithful are promised continued organic union with Christ the Vine.

The promise of continuity is not offered to any particular congregation or denomination or generation or family of church bodies or any passing period of history. No church in history is ever without error. Rather apostolic continuity is promised to the whole church to preserve her from fundamental error through the long course of history, that is, to the end (cf. Matt. 28:20). Due to the Spirit's steady guidance, all those called will not be allowed to err at the same time. Their way will be silently hedged by the truth.

While grace does not coerce, neither does it ever bat zero in any given liturgical season. It is unthinkable that God would create the church at great cost, only to let her fall finally into permanent or irremediable error. Meanwhile our communions remain vulnerable to all those hazards that accompany life in time. These perils call the churches to steadfast faith.

The Continuity of Witnesses

The continuity of the church in time is more a teaching of the power of the Holy Spirit than of the cleverness of human imagination or strategy. The Lord promises that the Holy Spirit "will teach you all things and will remind you of everything I have said to you" (John 14:26). Always some seeds of faith remain buried in the ruins and ashes even of the most divided or corrupt remnants of church organizations. Sometimes such seeds may seem to survive marginally as semi-endangered species, scattered thinly throughout the parched world, as vestiges of the covenant communities. Yet wherever Word and sacrament are being transmitted and delivered, they are never without some effect, for "my word," says the Lord, will "not return to me empty, but will accomplish what I desire"(Isa. 55:11). The time frame of this accomplishment is in God's hands. The part of the faithful is to believe the promise.

The foundation is standing sure, and the Lord knows who are his (2 Tim. 2:19). This is the theme of the confessing theologians' pastoral letter that follows. Whether in the Sudan, China, Cuba, or Lebanon, the embattled church continues to live by the Spirit.

Classic Christian teaching has healthily survived the hazards of modernity and joyfully flourishes amid these present perils, despite many failures in our faithfulness. Against all predictions of the once-confident secularizers, a disciplined Christian spirituality is being ever renewed by the Holy Spirit. Young people are rediscovering Holy Writ and its classic ecumenical interpreters. The historic wisdom of classic Christianity is becoming for them the basis for the rational critique of modern pretenses to moral superiority. The turning point they are celebrating is this: Classic Christian teaching, worship, the life of prayer, scholarship, hymnody, and institutional life have in fact outlived the dissolution of ultramodernity.

The Holy Spirit has promised to continue to give life to the body of Christ. It is only on the false premise of the possible failure of the Holy Spirit that the church imagines itself as coming to nothing. This is the least likely premise in the Christian understanding of history.

Those who willingly enslave themselves to passing idolatries should not be surprised when these temporarily alluring gods of narcissism and naturalism are found vulnerable. They have clay feet. When modern institutions are shaken, when current philosophies wither on the vine, those who have put their trust in them understandably grieve and feel angry and frustrated.

The Maturing of Minds

Loneliness and abandonment were once strongly felt among many orthodox and evangelical believers within the mainline. Confessing Christians are now learning to articulate what they hold in common. They are clearer about what needs to be changed. They are placing themselves and their churches before God. They are viewing their present circumstances from within the perspective of the unfolding history of salvation—the story of God with humanity. They acknowledge themselves to be under divine judgment—now and finally. They are committed to *inhabit the church's classical tradition for a sustained period of time in order to reform the church's present waywardness.* This habitation is required for those who conscientiously want to entrust their children to the churches.

These renewing churches, movements, and individuals have recently experienced, by grace, astonishing growth and vitality. They are no longer standing at a naive or immature beginning point. They are in a maturing stage of reflection. They are now confessing with other Christian believers the faith held by all believers everywhere. They are standing firmly now in the historic community of faith that provides the sure basis for dealing with whatever unexpected historical vulnerabilities may occur.

Confessing Christians are confidently taking the high ground in the debate on the destiny of the church. They are not focused on the manipulation of power, but on how persons are being actively empowered by the Spirit. They are not trapped in desperate egalitarian efforts to find an ever-illusive congenial balance of race and gender strategies, but they are becoming attuned to hearing the thundering truth of God's Word for church and society in our time.

The divisions we are experiencing in the mainline do not imply that the church is in irremediable schism or apostasy. *Not every division has been of the devil; not every union of the Holy Spirit.* Ruptures sometimes take place in the struggle to *reunite* the faithful. Again and again we have seen the leadership take the mainline to the brink of schism, and the laity pull it back to its classic center.

Getting in Touch after a Long Separation

During the long separations of World War II, people in my family had the habit of sending around handwritten circular letters over thousands of miles to keep each branch of the family in touch with the others. We called them "round-robin" letters. Trying to save valuable wartime paper, we sent them along from hand to hand to the next cousin or uncle after reading them. I vividly remember gathering around our dinner table and listening intently to these tattered letters that sometimes took weeks to make the circle.

We got news from or about my Uncle Ira in California studying at Berkeley, my aunt in Tennessee, and my cousin near Bastogne, who later was killed in the Battle of the Bulge. My mother's cousin was in a German prison camp where he painted scenes of his stalag with a brush made of his own hair. He survived. Once during the war we managed to scrape up enough gas ration stamps to bring most of the family together in Louisiana. Repeatedly we would coast down hills to save gas. Finally we met and saw our beloved cousins face-to-face.

Our current situation as confessing Christians in the mainline churches seems something like those memorable wartime attempts to communicate and these postwar family reunions. They have been struggling mightily in distant locales, but praying for each other, and sustaining each other in love. They have had only sporadic communication (between faithful Presbyterians, Methodists, Anglicans, etc.), often long-delayed, and usually fragmented. But they know they belong together.

This separation has dominated the confessing Christians of the mainline until their recent "family reunion." It happened in 2002, at Indianapolis, following decades of disconnection. Only then did they see each other face-to-face, feel the embrace, and experience the warmth of their family life together. They found that they had much to tell each other about their struggles and hopes, and much to learn from each other's stories. This is the situation of the confessing church today within the mainline.

Confessing Christians have been given the responsibility for speaking *to the church* in a time of its lost weekends, its amnesia. In speaking in their own voices, they have undertaken the special vocation of speaking *to* the contemporary church *for* the historic Christian *communio sanctorum* (communion of saints)—for classic, ecumenical Christianity, in a time when orthodox teaching has been neglected, despised, abused, discriminated against, and marginalized.

In this spirit, the sojourners gathered at Indianapolis were a cross section of orthodox and classic Christian believers of mainline Protestantism. How did they identify themselves? As "Evangelical, Confessing and Renewing Christians in the Mainline Churches of North America." They were learning that each one had more in common with believers in other mainline denominations than with skeptics in their own.

Revitalizing Ancient Ecumenical Teaching

Confessing Christians are united in calling for the vital recovery of ancient ecumenical teaching today. They are attempting to bring classic Christian teaching firmly back into mainline church leadership. They constitute living evidence that the Holy Spirit is calling this new reality—a new ecumenism—into being.

This new unity is appearing slowly but surely. It follows after the deterioration and collapse of the bureaucratic and ideological wanderings of the modern ecumenical churches of the last half century. Confessing Christians seek the recovery of doctrinal integrity throughout the mainline—in every church, within every intercession, through every gift, in every mission effort, and as the sure grounding for legitimate debates on public policy.

They are all engaged in similar struggles among their different churches for the recovery of theological integrity in their schools, congregations, boards, agencies, ministry, and leadership. They are seeking to learn from each other varied insights gathered from very distant quarters. This recovery is not a fantasy, but a palpable reality. This is happening. There is a thirst for truth-telling, and an end to evasion.

The Textual Evidence

In what lies ahead, we will gather a collection of confessional and teaching documents from numerous confessing and renewing movements, from their statements of faith and mission. Using these as a reference, the young leaders of the Confessing Theologians Commission have sought to bring together the core teaching of Confessing Christianity in a single statement. They have not created a consensus, but articulated an already existing consensus of mainline believers today. It reflects the worldwide classic consensus of believers of all times and places.

The heart of renewing and confessing Christianity remains committed to staying *within* the structures in which they now stand in order to transform them. They encourage confessing and renewing movements to remain steadfast, to hold firmly to their own baptism, with good conscience. They do not imply that leaving under any circumstances is by definition unthinkable. But in their common opinion, their own communions have not yet put them in the indefensible position of having falsely to deny the faith in order to preach the gospel. So they remain *in*.

The Emergence of a Deeper Ecumenism

As a result, the renewal and confessing movements constitute an emerging, potentially cohesive, ecumenical reality. They are no longer thinking of renewal simply within their denominational walls, without correlation with other communions. They are not making these statements to vent spleen, but to show their unity in the body of Christ, their ecumenical intent, its plausibility, and already emerging reality.

Ecumenical reality is no longer the private reserve of the *old ecumenical movement* (National and World Councils of Churches). Confessing Christians know that they are being offered the grace to address the churches of which they are a part, and to show resonances with other confessing Christians in our families of churches, who constitute a larger, more doctrinally sound, *new ecumenical movement*.

The declining twentieth-century ecumenical movement, having detached itself from the ancient ecumenical movement, must again become regrounded in apostolic authority and classic ecumenical wisdom. Only a new grounding in ancient ecumenical faith and moral teaching can avert and redirect the devastations of modern ecumenical leadership. Modern ecumenism rightly began in mission, but then lapsed into a merger mentality, then a defensive bureaucracy, and finally into unrepresentative forms of extreme politicization.

The new ecumenism (which is to say ancient orthodox ecumenism) is actively returning to the wellsprings of unity in apostolic truth and classic Christian teaching as basis for rebuilding. The mainline churches have given millions of dollars to an old, weak, failing form of confused liberal ecumenism. These worshipers are now asking how they can redirect their energies and gifts to more promising and grounded forms of Christian unity. A major practical objective of confessing Christianity is to detach their denominations from funding commitments to the organizational vestiges of the old ecumenism (WCC, NCC). These vestiges no longer have the moral authority to pretend to be the bearers of ecumenical teaching.

Confessing Christians are giving a larger voice to many previously disenfranchised and underrepresented evangelical and orthodox laypersons within the NCC member churches. Their pariah position is reversing dramatically. The Association for Church Renewal is the most evident instrument the Spirit has provided to reflect the views of the confessing and renewing movements within the mainline. The Confessing Theologians Commission of the Association for Church Renewal has answered their call. This study is one evidence of it.

5

Be Steadfast

Confessing Theologians Speak Out

The Association for Church Renewal is a coalition of chief executive officers from more than two dozen active renewing and confessing movements within mainline Protestantism. After years of planning, they have succeeded in bringing together the first national gathering of the grassroots membership groups of these movements. Together, these movements represent millions of orthodox and evangelical believers in constituencies of mainline denominations.

Distinguished young theologians were invited by the Association to speak to the confessing movements. They brought together leading young theologians from all these churches, especially those already well informed on church renewal issues and confessing movements, who have shown their resolution to speak out boldly even when there are strong social pressures to keep silent. Each Commission theologian has a demonstrated record of passionate and articulate engagement in the issues that actively occupy the renewing movements. Each has already provided useful counsel for confessing and renewing initiatives within their own communions.

In the following section they present seasonable counsel for the ecumenical phase of renewing movements. These theologians are well prepared to serve as biblical mentors for a unifying movement of renewal within all these churches. This is the first extensive effort to bring together leading theologians of mainline renewal groups along ecumenical lines. The gathering of these theologians has offered a valuable opportunity for the mainline faithful to receive biblical counsel and plan wisely for unfolding developments. The Confessing Theologians Commission was called together to advise these movements and their member organizations on theological integrity within mainline renewing movements. They represent widely varied renewal efforts within the mainline. Gathering at the invitation of Bishop James Stanton of the Episcopal Diocese of Dallas in September of 2002, they were asked to speak from the heart and from conscience in a way that is biblically informed while remaining grounded in their own confessional traditions.

The confessing theologians (whose formal confession is presented below) were asked to address three specifically targeted questions felt to be urgent issues in all mainline renewal movements. They were asked to provide reasoned arguments for (1) why believers are called to remain within mainline churches, so long as conscience allows, to renew and reground them; (2) why these renewing and confessing movements are now more than ever needed in the church today; (3) what the renewing and confessing movements can contribute to our society amid its present hazards and possibilities.

Their response is offered in the form of a pastoral letter. It seeks to guide study and prayer within these movements. Their report was addressed to the faithful of the renewing and confessing movements, not primarily to the press or to the culture. They were not trying to offer either sound bites to reporters, or grand programs for legislative action, but substantive theological reasoning for the grassroots lay-renewing movements. They sought to encourage renewal movements toward a realistic sense of confidence in the work of the Spirit, and to call upon the churches in our communions to make a deeper confession of their sins and their faith in Christ.

The ensuing letter sets forth key affirmations agreed upon by the Confessing Theologians Commission. Their discussion did not proceed by rules of parliamentary debate, but as a community of prayer and conviction seeking a consensus that would be serviceable to the churches. They sought to identify the doctrinal consensus that is currently consistent with the ancient *consensus of the faithful.* They intend modestly to express the underlying reasoning that is already present in the mainline confessing and renewing movements, not primarily their own individual opinions as such.

These eighteen confessing theologians are not risk-aversive. They teach in mainline seminaries, and many under adverse conditions. Each one has a steady record of courage under fire. This is an advocacy commission serving active renewing groups. Unwavering firmness of character and resolution has been required to speak up within these troubled communions. No theologian is serving in the confessing and renewing movements without cost, without professional risk of academic dismissal, or without social consequences.

Each of the confessing and renewing movements within the mainline has its own mission statement, and in most cases a confessional statement, newsletters, and publications. The eighteen theologians of the Commission represent renewing and confessing movements in eight mainline traditions: United Church of Canada, Episcopalian (ECUSA), Lutheran (ELCA), Presbyterian (PCUSA), United Methodist, American Baptist, United Church of Christ, and Disciples of Christ. No previous coordinating effort of this sort has been attempted either on the level of theological discourse or grassroots activity. They focused their attention on theological integrity within mainline Protestantism, but they voluntarily sought out consultative relationships with other orthodox theologians faithful to their traditions.

A Letter to Confessing Christians

A STATEMENT OF THE CONFESSING THEOLOGIANS COMMISSION OF THE ASSOCIATION FOR CHURCH RENEWAL

"Nevertheless, God's solid foundation stands firm, sealed with this inscription: 'The Lord knows those who are his,' and, 'Everyone who confesses the name of the Lord must turn away from wickedness.'" 2 Tim. 2:19 (NIV)

Sisters and brothers in the Lord:

God alone renews and continues to bless his people. God has not abandoned his church, and calls us to keep faith with him and those dear to him. We are called to be obedient to the faith once for all delivered to the saints.

In thanksgiving for God's promises fulfilled in Jesus Christ, we seek to humble ourselves before him, pray, seek his face, and turn from sin, that he may hear, forgive and heal. We all stand under divine judgment; we all are in need of divine grace.

We give thanks also for this, the first North American gathering of renewing and confessing movements. Your conveners have asked confessing theologians to address three urgent questions facing all mainline renewal movements.

Why should we remain in our churches?
Why do our churches need faithful confessors?
Why does our society need faithful Christian confessors?

1. WHY SHOULD WE REMAIN IN OUR CHURCHES?

The challenges facing our churches today are indeed immense. We have all seen declines in biblical and theological literacy, catechesis and spiritual formation. Our churches have experienced severe declines in numbers of congregations and in absolute numbers of members. We have also seen our churches rent by contentious argument, exhausted by never-ending conflict. Many grow weary, and wonder if they and their congregations should stay.

Our own experience speaks to this question, too. We have all passed through long seasons of anguish and travail, and we anticipate more. We are still here. The Holy Spirit has not abandoned our churches, neither will we.

Resignation, quietism and despair do not serve the church catholic and the communion of saints. We urge our brothers and sisters not to withdraw, but mutually to encourage one another in a struggle in which there is good hope. Our Lord reminds us, "God removes every branch in me that bears no fruit. Every branch that bears fruit, he prunes to make it bear more fruit" (John 15:2). We pray God give us courage, perseverance and mettle for the task.

Much work has been begun by the various renewal movements among our churches. We note with thanksgiving the revival of Bible study, renewed interest in evangelization, fresh seasons of prayer, and renewed concern with the plight of the poor. We have committed ourselves to the ongoing life of the churches in which God has placed us, and we pledge our best efforts as theologians of the church to those who are engaged in this divine work of reform and renewal.

It is a beginning, and must continue, commending ourselves and our denominational leadership to God with fear and trembling.

But ultimately the reason we cannot and must not leave our historic Christian communions is that the Gospel can still be freely proclaimed in them and the sacraments administered without hindrance. However true it may be that "other gospels" are also heard in our midst, none of our churches has legislated against the preaching of the Gospel of Jesus Christ. In such a situation it is unnecessary for congregations to turn their backs on their churches.

2. WHY DO OUR CHURCHES NEED FAITHFUL CONFESSORS?

Churches need faithful confessors for one essential reason: a church which is unable to confess its faith is a lame and withered church. The church needs faithful witnesses in order to be the church of Jesus Christ.

We believe that God's call to be faithful witnesses within the churches requires not only truthful confession, but also a long-term effort to reform our institutions. Our deliberative, legislative, administrative and educational structures in many instances do not faithfully serve the church's mission and pastoral obligations. The work and witness of faithful confessors helps to reclaim and redirect these institutions toward their proper ends. We therefore believe that confessing movements are necessary if the institutional forms of our churches are to be grounded in God's purposes for his church.

We note with joy how renewal movements in many churches have led to the discovery of a common bond in the faith of the church catholic and mutual encouragement in the Gospel. Across the renewal movements we rejoice in the recovery of sound doctrine, notably the doctrine of the Trinity, and the doctrine of the unique, saving significance of Christ's person and work. God has enabled many to recover their intellectual nerve.

God has also blessed our churches in other ways through the work of the renewal movements. In some quarters we see fresh vitality in worship and in preaching. In other quarters we witness new ventures in mission, the renewal of personal piety and an increase in enthusiastic discipleship. In still other places we see increased reading of Holy Scripture, deepened petitionary prayer, and a more profound embrace of God's concern for the poor.

God has given us a spirit of repentance and shed abroad his love afresh in our hearts. We expect further blessings in the years ahead, and we anticipate that God will continue to use renewal movements for the sustaining and furtherance of such blessings.

3. WHY DOES OUR SOCIETY NEED FAITHFUL CHRISTIAN CONFESSORS?

Faithful Christian witness humanizes society and heals the nations. St. Paul teaches, echoing Isaiah, "The root of Jesse shall come, the one who rises to rule the Gentiles; in him the Gentiles shall hope" (Rom. 15:12 NRSV). Confessing Christ requires the discipline of life, personal and corporate, private and public.

In the absence of faithful Christian witness, society establishes false idols. The twentieth century is littered with the victims of secular ideology. Nazi and Marxist ideologies produced Auschwitz and the Gulag. The North American threat comes from a more benign form of atheism that banishes Christian witness from the public square. Consumerism, materialism, individualism and hedonism rush in to fill the void. Dogmatic atheism brutalizes and destroys the church. The more benign and civil atheism seduces and marginalizes the church. Disoriented by the ideology of moral relativism, some church leaders haphazardly champion fashionable causes. In each case, the savior of the church and the light of Christ is lost.

In the mercy and power of God, a renewed church will reform life. Christian witness reminds government of its accountability to God and empowers the faithful to fulfill their duties as citizens. In teaching us to render to Caesar that which is Caesar's, the Christian Church supports space for political disagreement and debate. It endorses finite patriotism—loyalty without idolatry, criticism without cynicism. The Gospel champions the sanctity of human life, urging us to protect the weak, the vulnerable and the innocent. A robust faith teaches us that the fruits of our labor are a gift from God, to be used for the common good. Spiritual renewal engenders a right ordering of sexuality and family life. A confident orthodoxy fosters care for creation for its own sake and for the sake of human flourishing. Most importantly, even in times of great social crisis, the Lordship of Christ inspires a hope that will not despair.

In our zeal for justice, we must not confuse specific policy proposals for prophetic proclamation nor collapse the church into a chaplaincy for our favorite political party. Living in a powerful country, we must not exaggerate our ability to influence events for either good or ill. A renewed witness calls for appropriate humility, repentance, and self criticism.

These are our prayerful and considered responses to the questions that have been posed to us.

BE STEADFAST IN FAITH AND HUMILITY

We thank God for the hunger that he has placed in the hearts of people for reform and renewal, for clarity concerning the things of faith, for godly instruction and holiness in life. We rejoice in our work together for the faithfulness of Christ's church.

We know that along with God's great blessings in the work of the renewal movements come temptations to timidity, faithlessness, and presumption. Our work for renewal involves repentance and amendment of life as well as witness. The empowerment for our ministry comes from abiding in Christ the true vine, apart from whom we can do nothing.

Christ has told his disciples that persecutions will come, but as James reminds us we are to count it all joy when we meet various trials. In that joy, and confident of his great faithfulness, let us together proclaim the Gospel by which we have been saved.

May the grace of our Lord Jesus Christ and the love of God and the fellowship of the Holy Spirit be with you.

The following theologians have served as constituting members of the Confessing Theologians Commission:

Presbyterian (PCUSA): Diogenes Allen of Princeton Theological Seminary, Bruce McCormack, Princeton Theological Seminary, Roberta Hestenes of World Vision (formerly President of Eastern College), Mark Achtemeier of Dubuque Theological Seminary, and Andrew Purves of Pittsburgh Theological Seminary. **United Methodist**: William Abraham of Perkins School of Theology, Leicester Longden, Dubuque Theological Seminary, James V. Heidinger, Good News, President of the Association for Church Renewal, and Thomas C. Oden of Drew University School of Theology. **Episcopalian** (ECUSA): Bishop James Stanton, Diocese of Dallas, Philip Turner, former Dean of Berkeley Divinity School at Yale, Ephraim Radner of the Colorado diocese, and R. R. Reno of Creighton University. **United Church of Christ**: Donald Bloesch, Dubuque Theological Seminary. **Lutheran** (ELCA): Walter Sundberg of Luther Seminary, Russell Saltzman of Forum Letter, and Bruce Marshall, Perkins School of Theology. **American Baptists**: Scott Gibson of Gordon-Conwell Theological Seminary, and Donna Hailson, Eastern Baptist Theological Seminary. **United Church of Canada**: Victor Shepherd, Tyndale Seminary, Toronto. **Orthodox** consultant: James Kushiner of Touchstone.[1]

THE OTHER SIDE
OF THE
MAINSTREAM

The mainstream is the old ecumenism. We are visiting and describing the other side of the mainstream, which bears good news of a new ecumenism.

Mapping Our Way

To review where we have been, and where we are going: First we had to find our way back home to the scene of mainline Protestantism, observe what has been happening there, see and touch and smell the scene of the implosion. The next step ahead is to visit the surviving families in the neighborhood of the old mainline. From there we will go back to the old school ground where the coaches and teachers taught durable discipline and values. Then we come to a feast that draws all who love the place back together. And finally we venture into the examination of who owns the mortgage—the less pleasant arena of church discipline and judiciary bodies, and ultimately to the civil court where issues like disputed church property are being argued. So sink the boots firmly in the stirrups. The trip on the other side will be rough and rocky.

6

Redefining Ecumenism

The New Ecumenism

There are two contrasting ecumenisms, old and new. The old ecumenism is decisively wedded to the Geneva and the 475 Riverside Drive, New York establishments—the World Council of Churches (WCC) and the National Council of Churches (NCC). This is the familiar "old" ecumenical movement that everybody has known for fifty years. But there is today an emerging new ecumenism which, though embryonic, is yet sufficiently developed to be recognizable in its main features. These two views of the ecumenical reality have quite different commitments, interpretations, and manifestations.

The irony of the new ecumenism is that it is much older (by a millennium) than the "old twentieth-century ecumenism." The old (dying, modern) ecumenism has been intensively preoccupied with negotiating institutional structures seeking organic unity. The new ecumenism is seeking to restore and embody classic Christian truth within and beyond the old divisions.

The disappearing ecumenism is determined to create a unity by fudging Christian truth. The new ecumenism is determined to seek only a unity defined by truth. The new ecumenism has ancient ecumenical roots, which are proving to be ever more deep and vital than the political preoccupations of the old ecumenism with its decaying, modern roots. The ecumenical bureaucrats of the National Council of Churches are now struggling mightily with deficit spending and the threat of complete collapse. A new post-NCC ecumenism is already being shaped by the Spirit. Here is a brief glimpse of characteristic differences between the old and new ecumenisms:

The old (NCC) ecumenism is wary of ancient ecumenical teaching. The new ecumenism of orthodox confession is deliberately grounded in ancient ecumenical teaching. The vanishing ecumenism has a long record of accommodating modern biases. The new is critical of failed modern ideologies. The old is oriented mainly to Enlightenment assumptions, and the accomodative tradition following Schleiermacher. The new is constantly attentive to the word of Scripture, the wisdom of classic Christianity, and consensual conciliar teaching. The old ecumenism is fixated on manipulating and managing revolutionary pretenses. The new is patient amid historical turbulence, and does not pretend to be prepared to speak out loudly about every news alert. The old is trapped in outmoded revolutionary fantasies. The new has a gradual and organic view of historical change.

The old ecumenism is intensely preoccupied with ushering in rapid social change and itself being the foremost herald of that change. The new is keenly aware of sin's recalcitrance in all our pretensions about the heralding of radical social change. The old is ideologically drawn to the heirs of Marx, Freud, Darwin, and Nietzsche. The new is appalled at the colossal tragic consequences of Marx, Freud, Darwin, and Nietzsche. The old is bureaucratic stem to stern. The new is suspicious of top-heavy administration. The old looks at the world through a denominational lens that is preoccupied with defensive organizational structures. The new functions on the assumption that denominationalism is morose. The old is enamored with left-leaning, state-planning strategies and statist politics. The new is ready to make an articulate defense of a free and democratic society and a free market as instruments of social justice. The old has settled for a definition of unity characterized by shifting political alliances; the new experiences a unity already in Jesus Christ its head.

While the old bends every ecumenical effort toward negotiations leading to interinstitutional unity, the new ecumenism celebrates the real but imperfect unity that the faithful already have in Christ, based on classic Christian truth. The old is characterized by failure of nerve and is financially vexed by its lack of constituency support. The new is confident and growing in resources. The old is politics-driven; the new is Spirit-led. The old operates according to hierarchical business organization analogies; the new works by a nonhierarchical, grassroots encouragement of practical solutions on the ground, using a web-networking analogy. The old began in 1948 at Amsterdam. The new began in the council of Jerusalem, AD 46.

These patterns, not absolute distinctions but definable tendencies, overlap and interweave. They serve to point to characteristic differences of tone and trajectory.[1] The renewing and confessing movements give expression to this new ecumenical reality. The new ecumenism is not headquartered in any particular bureaucracy or establishment but is as diffuse as the uniting work of the Holy Spirit.

The Organic Union Fantasy

When the body of Christ is viewed as a matter of institutional merger or organizational fusion, everything depends upon human skills of negotiation. Too little attention is given to the Word of God as divine address. This bureaucratic union fantasy fosters a tragic diminution of the oneness of the body of Christ, which is found in shared faith, and shared participation in Christ's life.

The faithful are learning to resist this temptation. They do not thirst for the merger mirage. It is a limited and misleading illusion that tends to lead away from unity in Christ.

Rather what the Holy Spirit is doing in the world today is something very different from creating organic institutional unity through negotiation or strategic agreement or talk. The Spirit is eliciting faith. Faith is eliciting works of love. Those whose faith is active in love recognize each other as the family of God. This recognition is itself a gift of the Holy Spirit. While the old liberal ecumenists want to talk, talk, and talk some more, these believers want to experience behavior-transforming personal faith in Jesus Christ as Lord. Liberals want to find some way of negotiating toward outward unity of institutional entities. Believers have very little interest in this game of elitists and insiders.

Dialogue as an Instrument of Manipulation

The unity of believers can be achieved only on the basis of the truth. That truth is attested by the work of the Spirit. Our talk, however well intentioned, will not in itself suffice. Only the Spirit reveals the truth of our oneness in Christ. That oneness is recognized only by faith, not institutional manipulations. It is not talked into being or achieved on the basis of clever dialogue about that oneness, or by practical strategies for cooperation. That is not Christian unity. The unity of believers is found concretely in their here-and-now lively participation in the one body of Christ through faith. So dialogue on any other basis than the unique saving action of God in Jesus Christ, the authority of Scripture, and the consequent call to the holy life, is misdirected wheel-spinning.

The fantasy of achieving organic church unity through talk based on altruistic-humanistic dialogue has proven to be a chimerical dream. Claims to seek the visible unity of the body of Christ are often concealed efforts to frame the ecumenical task in terms of outward institutional coalescence, which evangelicals have repeatedly refused.

This is a hard learning that many of us who have been lifelong "ecumaniacs" have long resisted but gradually had to face: *Dialogue itself has often become an instrument of manipulation.* While dialogue based upon the truth of God's revelation is of the essence of Christian community, bare talk motivated by organizational merger is a diversion away from life together in Christ. This has been a reluctant empirical discovery of the confessing and renewing movements.

The liberal left always wants to dialogue, but typically with the intent of co-opting the faithful for political actions. Much time has been wasted seeking traction in this swamp. All parties have become worn out with dialogue. The partners shockingly missing in the supposed NCC dialogue are evangelicals in the mainline, especially those who do not easily pass politically left litmus tests (feminism, demythology, and leftist politics). The lowercase orthodox have had very rough sledding in modern ecumenism, even as have the uppercase Orthodox.

As a result, confessing evangelicals and orthodox Christians are less impressed by the promise of dialogue than by the promise of truth-forming faith through the Spirit. Dialogue and merger can become hidden traps of codependency. What the old liberal ecumenists seek, what they desperately yearn for, what they have a passion for, is the legitimization that appears to accompany what they call "organic unity." This is works-righteousness that appears to justify their existence. So if the WCC institution could be as embracing as possible (without any reference to sound doctrine), and as sprawling as the globe (but keeping at arm's length from evangelicals and traditionalists), and has the appearance of inclusiveness (however exclusive it may be), it appears to liberal eyes as if legitimized.

The desire underlying this ploy is the struggle for power and influence and public recognition, not gospel testimony to the whole needy world. Thus the old ecumenists have struggled desperately to achieve the mutual recognition of their leadership of their own demoralized institutions. They want institutional unity now, whether or not it manifests the living Christ. They want to congratulate themselves on having themselves achieved it, not receive it as a gift of the Spirit. This is just one more form of self-justification that they would have resisted if they had been more deeply grounded in Scripture. When they see that institutional union talks within Christianity are breaking down, they have a solution: expand the dialogue to include other religions.

The Premise of Moral Equivalence

The premise of moral equivalence is this: All viewpoints are presumed equally legitimate. This means all truth is relative. Everyone's view is equally weighted. The liar is given the same legitimacy as the truth-teller. That may seem truthful in the secular university, but it is not as applicable in the living body of Christ where the truth is valued more than falsehood, and where the truth is known to be revealed in history.

By means of this ploy, the faithful are often outflanked, baited, outtalked and often outvoted by the unfaithful or by the dubiously faithful, yet all in the name of a vague higher Christian unity. Permissive modern ecumenists no longer have an unquestioned right to present themselves with impunity as Christian believers when they are not. When any harebrained idea is considered equal in truth with God's revelation in history, then the integrity of faith itself is imperiled.

The result is a superficially democratic assumption that all views on any subject are of equal value. This absolute relativism is familiar to modernity but has been misnamed postmodernism. It is late in the day when a dying desperate ultramodernity gets the fanciful name of "postmodern." Sounds good? This is another deception of uncritical dialogue that wears the mask of scientific criticism.

In seeking to affirm the proximate value of all primitive cultures, egalitarian anthropologists have erred by placing excessive emphasis on the intrinsic value of each and every aspect of every culture. The implication is that all are morally equal. This is the premise of equivocation or "moral equivalence" that creeps into almost every ultramodern (or so-called postmodern) conversation. No one view or opinion has more to teach or learn than any other does. So they hesitate to judge Aztec or Punic infanticide as unworthy because it had a function in its culture. So there is nothing wrong with cannibalism, it is just different. Moral equivalence means that truth is given equal status with relativism. That view has entered so decisively into the ecumenical ethos, under the influence of misguided anthropologists like Margaret Mead, the iconic queen of the heyday of ecumenism, that it has become a normalizing assumption of ecumenical dialogue.

Should Unfaith Have the Same Legitimacy in Dialogue as Faith?

So should no voice be left out of the dialogue about what Christianity is? Answer: Those voices that do not know what Christianity is cannot rightly speak for Christianity.

Egalitarian argumentation says the contrary: So why shouldn't the Christian faithful sit down in dialogue with heretical Christians who are not faithful, and who intend to undermine the vitality of faith? Answer: Preserving the integrity of the truth is of higher value than the false pretense of premature agreement. Maintaining the continuity and integrity of the truth-telling community of faith is of greater weight than the false pretenses of "no offense" latitudinarianism.

When Dialogue Avoids Truth

Yet the old liberal ecumenical partners persist in coming to evangelicals and lowercase orthodox believers with a very dated call to dialogue. Now after all these years of demeaning evangelicals and classic orthodoxy, they finally seem ready to talk. About what? Their organization. Why? Because they see their own desperate efforts failing, while orthodox faithfulness is being blessed by the Spirit.

So now the liberals want to talk. But what they especially want to talk about is often little more than sociology and politics and strategy. This conclusion is drawn from long and tedious experience. They want to explore feelings, social location, comparative ideologies, quirky historical memories, personal stories of alienation, and narratives of social oppression. Thus the question of dialogue becomes shifted away from the truth of participation in Christ to some lengthy and chic sounding diversion. It is rare that they want to talk about how the living Truth, the risen Christ, unites believers. They do not often want passionately to be addressed by the living Word of God attested in Scripture, or hold their opinions radically accountable to that written Word. They are not inclined to ask how the truth of divine revelation impinges upon all their strategies and schemes. Classic Christian believers do not yearn for this sort of dialogue, but for the story of the divine-human dialogue that Scripture tells. They are ready to talk about how the Great Commission calls all believers to tell the whole truth of the gospel as revealed in Jesus Christ, and how the Spirit consequently creates unity through faith.

Lowercase orthodox believers are not seeking a debating society that would aspire to be a religious version of the United Nations. They do not see organic union as the final objective, especially if that objective is reduced to rhetorical evasion and organizational tinkering. What they want to see is the living confession of Jesus Christ transforming human, personal, and social experience. Wherever they see that, they know instantly from the heart their deep affinity with it. Wherever they don't hear that, they know inwardly how alien and distant are these temptations.

The seductions of dialogue typically draw believers toward subjective feelings, mutual congratulation, and institutional horse-trading. They thrive on negotiation or arbitration models of interaction. They thereby draw us far away from the truth that is declared in Jesus Christ in whom all believers are called to participate by faith. So it should not be surprising that classic Christian believers tend to regard undisciplined dialogue as a temptation.

It is undisciplined dialogue if not already ordered by the original apostolic witness. That requires taking the original witness with utter seriousness. It requires letting the text address us, rather than insisting that we ourselves are the judges of the authenticity of the text.

Confessing Christians have a long history of experience with the frustration and futility of such undisciplined dialogue not ordered under the written Word. It less often leads to the question of truth than to the question of how we "feel," and how we can accommodate or negotiate our competing interests. That is different from the question of the truth announced in the gospel, which alone engenders the unity of believers.

If the central question of Christian unity for classic Christian believers is the truth of the gospel, then the apostolic testimony made known in Jesus Christ is the first step toward unity. All other dialogue, however altruistic it may appear, is truly a diversion, a pretension of searching for truth, a ruse that substitutes narcissistic talk for integrity. What seems an innocent and generous invitation to dialogue actually amounts to a disposed predetermination to replace the truth question with what we "feel" about our own experience. In this way *dialogue becomes an instrument of manipulation* already shaped by wrong premises. Global orthodox believers seek unity in the truth, not unity apart from the truth, not unity as a substitute for the truth, but unity in the truth of the revealed Word.

Confessing Christianity in Public Life

There are two familiar, yet opposite charges that are frequently made against orthodox, evangelical, and classical Christian believers: that they are too *apolitical*, and that they are too *political*. Both charges typically come from highly opinionated political partisans.

First, the apolitical charge says that classical Christians privatize religion; they think only of personal salvation, not social change or public policy; by focusing on piety they neglect social process and justice. Second, the too-political charge says that classical Christians line up too easily with fascists and reactionaries who supposedly supply them with funding. Both charges are at a deeper level substantively the same: that classical Christians lack social conscience. Both charges are untrue.

Not only the words, but more so the deeds, of confessing Christians show otherwise. They have a clear record of giving more generously to relief work than do permissive secularists. They work harder at bread and soup lines. They spend more hours in prison ministry services. They are highly involved in acts of social responsibility, without being trapped exclusively in one party or another. Here is why:

The lodestar of confessing Christianity is the lordship of Christ over all of life. The faithful know that the classic Christian tradition has the most viable resources within failing modernity for rebuilding a just society. Believers understand that profound political implications abound in the orthodox Christian teaching:

> God alone is sovereign and worthy of worship.
>
> All persons are created in the image of God.
>
> Faith becomes active in love.
>
> Love is in search of public policy justice that proximately embodies God's love within the history of sin.
>
> The culture of death is contrary to the inestimable value God places upon life.
>
> Governments exist to guarantee freedom, not control it.

A church that faithfully proclaims and demonstrates these teachings will do much to sustain and spread democratic justice. All these are elementary and axiomatic for biblically informed, well-discipled believers. None of the above assertions is a partisan political position, but moral reasoning applied to public policy.

Nurturing Democratic Representation

Confessing Christians believe without apology that Western representative democracy needs to be regrounded in the best wisdom of classical Christianity. Among political systems of our time, representative democracy holds the most promise for a relatively just ordering of society. They are convinced that the church best serves democracy by simply being the church, true to its own calling in Christ.

They are aware that even today, despite all efforts to defend it, the worldwide health of democracy is far from assured. They empathize with and pray for Christians the world over who are faced with life and death struggles amid tyrannical and idolatrous regimes.

When the gospel message is met with religious persecution, confessing Christians have stood in solidarity with persecuted fellow Christians far more willingly than the permissive secularists, who have repeatedly aligned themselves with the old Soviet and Castro regimes and even the so-called Patriotic Movement in China. Meanwhile confessing Christians have, in many parts of the world, become the foremost champions of the human rights of all persons. They are calling for a basic public policy realignment within their straying churches that is more consistent with truly caring for the actual poor and alienated (not with an ideology of alienation)—with those who have suffered long from statist ideological abuses.

Confessing Christians resist an excessive dependence upon the state to solve all problems. They have a serious doctrine of sin both in personal and social life. They spurn the cultivation of divisive class identity politics. They are convinced that the most serious threat to democratic freedom comes from the fragmentation of the family, which is central to God's purpose for the protection of children and the well-being of society. They resist an extreme emphasis on the autonomous individualism, automatic historical progress, and the elevation of private rights over public responsibilities. Confessing Christians contest all attempts to relegate religious and moral truths to the realm of the purely personal and private. They seek to offer scripturally grounded wisdom for addressing social problems, rather than demanding that the secular state solve all personal and social dilemmas.

A large part of humankind still lives under regimes that violate these convictions. They rob vast numbers of people of their basic human dignity. By binding their people in political shackles, they also make it more difficult for them to rise up from poverty. Hundreds of millions of believers now suffer persecution or restrictions in the exercise of their faith. Islamist fascism (as distinguished from true Islam) is a growing threat to freedom and human dignity. There are far more regimes in the world that resist democracy than enable it. Dictators still limit free expression of interests, control the press, and espouse overweening statism in the name of economic justice. The press has shamefully colluded with these cultural disasters. Evil forces roam the earth devouring the innocent.

Never has there been a greater need for strong churches to become a crucial component of civil society. North American churches are called to serve. Needed: a fresh, spirited breath of Christian energy that transforms both individuals and cultures. Yet tragically, important segments of the North American mainline are spiraling into deep decline as they retreat from this task. They are locked into political agendas mandated neither by Scripture nor by ecumenical tradition. They have thrown themselves into partisan or utopian crusades—pro-abortion politics, radical feminism, coercive state regulatory practices, desperate and frustrated antiglobalization activism, statist dependency politics, class warfare rhetoric, unscientific visions of environmentalism, and permissive sexual liberation. Where these well–intentioned causes have gone awry, they have inflicted serious damage upon both church and society. In pursuit of extreme and highly idiosyncratic political agendas, these supposedly "prophetic" church leaders have pursued unwise policies, alienated believers, undermined church structures of openness and accountability, lost support, and rendered their own ministries ineffective.

Patient Regrounding of Social Witness

The Holy Spirit is guiding the faithful to call their churches to responsible social policy and compassionate action. Confessing Christianity seeks to supply them with the teaching and discipline, information, ideas, and tools necessary for transforming their beloved churches. Until recently they have largely lacked both voice and a network of fellow believers committed to the same values. This is changing.

Increasingly, confessing Christians are seeking less to critique what is wrong than to uplift what is truthful and good, according to Christian wisdom, and to rally others to these gifts and tasks. Some serve the function of watchdog on behalf of believers in surveilling unwise, biased, and dysfunctional public policy. Others monitor the statements of church leaders and the programs of church agencies, especially when they abandon classic Christian teaching. They speak up with frankness whenever such programs and ideologies depart from Christian teachings, whenever they demean lay wisdom, and whenever they do social damage and cause harm.

Confessing Christians have, despite resistances from their judicatories, attempted to provide an accurate picture of what is going on in the mainline. This has required careful research, investigative journalism, candid analysis, and courage. This task has been undertaken with very little money or support, and that mostly from small donors. Reform efforts are focused especially on those mainline Protestant churches where the problems are most outrageous. They seek to unite reforming voices within the historic Christian communions. They assist delegates at national church meetings in understanding where critical issues are arising, in drafting potentially useful legislation, in framing arguments for debate, and in organizing the faithful for concerted and effective action.

The ripple effect of confessing Christianity spreads not only in and through the churches, but further into the larger society. It is a demonstrable historical fact that faithful believers in past centuries have brought great gifts to failing cultures. Churches re-rooted in the gospel message will bring to bear the Christian teachings that wisely enrich the quality of public life.

There are many difficult political questions that do not have a single or simple answer. On such matters, the church does well to remain open to a diversity of Christian views, keeping premature conclusions tentative and open to correction. Confessing Christians seek to encourage local churches that are actively proclaiming biblical teaching with authority, and holding their leaders accountable to their own biblical teaching standards to which they voluntarily consented in their ordination.

Churches under gospel discipline are renewing their commitment to the Great Commission taught by Jesus. They understand that Christianity intrinsically makes a universal appeal to all humanity. They know that the human aspiration for freedom is not restricted to Western societies. The gospel announces freedom for all captives everywhere, wherever the forces of guilt, sin, and death hold the human spirit in bondage.

Why a Confessing Movement?

"Confessing" implies both confessing human sin and confessing Jesus Christ as Lord. But some will argue that mainline Christianity already confesses sin every Sunday in common worship, and confesses Jesus Christ as Lord. Indeed many Protestant laypersons confess their sin and Christ's lordship daily from the heart. But this confession does not adequately find expression in governing councils or elite governing boards and politically oriented agencies, to which lay believers commit funds and support.

Confessing Christians have waited patiently for many years, even decades, for the mainline church leadership to take seriously their own solemn teaching office as assigned to them by their voluntary ordination. Now they are calling upon them to do this honestly and without any evasion. The churches have suffered from attempts to base Christian teaching on experience alone, or worse upon the modern experience alone, or upon class or gender identity alone, or particular political ideologies, as if apart from the instruction of the written Word. The mainline elite has become so fixated on friendly sentiment, hypertoleration, and superficial unity that it has tended to brush under the rug all norms except egalitarian political correctness. Much liberal leadership has become so narrowly politicized, and so out of touch with the lay constituency, that the faithful no longer can take at face value any of the facile promises of the leadership. There is serious doubt as to whether that leadership knows how, even if it desired to do so.

What will it take to transform the Protestant mainline into theological accountability? At the very minimum it will take a new seriousness about the Bible as the norm of Christian doctrine. This norm was central to Luther, Calvin, Cranmer, Wesley, and all the leading progenitors of the Protestant traditions. It is specified in the established doctrinal standards of all these church bodies. The theological method of orthodoxy is centered in Scripture, viewed in the light of the classical Christian tradition, made plausible through rational argument, and the experienced presence of God in our lives. The Protestant traditions of spiritual formation have historically offered disciplinary guidelines for engaging in this reflection of Scripture, utilizing the wisdom of the whole historic church tradition, under the guidance of sound reasoning.

7

The Deepening Tide of Confession

The place to look for vitality in confessing Christianity is the grass roots. You will not find it primarily in bureaucratic offices or legislative halls, but in modest Bible studies, small prayer groups, active food relief, soup and street ministries, and urgent-need missions. This chapter provides on-the-ground descriptions of laypeople caring about the church enough to embody its mission and seek its reform.

Grassroots movements of confessing Christians have formed in every nook and cranny of the mainline Protestant denominations. What follows is a sampling of the varieties of renewing and confessing movements currently active, now becoming more articulate and ecumenically coordinated. These movements are quietly and passionately at work. Their mission statements clearly define their politically transpartisan commitments, tenacity, and faithfulness.

The following inventory of grassroots activism is to my knowledge not available anywhere else. Only a sketchy outline is found in my book *The Rebirth of Orthodoxy*. Here I will explain further the social location of these movements within their communion's milieu. This will be useful especially for those who may recognize small pieces of the puzzle, but have had no opportunity to envision the whole, and for journalists altogether unfamiliar with evangelical Protestantism. It may also encourage isolated worshipers who at times feel quite abandoned in their lonely, local church identity struggles. The first focus is on transdenominational coordinating efforts, followed by denominational renewal efforts.

Confessing Movements Spanning the Mainline Denominations

The place to begin is with a description of confessing Christians working *interdenominationally*, transcending barriers, seeking coordinated accountability with other confessing Christians. These movements are not merely seeking to reform their own denomination, but to also connect realistically with reforming initiatives in other denominations. They are attempting to embody the unity of the body of Christ as ecumenically and consensually understood over all Christian centuries, not just in the present.

Most crucial for the coordination of mainline renewal movements is the *Association for Church Renewal*. It works to unite the efforts of some three dozen renewing and confessing movements in these historic churches related to the World Council of Churches. It constitutes the major nexus of orthodox and evangelical renewal leaders from mainline churches in North America. All are committed to realigning the mainline toward classic Christianity. It is composed of executive officers from these renewing and confessing movements, bringing them together and coordinating these movements.[1] The combined popular strength of these confessing movements is noteworthy, amounting to perhaps a million active participants, and several million interested sympathizers.

The physical location where most of the coordination takes place is in Washington DC, at the *Institute of Religion and Democracy*. It is an ecumenical alliance of North American Christians working to reform their churches' social witness in accord with biblical and historic Christian teachings, thereby contributing to the renewal of democratic society at home and abroad. Building on more than two decades of forthright advocacy, the Institute of Religion and Democracy is uniquely situated to gather together and synchronize the work of widely scattered movements.[2] It offers a cohesive vision for the church's contribution to democracy in a pluralistic society, along with practical programs and efforts to support that vision. It is playing a pivotal role in the new ecumenism as a movement for Christian unity in the service of Christian witness. The Institute publishes *Faith and Freedom* and sponsors the Ecumenical Coalition on Women and Society, as well as renewal initiatives among Anglicans, Presbyterians, Methodists, and Lutherans. Leading Catholic scholars (George Weigel, Michael Novak, Robert George, J. Budziszewski, Richard John Neuhaus) contribute significantly to the IRD leadership.

The journal that best gives voice to many aspects of the new ecumenism is *Touchstone*, a magazine of "mere Christianity," published by the Fellowship of St. James.[3] *Touchstone* is a Christian journal, conservative in doctrine and eclectic in content, with editors and readers from each of the three great arenas of Christendom—Protestant, Catholic, and Orthodox. The mission of the journal is to provide a place where Christians of various backgrounds can speak with one another on the basis of shared belief and the fundamental doctrines of the faith as revealed in Holy Scripture and summarized in the ancient creeds of the Church.

The Center for Catholic and Evangelical Theology is an ecumenical initiative that seeks to cultivate faithfulness to the gospel of Jesus Christ throughout the churches. It encourages theological inquiry that is at once catholic and evangelical, obedient to Holy Scripture and committed to the dogmatic, liturgical, ethical, and institutional continuity of the Church. Its use of the terms *catholic* and *evangelical* extends beyond both Roman Catholic and generic American evangelism, yet is respectful of both sides of that divide. The Center challenges the churches to claim their identity as members of the one, holy, catholic and apostolic Church. It affirms the Great Tradition and seeks to stimulate fresh thinking and passion for mission. To achieve this goal the Center sponsors projects, conferences, and publications. *Pro Ecclesia* is the superb journal of theology published by the Center.

The Center of Theological Inquiry encourages advanced research into the content and significance of Christian theology and its critical engagement with nontheological disciplines.

Religion and Public Life is an interreligious, nonpartisan research and education institute whose purpose is to advance a religiously informed public philosophy for the ordering of society. It does not correspond to the profile of what we are here calling confessing and renewing movements within mainline Protestantism, but under the leadership of Richard John Neuhaus, it has succeeded in bringing many leaders of confessing Christianity into a vital conversation with Catholic and Jewish leaders on points both of diversity and similarity.

A major arena where Reformed theologians converge is in the *Alliance of Confessing Evangelicals*, the publisher of *Modern Reformation*. They sponsor Reformed Theology Conferences and the radio ministry called *The White Horse Inn*, which provides "a forum for confessional theologians to discuss the possibilities, strategies, and proposals for a vigorous initiative in relating orthodoxy to contemporary challenges and opportunities."[4] Similarly, *Reformation and Revival Ministries* (publishing the *Reformation & Revival Journal*) seeks to encourage reformation in the local Christian churches worldwide. It aims to promote the cause of revival and spiritual awakening through prayer and the provision of resources to aid Christian leaders, standing in essential agreement with the confessional statements of historic Reformation theology.

A related initiative is the *Renewal Fellowship*,[5] whose mission is to create a network of individuals and congregations committed to the renewal of their local churches, defining a renewal church by these essentials: biblical teaching, Christian fellowship, worship, caring for needs, the empowerment of the Holy Spirit, and evangelism. Their journal is *RenewaLife*. The Fellowship serves as a transdenominational association of evangelicals seeking to restore the biblical roots of the Reformed, Congregational, Evangelical, and Christian heritages.[6]

Two transdenominational movements serve as ministries to those struggling with sexual identity. First, *Transforming Congregations* offers help to all persons affected by relational brokenness resulting in sexual sin.[7] Transforming Congregations is a movement among mainline denominational churches to affirm that those who deal with homosexual temptations are loved creatures of God, and that Christ can and does have power to change those who are trapped in unwanted sexual behavior patterns. They affirm the biblical position that God loves all persons, that homosexual practice is one sin among many, and that the Holy Spirit is available to transform all persons—including homosexual persons. They minister also to the families of those struggling with homosexuality, and all others affected by sexual identity struggles, as partners in Christ's work of healing. They call the church to recognize its need for repentance and healing of both its homophobic and its uncritical and uninformed responses. They seek to integrate all persons striving to live as faithful disciples of Jesus Christ into full membership in the local church.

Second, *Regeneration* is a biblically based, Christ-centered ministry helping men and women seeking to overcome homosexuality. They also work with individuals dealing with other forms of sexual brokenness, with family members, and with churches. Established in 1979, Regeneration is a part of the worldwide Exodus International network, a coalition of Christ-centered, biblically based ministries to homosexual persons. These ministries are equipped to help homosexual men and women seek healing, to minister to family members, and to help churches deal pastorally with homosexuality.[8] Regeneration Books is a part of the ministry established to make readily available the best Christian Books dealing with healing for homosexuality. This ministry strives to review all relevant books and to make the best available to the Christian reader. Their online resource center offers reference services on the Web.

Several websites provide excellent information on many of the varied renewal ministries within the mainline. One of the best is that of Christopher Hershman, a Lutheran pastor who watches mainline stories like a hawk, and distributes them through the net.[9]

All of the above efforts are ecumenical or cross-denominational expressions of confessional Christianity. Now we turn to brief thumbnail sketches of renewal movements that lodge within particular denominations.

Confessing Christians
in the United Church of Canada

The United Church of Canada is not imploding; it has already imploded. It's not as if it is awaiting a slow self-immolation—it is already well along that process. It is increasingly powerless to exercise discipline or authority within its own congregations. It is in deep trouble financially. Its membership losses are incredible. Although its growing churches are almost all evangelical, they are often treated as pariahs within the denominational offices.

But there is active ferment and hope within the United Church of Canada. Its own renewing groups view it as standing in the midst of its most serious crisis of identity and mission in its history. There are four major renewing movements within the United Church of Canada:

The purposes of the *Community of Concern*[10] are to promote within the United Church of Canada greater adherence to the Twenty Articles of Faith in the Basis of Union, understood in the light of the Apostles' and Nicene Creeds and their Reformed, Wesleyan, and Congregational heritage. They seek to encourage within the United Church a theological renewal grounded in the Scriptures, Christian tradition, and the Articles of Faith. They seek the biblical and theological wisdom requisite to speaking to society with a clear, consistent, informed voice on matters of public justice. They seek a continuing process of reform through which Jesus Christ is clearly confessed as Lord both in word and action, in accord with a balanced understanding of Scripture and in continuity with the tradition of both the Reformed Churches and the whole historic ecumenical church. They urgently seek more fairness in Canadian church decision-making processes. They seek the reform of theological colleges and church-related education, as well as United Church structures, procedures, and leadership. They help congregations to recover their historic Christian identity. The Community of Concern seeks the strengthening of family life and values among the membership of the Canadian churches, and to reawaken the recognition of the family as the fundamental unit of society and the key to its well-being. They are convinced that the biblical intent for healthy and fulfilled sexual relationships is loving fidelity within marriage and celibacy in singleness. They sponsor theological conferences in support of these objectives and seek to maintain worldwide contacts with other groups and organizations having similar concerns. They intend to pursue a positive and healing ministry throughout the Church, encouraging members and congregations to remain within the United Church, working to resolve conflicted issues. They provide financial, legal, and spiritual support for individual members, ministers, and congregations in their efforts to work within the church law of the United Church of Canada to achieve these objectives.

The distinctive mission of *Church Alive*,[11] a closely allied ministry within the United Church of Canada, is to make plausible a clear biblical witness to Jesus Christ crucified, risen, and exalted. It wants to encourage rigorous theological enquiry and discussion; to challenge doctrinal inadequacies; to encourage spiritual growth through prayer, Bible study, sacramental worship, and other means of grace; and to encourage a truly prophetic approach to contemporary culture. Their journal, *Fellowship Magazine*,[12] is cosponsored by the Community of Concern of the United Church of Canada, Church Alive, and the National Alliance of Covenanting Congregations of the United Church of Canada.

The National Alliance of Covenanting Congregations gathers local congregations of believers into a fellowship that sustains them in their respective ministries, and in their involvement in the legislative halls and courts of the church, where there is a need to "uphold historic Christian faith and traditional Christian morality."[13] They seek to gather clergy and church leaders together in fellowship and mutual support. They help congregations of the United Church of Canada make a public witness of beliefs affirmed by the majority of its members, and so hold its people together within the United Church of Canada with integrity.

The Evangelical Fellowship of Canada, which publishes *Faith Today*, is "committed to bringing Christians together for greater impact in mission, ministry and witness."[14] It exists to be a public advocate of the gospel of Jesus Christ, provide an evangelical identity that unites Canadian Christians of diverse backgrounds, express biblical views on the critical issues of the present, and to assist individuals and groups in proclaiming the gospel and advancing Christian values in the nation and around the world.

These are the major renewing and confessing movements within the mainline Canadian church except for Anglican and Lutheran movements addressed below. Now to movements based chiefly in the United States of America.

Implosion and Renewal
in the United Church of Christ

The United Church of Christ (UCC) is on the frontline of the ideological conflict that is affecting virtually every local church in the mainline. They are among the most beleaguered of the mainline denominations, burdened with faltering morale, diminishing congregations, church closures, property abandonment, and precipitous rates of membership decline. Many of the clergy (though not the laity as a whole) of the United Church of Christ are among the most liberal of the mainline denominations, though in many local instances moderate and conservative congregations do exist. On first glance it might seem hopeless to undertake major efforts at evangelical renewal or orthodox confession. Yet the UCC has very active renewal movements that have proved very effective and tenacious.

The six thousand historic UCC congregations often stand at the very center of their communities and are the historic founding churches of their towns and villages. The spiritual state of these congregations continues to shape the spiritual state of these communities. They are aware that no new church starting without the potential advantage of two centuries of community presence may be as capable of attesting God's presence as the church that has grown up with that village or city from its beginning. This is especially true in New England, where Congregational churches were founded as early as the 1600s in villages and town centers. There remains a faithful core of believing Christians in every local church. This indicates that the Holy Spirit has not abandoned these churches.

The Biblical Witness Fellowship describes itself as "a confessing church movement in the United Church of Christ." It publishes *The Witness*,[15] and sponsors Mission Renewal Network, which seeks to "mobilize missions among Churches serving Christ in the Evangelical, Reformed and Congregational Christian Heritage."[16] There are now more missionaries connected with the small donor-funded Missions Renewal Network ministry of the Biblical Witness Fellowship than there are part- and full-time missionaries funded by the entire UCC denomination. The Fellowship is capable of wisely assisting churches in the stay/leave decision, and in locating and placing godly pastors. The Fellowship has poignantly addressed the question of "why we stay," arguing that withdrawal amounts to dodging responsibility for the ensuing generations. They have remained faithful and confident in God's call to reformation and renewal within the United Church of Christ. The Fellowship especially criticizes the denomination's sexuality curriculum for having given religious dress and respectability to a pervasive political and ideological effort to sexualize the next generation of children, redefine marriage, and destabilize the family as the central unit of society.

Confessing Christ[17] is another quite different renewal initiative that works within the United Church of Christ to reassert the authority of Scripture, the centrality of Jesus Christ, the confession of ecumenical creeds, the Reformation confessions, and covenants, and to interpret them for people today. Its members observe an order for daily prayer, Scripture reading, and confession of faith, with intercession for persons who are suffering for their faith. Their website opens the door for conversation with many others who are coming to faith. Confessing Christ views itself as "centrist" in spirit, believing that the polarization between the "left" and the "right" in the church leaves out of account a vast silent center of clergy and laity who do not fit into polar categories. Their witness is first and foremost to Jesus Christ, the center, seeking to reclaim the centralities of Christian belief (the Trinity, the incarnation and the atonement, salvation) and to relate these convictions to pressing ethical issues, as well as to evangelism.[18]

Advancing Churches in Mission is "a movement committed to awakening and equipping the local church for accomplishing God's global purpose."[19] What began as the Fellowship of Charismatic Christians in the United Church of Christ is now called *Focus Renewal Ministries*,[20] long active in the coordinating efforts of the Association for Church Renewal.

Lutheran Confessional Movements

The Evangelical Lutheran Church of America (ELCA, as distinguished from other large Lutheran bodies such as the Missouri Synod) remains a member church of the National Council of Churches, but only ambivalently so. Underneath the surface very different sorts of movements seek to renew and reform the ELCA, and in some cases to resist uncritical liberal ecumenism. They do not share the same views on polity questions and ecumenical discussions, but all are basically committed to a deepening of classic Christian teaching within the Lutheran tradition.

The Confessional Lutheran Divide

Among the Lutherans (ELCA) there remains a widening gulf between confessional Lutherans and liberal Lutherans. Further, the renewing and confessing Lutherans are themselves deeply divided on liturgical and polity convictions. Some, such as those Lutherans active in the Center for Catholic and Evangelical Theology, are deeply invested in Lutheran-Catholic dialogue, while others, such as Word Alone, are fiercely resistant to the direction of those dialogues.

Major differences of opinion exist as to whether the future of organic ecumenism will be a sound or even marginally acceptable course for Lutheran churches. This has come to a head with the ongoing directions of the Lutheran-Catholic dialogue on justification, and in the Lutheran-Episcopal dialogue on ministry. The vision of organic visible union of the body of Christ, which ultimately implies merger of now-separated bodies, remains a sociological objective and outcome of this ecumenical vision. Opposed to this view, many conservative Lutherans have expressed serious resistance regarding two points in particular: First, the teaching of justification by faith—that is the article which virtually all Lutherans affirm, upon which the church stands or falls—has been obscured in the Joint Declaration of the Lutheran World Federation and the Roman Catholic church. Second, the notion of church government that takes the literal historic line of succession of bishops as a rigorous premise has been rejected by many confessional Lutherans.

Other issues cling like barnacles to the Lutheran ship, but these are the two most vexing. Both positions would agree, however, that the Achilles' heel of ELCA Lutheranism is liberal ecumenism gone wild: feminist, bureaucratic, and disconnected with the grass roots.

Varied Lutheran Renewing and Confessing Initiatives

The American Lutheran Publicity Bureau, established in 1914, is a nonprofit organization independent of official church control, linked by faith and confession to the church it serves. They publish a substantial journal, the *Lutheran Forum*.[21] They are committed to an understanding of Lutheran tradition as evangelical and catholic. They point to the church's scriptural and confessional foundations as the basis for fostering renewal not only within the present Evangelical Lutheran Church in America, Lutheran Church-Missouri Synod, and Evangelical Lutheran Church in Canada, but also Lutheran churches abroad and the wider ecumenical setting. They seek to make accessible the theological, liturgical, and devotional resources of their own confessional heritage within ecumenical dialogue.

Word Alone is a nationwide, grassroots Lutheran network of congregations and individuals committed to renewing the Evangelical Lutheran Church in America, in order that it may be fully grounded in God's Word and in the Lutheran confessions, and more truly centered on making disciples of Jesus Christ of all nations. The mission of Word Alone is to build an evangelical, confessional Lutheran future in America, not to spend Lutheran capital in organic church union dialogue. They seek to reform and restructure the church's polity so as to elicit more representative governance throughout the church with checks and balances on the authority of church-wide legislative and polity structures. Their current central concern is ordination, especially in the light of what they regard as a diminution of the universal priesthood of all believers.

Word Alone was preceded in its founding by *The Great Commission Network*,[22] which has sought to unite evangelical and confessional pastors, laity, institutions, and congregations of the Evangelical Lutheran Church of America into a network for the purpose of prayer, evangelism, global missions, and ministry by calling for a renewed commitment to biblical and confessional authority.[23]

They seek to encourage and support the leadership of ELCA in those ministries and programs that are faithful to the Church's biblical and confessional stance, but to speak out boldly on ministries and programs that stray from the historic biblical and confessional stance of the Lutheran faith. Their central purpose is to encourage Lutheran leaders, pastors, and laity to help fulfill the Great Commission. They have stated goals of evangelizing a minimum of one million new believers who will become disciples of Jesus Christ and active members of the Church by AD 2010. They hope to send out a minimum of five thousand missionaries by the year 2010 with the prime directive of making new disciples of Jesus Christ, to plant new churches, and to be partners in support with the existing churches throughout the world. They encourage hospice ministries in congregations to minister to those living with AIDS, cancer, and other life-threatening illness. They encourage opening their hearts, homes, and finances to refugees, the homeless, unwed mothers, and those victimized by rape, domestic abuse, and abortion. They have established a nationwide prayer network to help strengthen individuals and families in faith.

American Baptist Renewal Initiatives

Among renewal initiatives of American Baptists are the *American Baptist Evangelicals* (ABE) who are committed "to serve the renewal of American Baptist churches by building partnerships to serve, connect, nurture, and grow healthy congregations,"[24] as well as the pro-life American Baptist Friends of Life, and the *American Baptist Fellowship Newsletter*. American Baptist Evangelicals seek renewal within the American Baptist Church-USA, working actively to offer positive directions for the local, regional, and national church and for society. ABE members covenant to begin renewal within themselves and in their own churches; to stay informed as to denominational issues, and to act responsibly on them; to pray for their denomination, the American Baptist Church-USA; to affirm ABE's statement of faith; and to support ABE financially. Founded in 1992, the group has felt an urgent need to affirm scriptural authority, the uniqueness of Christ, and the centrality of the gospel, and to address polity and disciplinary issues among American Baptists. The movement has spread to almost every region in the United States. They desire to be used of God as a positive spiritual movement of reformation, renewal, and revival within their denomination. They strongly affirm the uniqueness of Christ, and stand against moral relativism. At the heart of their renewal movement is a deep concern to bring Christ, the gospel, and biblical authority to the center of Baptist life. They call for a return to the Word of God and the principle of *sola scriptura*. It is their intention to ground everything they believe, say, and do as a denomination in thoughtful, careful, prayerful submission to the Word of God under the guidance of the Holy Spirit. They commit themselves to pursue renewal in love, kindness, compassion, integrity, and humility. They express a concern for the truth, a commitment to listening and dialogue, and above all, a desire for God's will, reign, and glory. They describe themselves as a movement of prayer, believing that only God through the power of the Holy Spirit can bring about the genuine biblical and evangelical renewal they pursue. They recognize that there is and will be serious opposition to this kind of biblical and evangelical renewal. This resistance is found not only in believers themselves, but also in institutional recalcitrance, and in the evil spiritual forces that always seek to overturn God's work. They focus on the biblical calling for the people of God: worship, evangelism, discipleship, community, and mission.

Careful readers will note here the absence of discussion of renewing movements within the Christian Churches—Disciples of Christ. Many of the congregations formerly related to the *Disciples Renewal Fellowship* have pulled out of the communion. This means that the rapid decay of the liberal denomination's cohesion has left the task of renewal largely up to local and congregational initiatives without much national coordination. Thus there is as yet little evidence of a viable national movement to resist the Disciples' implosion, which is very far along, and some think, irreversible. While the congregational traditions may be less vulnerable to bureaucratic imperialism, they remain more vulnerable to anarchic forces.

8

....

Core Movements
of Confessing Christianity

The largest movements of renewal in North American Christianity are among the Anglicans, Presbyterians, and United Methodists.

The Anglican Implosion and Realignment

The most confusing and decisive implosion is found in the ordinarily calm and irenic Episcopal Church USA (ECUSA), the American branch of Anglicanism. Having recently elected an avowed homosexual bishop despite clear protests from the vast majority of world Anglican primates, the American denomination now faces the threat of official censure or at least ongoing disapproval from the world Anglican Communion. The word "Episcopal" has become so tainted in some quarters that confessing and renewing North American Anglicans are less likely to speak of themselves as Episcopalians and more likely to identify themselves as simply Anglican, so as to identify with the world Anglican majority and distance themselves from the American Episcopal minority.

How American Episcopalian Nonconformists Deserted Worldwide Anglican Tradition

The longstanding posture of Anglicans has been open, nonjudgmental, and accepting. Lacking clergy discipline, the undisciplined have dug for themselves a deep hole.

The implosive divisions within the Episcopal Church USA are easier to describe because the crisis is radically focused on an absolutely clear dilemma: the Episcopal ordination of a divorced man who has "come out" as an openly declared homosexual. Most worldwide Anglicans, however, view the legitimization of homosexual unions as a denial of classical Christian teaching on sexuality. They point particularly to Jesus's teaching that one man and one woman are called to live in a covenant of sexual fidelity. This is the pattern of sexuality created and blessed by God and honoring to the holiness of God.

More than half of the Anglicans in the world live in Africa and Asia where evangelical faith is strong. Only a small minority of Anglicans live in North America. But their wealth tempts them to presume they still have legitimate control and buyout power over the organizational apparatus of the entire worldwide Anglican Communion. This leverage is suddenly without authority and prestige. The crisis has been focused on the presiding Episcopal bishop, Frank Griswold, long prominent among "gay" cause advocates, and even the Archbishop of Canterbury himself has a controversial record of gay-friendly symbolic actions.

The Schismatics Are Those Who Abandon the Faith, Not the Faithful

The result is the real possibility of tearing apart the Anglican Communion. This would not be a split between the withdrawing faithful and remaining unfaithful, but rather the steadfast faithful refusing sacramental fellowship with a self-censuring minority, while yet seeking penitent reconciliation where conscionable.

So the Diocese of New Hampshire, where a willful sexual revisionist was noncanonically elected bishop, risks now being censured by the worldwide communion as openly schismatic. If the Episcopal Church USA (ECUSA) leadership had not publicly confirmed V. Gene Robinson's election as if it were legitimate, it would not be so blatantly in default of the confidence of the wider world communion. But ECUSA has thus far acted defiantly to offend the vast majority of the worldwide Anglican faithful and bypass their repeated admonitions.

This is a heavy-laden decision that will influence the direction of other confessing movements. It is important to establish clearly that the permissive sexual revisionists are the ones breaking away from the Anglican Communion, not those who remain faithful to Anglican teaching. The schismatics are those who have rejected the ecumenical Christian teaching of creation, the sacrament of baptism, the marriage vows, and two thousand years of tested, traditional sexual morality.

It must not be concluded that the schismatic partisans are the traditional Christians. Such conclusions by the popular press must be challenged at every point they are asserted. Schism is caused by arbitrary acts of rejection of the unity and holiness and peace of the church. The defenders of classical Christian teaching are the valid recipients of the apostolic tradition, holding firmly to the *consensus fidelium*. Those who do not hold to that firm consensus may become hell-bent on schism, and some do not mind seeing the church split wide open on the single issue of libertarian sexuality.

It is necessary now to put the moral spotlight on precisely who would be responsible for such a schism before it becomes irreparable. The case is confused by the fact that the sexual schismatics are so often portrayed by a biased liberal press as if they were the true faithful, while the churches, dioceses, and congregations who are steadfastly faithful to the apostolic tradition are portrayed as if they were breaking away or causing the schism. That is precisely wrong, both from the viewpoint of Anglican canon law and classical Christian teaching. It is a press ethics scandal to falsely portray the conflict as if the faithful were the schismatics. This twisted spin pervades far too much reportage. Yet there are few signs of willingness in the press to amend its biases or correct its unfairness. This is an issue of journalistic integrity: editorial opinion is being reported as fact. The fairness of the press is tarnished.

The Anglicans of Africa and Asia are the burr in the saddle of modern liberal North American Episcopalian revisionists. Worldwide Anglicans have not and will not welcome the revisionists back into the fold without repentance. The Anglican primates of the majority South are no longer willing to suffer fools gladly. The fools in this case are national leaders who have colluded with the foolishness of the New Hampshire diocese in confirming their folly. According to canon law they can be welcomed back to the communion without being formally excommunicated if they show evidence of repentance.

This crisis has reverberations at every level of Anglican life. Whether it will require the discipline of the revisionist bishops or dioceses is yet to be seen. It risks causing the censure of the American liberals by the world communion. But that act of discipline need not be a church schism but a measured act of firm but gentle discipline seeking repentance and reconciliation. Yet some appear determined to choose their own way (*haeresis*), their own self-assertive view over against the historic Christian consensus. The Greek word means to willfully go your own way despite instruction and admonition. The need for discipline of *haeresis* is being felt in all quarters of the imploding mainline, whether in cases like Beth Stroud of the United Methodist Church, John Shelby Spong of the Episcopal Church, or the Presbyterian advocates of live-baby, partial-birth abortions.

The Eames Commission appointed by the Archbishop of Canterbury recommended an apology by the ECUSA for its unilateral action in elevating Robinson, a moratorium on electing more gay bishops, and called for the Episcopal bishops who participated in Robinson's confirmation to withdraw from Anglican Communion functions unless they apologize.

The latest development to be reported at this date is the Nassau conference held July 6–8, 2005, which gathered dozens of leaders from across North and South America and the Caribbean to announce the formation of a new body committed to the historic Anglican faith and formularies. Inspired by the effective witness of the Council of Anglican Provinces of Africa (CAPA), Archbishops Drexel Gomez and Gregory Venables, Presiding Bishop of the Southern Cone (South America), the Right Reverend Robert W. Duncan, Moderator, Anglican Communion Network, and the Right Reverend Donald F. Harvey, Moderator, Anglican Network in Canada, announced plans for the formation of the Council of Anglican Provinces of the Americas and Caribbean (CAPAC).

Whence Anglican Renewal?

Although the confessing and renewing movements within the Episcopal Church were active long before this crisis, they have become mobilized by it as never before. There have been active organizations and initiatives in the ECUSA that have been urging the restoration of classic Christian teaching long before the recent focus on sexuality.

Prominent among North American Anglican renewal movements is the *American Anglican Council* (AAC), which publishes *Encompass*, "to fulfill the Great Commission through mission, proclaim the biblical and orthodox faith, transform the Episcopal Church from within."[1] The American Anglican Council is a network of individuals, parishes, specialized ministries, and Episcopal bishops who affirm biblical authority and Anglican orthodoxy within the Episcopal Church. They covenant to strengthen people of biblical faith, who stand together amidst the challenges of contemporary culture and false teachings within the church. They seek to provide for the recruitment, formation, and deployment of a new generation of church leaders and to make the Great Commission (Matt. 28:18–20) the measure of every aspect of the church's life.

An earlier and corollary effort, *Episcopalians United*, has for years sustained a network of concerned individuals and groups, providing educational resources, encouraging spiritual growth, and influencing decisions of the church—all through concerted prayer, Bible study, seminars and conferences, publications, and the work of local chapters. They stress a willingness to seize the initiative rather than merely react.[2]

Concerned Clergy and Laity of the Episcopal Church (CCLEC) invite all believers to join in restoring the pure faith of Christ in their church and seek to return the Episcopal Church to its historic foundations. They are keenly aware that the attack on the foundational doctrines of Christianity is coming not from the external secular culture, but precisely from within their own church. Their mission is to turn the hearts of the faithful toward the Word.

SEAD stands for *Scholarly Engagement with Anglican Doctrine*, which brings together Anglican biblical scholars, historians, theologians, ethicists, and church leaders who are committed to bringing their church closer to the Anglican tradition, and to classical Christianity. They have assembled leading scholarly voices from both North America and the United Kingdom to take more seriously the patristic and confessional commitments of Anglican life. Also, the signers and supporters of the Baltimore Declaration,[3] and the contributors to Mission and Ministry,[4] are to be numbered among key renewing influences in the Episcopal Church USA. There are also a number of highly effective mission and renewal efforts such as South American Mission Society, and NOEL, the National Organization of Episcopalians for Life, publishing *NOELNews.*[5]

The *Anglican Mission in America* (AMiA) seeks to develop an alternate American Anglican province, led by Missionary Bishops of the Province of Rwanda, Charles H. Murphy III, and John H. Rodgers. Their consecration as bishops was confirmed by two Anglican primates in Singapore. It is held accordingly that there are two Provinces of the Anglican Communion in the USA—the present ECUSA, and the new American Anglican Province (exiles from the ECUSA).

Presbyterian Confessing and Renewing Initiatives

Numerically the largest renewing and confessing movements are found among the Presbyterians and Methodists. Struggling against heavy opposition only a few years ago, they both have gained increasing voice and influence, have had decisive legislative achievements, and have won highly contested confrontations.

The reverberations of the Presbyterian leadership implosion are being heard at all levels of church life. Each time the General Assembly meets to hear controversial reports of extended and expensive studies on fiscal responsibility, ecumenism, marriage and family, and social witness, the implosion goes deeper. Presbyterians have had a fixation on repeatedly funding painful, unresolvable, poorly represented, and tendentious studies that intensify division. The ricocheting sounds of the implosion are most pronounced in the denominational headquarters in Louisville, but their consequences echo throughout all their synods. The general will is sorely tested every time the liberal leadership wants something that must be approved by the synods, and overconfidently thinks they can get it. The synods have a way of repeatedly overturning the most determined efforts of the left-leaning bureaucratic consensus.

The power of the pocketbook revolution is better seen in the Presbyterian Church USA than anywhere else. The laity have learned simply to refuse to support financially the programs that deeply offend the conscience of evangelical and traditional and orthodox Christians. The result has been costly for the judicatory leadership, both in attempted programming and in funding. Here are nine of the major voices of Presbyterian renewing and confessing movements:

The Struggle for Renewal in the Presbyterian Church USA

First, *The Confessing Church Movement* was founded only in 2002 but its growth and influence have been exponential. This grassroots renewal began with a Pennsylvania local church making this straightforward affirmation: "Jesus Christ alone is Lord of all and the way of salvation; Holy Scripture is the triune God's revealed Word, the Church's only infallible rule of faith and practice; God's people are called to holiness in all aspects of life. This includes honoring the sanctity of marriage between a man and a woman, the only relationship within which sexual activity is appropriate."[6] On this guileless foundation a spontaneous movement has emerged that now encompasses 1,310 congregations with a total membership of more than 430,000.

Second, *Presbyterian Action* provides a rigorous critique of the public policy decisions made by the agencies of the Presbyterian Church USA. Presbyterian Action for Faith and Freedom publishes *Presbyterian Action Briefing*.[7] Its focus is on the church's social witness, respecting democracy, and economic freedom. Presbyterian Action defends and promotes biblical values within the Presbyterian Church USA, encouraging a Presbyterian social witness that is more clearly centered on basic biblical teachings. It seeks a public witness that is more consistently derived from an open process by which church members discern how those biblical teachings apply to social witness, and how they might be more fully expressed in the lives of the 2.6 million Presbyterian members. Presbyterian Action challenges national church pronouncements when they are unbiblical, unwise, or unbalanced. Their conviction is that the most powerful social witness of Christianity is simply the gospel of Jesus Christ, and not a partisan political agenda. Presbyterian Action speaks out forthrightly at the General Assembly for the many Presbyterians who feel excluded by the previously dominant activist circles of the left. Presbyterian Action sees itself as part of a larger movement of renewal, and is affiliated with the Institute on Religion and Democracy, an ecumenical think tank in Washington DC that seeks similar goals in other denominations.

Third, whether the discipline of the Louisville bureaucracy is possible is still felt as dubious among many Presbyterians. The nemesis of Presbyterian institutional centrists is a journal called *The Layman*, a lay publication of a lay movement not under the control of any synod or judicatory. The most thorough investigative journalism in the renewing movements is found in this journal, which reaches stunning numbers of laypeople. *The Layman* reports stories that are ignored and barely mentionable within the halls of the bureaucracy. It is an unrelenting thorn in the side of the establishment. *The Presbyterian Lay Committee* sends the Presbyterian Layman newspaper to about a half million persons. They urge that official church bodies refrain from issuing pronouncements or taking actions unless the authority to speak and act is biblical, the competence of the church body has been constitutionally established, and all viewpoints have been fairly considered.[8] They have been working within the Presbyterian Church since 1965 to put greater emphasis on the teaching of the Bible as the authoritative Word of God in their seminaries and churches. Their mission is to inform and equip God's people by proclaiming Jesus Christ alone as the Way of salvation, the Truth of God's Word, and the Life of discipleship. They emphasize the need for presenting Jesus Christ as the Lord and Savior through preaching, teaching, and witnessing with evangelical zeal. They stress the need for substantive Bible study and a life of prayer. They encourage individual Presbyterians to take their place in the public square, as led by the Holy Spirit, speaking out thoughtfully on social, economic, and political affairs as believing Christian citizens. They provide some of the most pertinent and reliable information on significant issues confronting the church, including those being proposed for consideration at General Assembly or other governing bodies, to enable Presbyterians and others in the Reformed family of faith to express informed reasoning.

Fourth, *Presbyterians for Faith, Family, and Ministry* is a ministry of Presbyterian women and men, clergy and laity who believe that *Theology Matters* (the name of their journal) and that what people believe has consequences. They are working to restore the strength and integrity of the witness of the Presbyterian Church USA to Jesus Christ as the only Lord and Savior, and by helping individual Presbyterians develop a consistent Reformed Christian worldview. They are committed to the restoration of Reformed theology as taught in Scripture and expressed in the Confessions. They demonstrate their commitment to the doctrines of Reformed Christianity by contrasting them with false teachings and distorted worldviews. They regard the primary attack on Christian faith today as that coming from the church's own willful accommodation to the false religion of secularist ideologies, including New Age, neopagan, and Wiccan teachings. They live under the conviction that a responsible Christian understanding of family and ministry can grow only out of a faith in Jesus Christ that is based on Scripture and the Confessions and is free of compromise with false ideologies.

Fifth, *Presbyterians for Renewal* believe the Lord has called them to serve in the renewal of their historic communion. While they criticize the larger church and call for change, they recognize that they are bound by their vows as well as their love of the church to work and minister in and through the given structures of the existing church's governing bodies, disciplines, and rules. As a special organization within the Presbyterian Church USA, they are committed first and foremost to ordering their lives and mission under the lordship of Jesus Christ. They have sought to encourage participation at every level of the church's life as faithful members and presbyters under the lordship of Jesus Christ. They seek to be supportive rather than critical; to be advisory rather than adversarial; to encourage rather than undermine support of Presbyterians for the national church; to work within or beside the national structure rather than working around it; and to work within the theological and organizational tensions of the denomination in a manner that helps others discern the nature of faithfulness to the historic Reformed faith. Since its inception in 1989, Presbyterians for Renewal has understood itself to be an organization that desires to serve the church rather than run it, to be a partner in the life and mission of the PCUSA rather than play the role of loyal opposition. Presbyterians for Renewal publish *ReNEWS*.[9] As followers of Jesus Christ, seeking to conform their lives and beliefs to the Word of God, their mission is to participate in God's renewing, transforming work in the Presbyterian Church USA. They describe their key values as "*obedience*: submitted to the Lordship of Jesus Christ; *faithfulness*: anchored in God's Word and the historic Reformed faith; *conviction*: passionate about shaping the church's life and theology; *engagement*: involved positively in the structure and politics of the PCUSA; *collaboration*: working with others who share their mission and vision; *servanthood*: committed to ministry that reflects the graciousness of Christ; and *prayer*: depending upon God's direction and power." Their vision is of a Presbyterian Church

that boldly proclaims Jesus Christ the incarnate Son of God and the only Savior and Lord of the world;

that confidently relies upon Scripture as the authority for our faith and life;

that effectively equips disciples to live abundantly in Christ;

that intentionally develops godly leaders for future generations;

that consistently supports congregations as the primary agents of God's mission in the world;

that willingly relies upon healthy governing bodies for accountability, mutual encouragement, and shared witness;

that courageously embraces action for social justice and evangelism as essential dimensions of their primary task, to proclaim the Good News;

and that faithfully lives with holy abandon in the power of the Holy Spirit, willing to risk all and serve all in order to show the love of Christ to all.

Sixth, *The Network of Presbyterian Women in Leadership* is sponsored by Presbyterians for Renewal. It offers resources, publications, and conferences for clergy and nonclergy women who are leading congregations, study groups, committees, Sunday school classes, and other programs. They sponsor a seminary ministry that combines a theological journal, campus visits, an annual Seminarians Conference, doctoral fellowships, email networking, and other resources for encouraging students and professors who share their renewal mission, values, and vision statements. They sponsor a youth ministry that seeks to introduce young people to Jesus Christ and help them become faithful disciples. They pursue this goal through camps and conferences, mission trips, and a variety of other programs, as indicated in the events reported in the Youth Ministry website.

Seventh, *Presbyterians Pro-Life* is the major prolife witness in the PCUSA. They publish *Presbyterians Pro-Life News.*[10] Sanctity of life concerns are among the highest priorities of virtually all renewal and confessing movements. This priority stands in the face of much of the established denominations' bureaucratic leadership, which has often supported abortion on demand and live-birth abortions, much to the consternation of many believers. Presbyterians Pro-Life seeks to be a prophetic witness to Presbyterians in upholding the sacred value of human life and the family. They have been forced to speak out to counter supposed official Presbyterian endorsements of NARAL, the National Abortion and Reproductive Rights Action League, whose hard-line abortion advocacy has made it necessary for the faithful to respond. Scriptural teaching requires the church to be committed to protecting the right to life of every human being from the moment of conception to the moment of natural death. In decisions about life and death, the sanctity of life of both mother and child must be respected, and every effort to preserve life must be made. They struggle for the culture of life and against abortion, infanticide, euthanasia, and any other practices that would devalue human life. They argue that the biblical teaching of the family is essential to recovering respect for the sacred value of individual human lives. God has ordained the family, the basic social unit of all human institutions, to propagate, protect, and nurture human life.

Eighth, there is a constellation of ministries called The Presbyterian Coalition, whose executive director is Terry Schlossberg in Washington DC, composed of sixteen renewal partner organizations, some of which have already been noted above. Information on the full list of these partner organizations can be found on their website.[11] It includes Evangelical Pastors Fellowship, Knox Fellowship, Literacy and Evangelism International, OneByOne, Prespyterian-Reformed Ministries International, Presbyterian Center for Mission Studies, Prespyterian Elders in Prayer, Presbyterian Forum, Presbyterian Frontier Fellowship, and Voices of Orthodox Women.

Finally, the New Wineskins Initiative has had an explosive beginning, bringing together more than five hundred leaders to their first convocation in Edina, Minnesota, in June of 2005. They include world Presbyterian church leaders from East Africa, Egypt, and South America, where churches are growing by leaps and bounds, yet who seek to "stop the infection" of the North American Presbyterian Churches on ordination standards and scriptural authority. Three "breaking points" would be the repeal of the fidelity-chastity ordination standard, or the removal of the Authoritative Interpretation that undergirds that standard, or a dilution of Christology. Plan A would be to convince the 2006 General Assembly to move for a bottom-to-top transformation, theologically, ethically, and bureaucratically. Plan B could eventually trigger pulling out of the PCUSA.[12] Confessing and Renewing Movements among Presbyterians are increasingly emboldened, active, and growing at this time of publication.

United Methodist Confessing and Renewing Movements

The Vehicles of United Methodist Renewal

The largest grassroots renewing movements in the mainline are within the United Methodist Church. The Methodists have more than two dozen renewing organizations that have provided a loyal opposition and a shadow-cabinet function within the hollow, deteriorating bureaucracy of liberal Methodism. There is an alternate Mission Society. There are alternate church school education and discipling materials, and even alternate seminaries. There are alternative efforts in social witness. And there is emerging within these renewing and confessing church movements a vision for the future.

Good News is the senior renewing movement within United Methodism. It describes itself as "A Forum for Scriptural Christianity Within the United Methodist Church." It publishes *Good News—The Magazine for United Methodist Renewal*, which has a large number of faithful subscribers and supporters.[13] The Good News movement is a voice for repentance, an agent for reform, and a catalyst for renewal within the United Methodist Church.

They seek, by God's grace, to proclaim and demonstrate the power and effectiveness of historic Christianity as emphasized in Wesleyan doctrine and practice. Scriptural Christianity in this tradition requires disciplines for holy living. They nurture evangelical fellowship within a worshiping, caring, and inclusive community. They seek diligently to be faithful and challenge unfairness wherever it is found in the church, to inform and educate United Methodists about issues challenging the church, and to assist in creating alternative church structures if necessary. Its goals are to encourage evangelicals to witness effectively for Christ within United Methodism, to proclaim biblical truths, to sound the alarm about unbiblical ideologies seeking to take charge, to seek honesty in the administration of discipline that is grounded in classic and contemporary church consensus, and to provide much needed fellowship among often-isolated evangelicals within their congregations and conferences.

The *Renew Network* is a ministry to and for women spawned by Good News, that seeks the reformation and renewal of United Methodist Women. The Network publishes the *Renew* newsletter.[14] They provide a lively network for renewal: to encourage women to establish and maintain a growing, intimate, personal, and vital relationship with Jesus Christ; to help provide a firm scriptural foundation for discernment in their faith; and to encourage, equip, and impassion them for discipleship and witness in family, church, community, and the world. They exist as a ministry to and with women of the United Methodist Church. They serve as a concerted voice seeking reform of and accountability from the well-funded and highly politicized Women's Division, the official women's organization of the United Methodist Church. They provide a support network for evangelical, orthodox women within the church, a voice for their concerns, supplemental resources for their program needs, and a place for them to share ministry with other women.

The Confessing Movement Within the United Methodist Church, which began modestly with 92 church leaders in 1994, convened by the late bishop William R. Cannon, theologian Maxie Dunnam, and this writer, now has a constituency of over six hundred fifty thousand, including more than three thousand Confessing Churches. "Confessing Jesus Christ as Son, Savior, and Lord, the Confessing Movement exists to enable the United Methodist Church to retrieve its classical doctrinal identity, and to live it out as disciples of Jesus Christ." They publish *We Confess*.[15] The purpose of the Confessing Movement is to call The United Methodist Church, all its laity and clergy, to confess the person, work, and reign of Jesus Christ. From the outset there has been a strongly declared and firmly held conviction to stay within the United Methodist Church. The Confessing Movement Within the United Methodist Church is still deeply committed to reforming rather than to leaving United Methodism. There is a strong determination not to leave imploding liberalism to its own self-destructive devices, but to reclaim its institutions, its libraries, its seminaries, its episcopal order, and even its way-ward bureaucracy for the purpose for which that bureaucracy was created, namely the Great Commission—proclamation of Jesus Christ and the life of service and holiness that emerges out of that proclamation.

Here are other evidences of active renewal and confessing movements within United Methodism: *The Taskforce of United Methodists on Abortion and Sexuality* is the prolife witness among the Methodists. They publish *Lifewatch*.[16] *Bristol House* is an alternative publishing operation that pub-lishes the popular series "We Believe" and other curriculum materials for the renewing and confessing churches.[17] *The Mission Society for United Methodists*[18] funnels resources to preaching and compassion ministries all over the world, far more extensively than the well-funded General Board of Global Ministries. The *John Wesley Fellows* is a scholarly society that seeks to support Ph.D. education in premier world universities for young evangelical scholars in the United Methodist Church who are committed to its doctrinal standards and to integrity in theological education.[19] *The United Methodist Renewal Generation* publishes Josiah Journal.[20] *Aldersgate Fellowship* holds conferences and publishes a newsletter. *Concerned Methodists* publish *The Christian Methodist*.[21] *The Foundation for Evangelism*[22] publishes *Forward* and funds evangelical chairs in United Methodist theological schools.

United Methodist Action is engaged in active advocacy and investigative journalism in defense of traditional Christian beliefs and social witness in the spirit of John Wesley. UM Action goes to church agency meetings, studies church publications, and interviews church officials, publishing its findings in news publications as well as in its own *UM Action Briefing*.[23] The *Briefing* not only provides reports of good and bad official policy and fund-ing decisions that affect United Methodists, but also recommends specific action items to elicit positive change and reform. Their Reform Agenda for United Methodists outlines specific proposals for the Reform of the United Methodist Church. UM Action, like Presbyterian Layman, is providing oth-erwise unavailable information, undisclosed in the official denominational bureaucracies and publications.

Among all these renewing and confessing groups, many came together to form Coalition 2000 at the quadrennial General Conference, which re-appeared in the 2004 General Conference and scored crucial legislative victories.

The Liberal Methodist Leadership Implosion

Since the United Methodists have the largest and most vigorous renewing and confessing movements in the mainline, it is useful to provide a further description of these dynamics.

Only a half-century ago, no one expected an internal collapse of a leadership that seemed to be the financial and institutional envy of mainline Protestant bureaucrats. It was a highly reliable organizational structure that everyone thought would carry the United Methodist Church well into the twenty-first century. Its colleges and universities, seminaries, mission agencies, and institutional stability were generally well funded and secure. So what happened? A combination of denominational introversion, doctrinal forgetfulness, political idealism, "no offense" Christianity, and disciplinary neglect—all at the same time—peaked in the late 1960s and moved slowly toward a fateful implosion that was not really evident until the late 1990s.

Just as with the rest of the mainline, there is an ever-increasing ideological distance between congregations and clergy, and between both of them and their agency and episcopal leadership. This distance is especially felt in the most vital and growing congregations, which are almost all evangelical. The elite liberal leadership could not grow churches. They leave behind a weak record of preaching. They wanted desperately to play the role of heroic social reformers. As a result, there is no longer a viable level of trust between liberal clergy and conservative laity that would have been assumed fifty years ago. That has simply disappeared. Its moral capital is spent.

The liberal hegemony that was on the ascendancy from 1950 to 1970 has been on the descendancy from 1970 to the present. This is roughly parallel to the rise and fall of the liberal ecumenical (WCC-NCC) hegemony. By the 1990s this elitism was showing signs of desperation, and by the turn of the millennium it was an altogether spent force, unable to reduplicate itself through another generation.

Meanwhile, as the hemorrhage of membership continued in liberal churches, evangelical churches were growing exponentially in almost every region. The once self-assured moral high ground of the political left was suddenly unveiled as hollow, and sometimes even as a shameless attempt to preserve power. It often grasped for almost any moral rationale available, mostly without Scripture, and mostly without the political influence it so much desired. Its intellectual assumptions were in time shown to be false and based upon poorly researched, ill-grounded ideological fantasies and upon a regulatory political mentality.

The knowledge elites that once controlled the United Methodist public face in Washington DC are in disarray—the social action agencies in the Methodist Building, and in New York City, the General Board of Global Ministry. The most expensive real estate Methodists own is the Methodist Building in Washington, which by deed and charter was deliberately designated for ministries of temperance and alcoholism. But by 1970 it had become an ingrown nest of ideological radicals not only committed to pacifism, the Nicaraguan Socialist revolution, Cuban advocacy, and abortion rights advocacy, but to presenting these causes as if representative of United Methodist laity. Accountability to donor intent is currently being legally challenged to discern whether the original charter has been violated.

The Default of Mission

The same disjunctions were everywhere evident in the waning decades of the twentieth century, but nowhere more dramatically than in educational institutions and mission agencies. The richest agency of the United Methodist Church is the General Board of Global Ministry, the chief administrative unit for funneling Methodist lay dollars into relief work and world social justice efforts. The agency's accumulation of wealth is astonishing: a half *billion* dollars in total assets by the end of the twentieth century.

For more than 150 years this agency has received from small, lay benefactors weekly sacrificial donations intended for worldwide preaching missions and social relief. Methodist foreign mission work began to take shape in the 1840s to Africa, China, and South America. The mission efforts that were started then became the most trusted and widely supported institution in Methodist history, and this trust was largely engendered by faithful women, giving monthly small sums for evangelical mission work abroad. Yet their agency, United Methodist Women, was early very welcoming to pacifist and socialist politics, and in time became an ideological haven for leftist activists. So this agency fell from being the most trusted and the most generously funded to being the most distrusted bureaucratic operation in Methodist history.

It is ironic that precisely because the mission board is so heavily endowed, it felt it could afford to remain aloof from populist influence, negligent of the Great Commission to preach the gospel to all nations, and ignore the will of local supporters, their prayers, and sacrificial giving. With plenty of endowed resources stored away from Manhattan to California, it did not feel the need to refer its decisions to the worshiping communities, who were viewed from Riverside Drive as benighted and in need of a much more thorough liberal education. This was the beginning of its downfall.

Methodist missions became a social service agency focused on grant-making social project administration. Virtually no attention was paid to preaching. All eyes were on supposedly bold social action and rapid social change, as their literature of the last five decades makes entirely evident. Yet it was the givers' biblical faith and commitment to the Great Commission that motivated their sacrificial giving. The resulting bureaucracy arrogantly reinforced the distance between the wayward decision-makers and the sources of their ongoing support. Their capital quickly spent, these bureaucracies were judged to be unworthy of the kind of sacrificial giving that had characterized the generation of their mothers and grandmothers.

By now they have belatedly realized that they have only fragmented and tainted their moral authority in many local churches and increasingly among their core base of women supporters. This has amounted to a self-willed, almost suicidal implosion of Methodist missions. They now dwell in encapsulated fortress bureaucracies. They desperately need self-esteem and get it only from those who are still enamored by class warfare politics, feminist radicals, socialist illusions, and left-wing permissiveness advocates. This is why they have been ignored, bypassed, and largely dismissed. The faithful women that have long been the backbone of missions have increasingly felt disillusioned with the Women's Division of the General Board of Global Ministry. Scrapping these unworthy channels, the evangelicals created an entirely different alternative: the Mission Society for United Methodists.

While the mission and social action bureaucracy could stand being ignored by the laity, it is much harder for them to abide being ignored by the politicians and public policy legislators. They had placed all their eggs in one leftist basket just when the legislators were becoming aware of their diminished influence. Now legislative and executive governmental functions that once were thought to pay serious attention to Methodist agencies and social justice experiments are quite inattentive. Congress yawns when outrageous paper declarations pour out of the Methodist Building. The issues of live-birth abortion and homosexual legitimization have brought the last stages of alienation. The politicians have learned that the emergent growth and dynamism within the United Methodist Church lies not in its bureaucratic agencies or Council of Bishops, but in the populace base that is far more reasonable, traditional, and confident than its entrenched, aging, and myopic leadership.

The liberal Methodist implosion was anticipated in the late seventies, but first began to be noticed by the leadership belatedly at the Cleveland General Conference of 2000. Its implications were not sufficiently grasped, however, until the Pittsburgh General Conference of 2004. Subsequently liberal Methodism has been characterized by almost hysterical fear on the part of the defensive bureaucracy that somebody is going to expose their hidden machinations, intrude into their organizations, their pensions, their money, their institutions, and their seminaries. They are ready to do or say almost anything to preserve the continuity of their ideology, to save face, to put a rosy spin on an already imploded leadership. They sense that this is about to happen, and they are desperately afraid of it.

That is the implosion. But there are visible signs of reversal. These modest signs do not imply that every quadrennial General Conference in the future is likely to be ever more conservative or traditionalist or evangelical than its 2000 and 2004 predecessors. But they do mean that the momentum of Cleveland and Pittsburgh will have to be reversed if the older liberal bureaucracy is to get a grip.

The Achilles' Heel of Liberal Methodism

The center of vulnerability of liberal Methodism is the issue of local church property. This is why we will pay special attention in the last part of this book to this dilemma, which has analogies in all other branches of the mainline. This issue reveals a special irony: For it is written into the property deeds of the United Methodist Church that they *must* be legally accountable to the doctrine and Discipline. The Discipline has as its first constitutional rule the protection of classical doctrinal standards. What this means is that any local church that defies the doctrinal standards is subject to charges and potential litigation with respect to its abuse of its local deed of property. This constitutional mandate is only gradually being recognized.

The brief version of this story, told in more detail in part 6, is this: In attempting to protect the Wesleyan chapels in England from the preaching of doctrines contrary to those of John Wesley, a model deed was set up which defined Methodist doctrinal standards. These include the standard sermons of John Wesley and his *Explanatory Notes Upon the New Testament* as exemplary expositions of biblical teaching. The same formulas that appear in the model deeds were passed on to the American churches. Between 1784 and 1808, when the Methodist Church was forming its constitution, which is still in full effect, the property deeds were especially respectful of the doctrinal standards. What happened in 1808 was that these doctrinal standards were written into the Constitution in such a way that makes them virtually impossible to amend. These doctrinal standards have been clearly defined over almost two centuries and have been reconfirmed in the 1988 and all subsequent General Conferences. The same doctrinal standards appear in every United Methodist Discipline. If a local church is unwilling to follow those doctrinal standards, then its local deed of property is subject to challenge, according to church law. Although it has yet to be fully tested in civil law, this is the challenge ahead for the United Methodist Church. How will it defend itself against church after church challenging its conferences as to their legitimacy in the stewardship of their property according to the United Methodist Constitution? That may seem abstract, but it is a cloud the size of a man's hand, to use Elijah's servant's phrase (1 Kings 18:44). There is only one clear solution to this dilemma, and that is that conferences and local churches should simply follow the doctrinal standards of the Discipline, and not to defy or inveigh against them. If they defy them, they may be subject to judicial action, first in the church courts and then, if unremedied, quite likely in civil courts. The financial consequences of this are enormous, since attorneys are the only beneficiaries of extended litigation, but that litigation will be forthcoming if the Annual Conferences themselves do not voluntarily assent to protecting their own constitutional standards. So this is the Achilles' heel of the liberal United Methodist Church leadership.

It is the leverage wisely provided by John Wesley himself in the model deed and deed of declaration that patterns every modern United Methodist local church property deed.

Recent Achievements

In the recent General Conferences of 2000 and 2004, confessing Christians achieved important legislative majorities on many of these most crucial issues. They partially limited the power of the bureaucracy to raise unsurveilled funding from the conferences. They made more fair the representational process by which the larger, growing, traditional, and evangelical United Methodist congregations and churches in the conferences will have relatively more voting power in General Conference legislation—in contrast with the previous imbalance that favored liberal jurisdictions and entities. These conservative majorities have increased from 62 percent to 74 percent in the last two decades on sexuality issues and by even greater majorities on issues of fiscal and representational fairness.

The momentum of orthodox and evangelical reform within United Methodism is best seen currently in the Judicial Council where, in one of its recent declarations, one liberal Conference was reprimanded for its abuse of church law by failing to investigate and failing to discipline a clergy member who repeatedly defied the sexuality standards for clergy. But the enforcement of this discipline has proved vexing.

This chapter has provided a bird's-eye view of many of the major renewing and confessing movements in the North American mainline. But how are these movements to be coordinated into an ecumenical voice?

9

Truth-Driven Unity

No movement in post-Reformation Christianity has been more divisive than the modern ecumenical movement. With all its idealized intentions to unite churches, modern ecumenism has been extremely divisive because it has distanced itself from the truth of ancient ecumenical teaching. Its political activism has alienated its own worshiping communities. Its negotiation schemes have been pretentious. Its visions of the future have been utopian.

Renewing ecumenism of the third millennium does not any longer yearn despairingly for a single monolithic institutional embodiment of nominal faith in Christ. It celebrates the varieties of genuine faith that the Holy Spirit is creating. The conciliar spirit of ancient Christianity, despite the institutional fragmentation of the Reformation, remained intact in the teaching of Luther and Calvin, and survived especially in the evangelical revivals' attempts to bring gospel ministries together. Confessing Christians share that conciliar spirit. Confessing Christians are rediscovering a deeper level of ecumenism than has been engendered by modern or oldline ecumenism.

Distinguishing Truth from Opinion

A distinction was made in cooperative evangelical revivalism of the eighteenth and nineteenth centuries between apostolic *truth* and ancillary *opinion*. Eighteenth-century evangelicalism anticipated the explicit evangelical ecumenism that developed in 1846 and the following years. Accordingly, it was prudent that the assertion of many contested ancillary opinions should be respectfully constrained in order to hold fast to the essential truth of the gospel. Gospel ministries attempted to come together on the mission field not on the basis of opinions but on the basis of the core of Christian truth. Matters of varied polity, ministry, church order, and worship practices did not divert them. Confessing and renewing movements in the mainline are rediscovering this.

Liberal constraints and social pressures over several decades have previously cowed believers into silence. They have learned to be embarrassed at being perceived as too sure of what the faith is. That has caused them to back away from any confession that others might interpret as doctrinally limiting or narrowly dogmatic. Any language that might have the appearance of offending anyone is ruled out. Often only those who hide their liberal dogmas in the garment of tolerance are given influential voice.

The Forgetfulness of Ancient Ecumenical Teaching in Modern Ecumenical Dialogue

Most of what today is called "ecumenical dialogue" is neither truly ecumenical nor candid dialogue. It is not ecumenical, because it has systematically forgotten the classic ecumenical criteria for truth. Nor is it dialogue, since dialogue requires a serious listening and speaking on behalf of the truth, not merely listening to cultures and opinions explaining themselves.

This is why confessing Christians are no longer at ease with the assumption that what is needed is simply more of the old so-called ecumenical dialogue. Less is needed if what has passed for dialogue is to be the norm. What is needed more is rigorous search for truth, the truth of God's revelation, as mediated through an intergenerational and multicultural tradition of canonical interpretation that reasons consistently from Scripture, as confirmed by centuries of Scripture-bearing tradition. Confessing Christians are becoming aware of the haunting irony that maybe they are being led further away from the truth merely by seeming to come nearer one another in order to talk more about less.

However much the faithful may yearn to be tolerant, they know, for example, that exploiting children for sex is simply wrong. It is sinful. Now we hear gasps, for "sinful" is not a word that belongs in a politically correct, tolerant, modern conversation. Why? Is it because pedophilia is not really a sin? Is it merely a disturbing social influence or bad habit formation? Hardly. Anyone who thinks seriously about the defense of children understands that the sexual exploitation of children is morally wrong, entirely out of bounds. No matter how much dialogue ensues, this behavior cannot set forth sufficient reasons to gain moral equivalency with truthful speech. Most lay Christians are quite clear about this. Few except clergy are confused.

Reasonable persons have a moral self-awareness called conscience that tells them most certainly that pedophilia is wrong. Those who practice it are degenerate and wicked, and must be constrained by law. Yet our society has gone through a long "lost weekend" of hypertoleration in which pedophiles have been given special legal protections. Even some Christian ethicists have provided tortured moral and religious justifications for their behavior. The faithful have been asked to view them sympathetically, not as wicked, but as simply in need of therapy or social reconditioning, or to be pitied because of their parents' mistakes. But obsessive pedophilia is not just stupid or morally debatable. It is wrong. It is based on perverted and dangerous misconceptions of humanity and justice and sexuality and of the relation of adults and children. These misconceptions must ultimately be challenged, preferably sooner than later, when irreparable damage may have been done to the innocent. Children must be protected against pedophiles who would use them for their own evil purposes. This is a moral requirement only because it is true. There is no moral equivalency between acquisitive pedophiles and caring parents.

Yet the call for dialogue often means accepting the premise of moral equality as the basis for entering the dialogue. Even though we may agree that pedophilia is wrong and protecting children is right, we hesitate to speak out loud with any certainty when it comes to Christian truth. It is safer just not to talk about the order of creation or guilt or incarnation or resurrection or final judgment. We are afraid we might offend people or make them nervous. And if we do talk about these things, we often intentionally do not speak with an air of confidence, but only with a thousand apologies and qualifiers, for we know we will have to face those who say: How do you know what you think you know? What about all those subcultures that would challenge what you say? It is as if the question of truth were merely a question of social location or counting votes.

It is easy to use toleration as a psychological bludgeon to silence anyone asserting anything about the revealed truth attested in Scripture. It is interesting to investigate the psychological and sociological dynamics of feeling responses as long as the investigation is based on the premises of cultural relativism and the moral equivalency of all ideas. But questions of apostolic truth require openly attesting the history of God's coming to save us from sin. This is not politics or psychology or sociology as such. It is the truth about God's actual coming among us in history. It has to do with scriptural authority, doctrinal integrity, and the truth of Christian testimony.

The Tyranny of the Absolutely Tolerant

Those who seriously seek Christian unity are satisfied only with that unity that is based on Christian truth—not feelings, not social pleasantness, not agreement, not negotiations. Those who are made uncomfortable by this stance have backed away from the very ground and source of Christian unity, which is Christian truth. Those who put on the face of being absolutely tolerant are unintentionally undermining the unity of the church by undercutting the question of truth.

Even the absolute toleration of deception and self-deception appears to be a virtue in some circles. Whenever deception is given the same legitimacy as truth-telling, any rational, moral creature must object. This fantasy of absolute toleration is revulsive to serious believers, and the more serious the more revulsion. Conformists are tempted simply to withdraw from any effort to offer any rational and scriptural arguments for the truth of Christianity. They do not want to be associated with anyone who might undermine their secular fantasy of their misconception of human unity, much less the unity of believers. So they are silenced, for fear of embarrassing someone who might feel misunderstood or neglected. This is the tyranny of the tolerant. The fantasy is that if we tell the truth of God's coming and saving, we risk offending sensitive ears. Imagine Paul or Athanasius bowing to this fantasy.

The irony is that the faithful are scared away from asserting truth by the threat of offending the unfaithful. They are intimidated. Many have not studied Scripture or ancient ecumenical teaching sufficiently to speak in a distinctly Christian voice.

Those who are perceived as so insensitive to assert that something is certainly true are, in the "best circles," ostracized, bullied, and assumed to be wrong even if no one is willing to say what "wrong" might mean. No one can honestly hold a conception of wrong without a conception of right, or an idea of injustice without an idea of justice, or of error without truth. But in modernity, where no miracles are supposed to be happening, at least this one has apparently occurred: without any notion of wrong or anything that even could be wrong, the intellectual elites have created what is right. Lacking moral criteria, they have created a new morality. It is a creation *ex nihilo*! Under the assumption of dialogue as truth in process, they have given birth to moral anarchy. Quite a historic achievement.

Awaiting a Majority

Cultural relativism has used this deceit to gain power. The absolute relativists want to assert their sincere desire for dialogue *until* they become a majority. Then they often want to settle issues by either exclusion or coercion. They first argue for democratic fairness, but when they acquire their majority, they are tempted to turn immediately to a triumphalism that assumes that liberal justice has triumphed. From then on, dialogue about truth is forbidden, and about absolute truth is absolutely forbidden.

One who asserts that deceit is on equal footing with honesty cannot be trusted to say so honestly. It is implausible to argue honestly that dishonesty is good. This confirms the intrinsic inconsistency of the arguments of cultural relativism that any opinion is just as good as any other. This view amounts to giving up already on the search for truth. Such a person is no longer searching for the truth, but only for self-expression.

Those in favor of regulatory politics or the legitimizing of sexual experimentation say they want dialogue with traditional Christians. They desperately want dialogue—right up to the precise point where they have legislative majorities and coercive judicial victories. Then they want to close ranks and consider the dialogue over. They want to achieve institutional reintegration, because what they are most afraid of is institutional disintegration.

These are the voices that restrict questions of ecumenism to questions of organic and institutional unity. This is the most counter-ecumenical of all modern ecumenical habits. They habitually want to continue dialogue, but only so long as deceit is considered morally equal to truth-telling. If both truth and falsehood have precisely equal footing in the dialogue, they are happy to string it out.

The Necessity of Properly Naming Heresy

The new (classic, orthodox) ecumenism differs from the old (liberal, bureaucratic) ecumenism radically by insisting that heresy must be taken seriously. Yes, it is permissible actually to use the "h" word, provided its meaning is understood. It means "something *other than* that which the apostles taught." If the distinction between falsehood and Christian truth is never made, or in principle not even able to be made, then the truth cannot be discerned or distinguished from falsehood. Christian unity, however, must be based squarely upon that known truth openly proclaimed and shared by all Christians of all times. That is the key mark that distinguishes the dying ecumenism of the twentieth century from the emerging ecumenism of the twenty-first.

The ancient ecumenical tradition knew that one could not be a Christian and an Arian at the same time. Arians say Jesus is not quite God. Christians everywhere and of all times say with one voice that Jesus is truly God, not less than God, without ceasing to be a man. They have confirmed this ever since the writings of the apostles John and Paul. This makes a huge difference. The rejection of Arianism was precise and well-grounded scripturally, and decided through rigorous exegesis and repeatedly reconfirmed. This confirmation allows every future believer to know, for example, that Arianism is not just an innocent mistake or bad exegesis, but counter to apostolic teaching as understood by the whole church in all times and places.

Arianism is not simply based upon a lack of good feeling or rebellion against an institutional process, but it is in error by denying apostolic truth. This is demonstrated in the written decisions of the early ecumenical councils. Their very purpose was to distinguish between orthodoxy and heresy, so as to put clear limits on what can be legitimately called Christian truth. There a well-marked boundary is drawn and posted for all to see. Beyond this point, the frazzled edge of the big tent ends. Others outside have themselves chosen to live there. Those who ignore this boundary have not historically been welcomed to the Lord's Table without repentance. In fact, no one is ready for the Lord's Table without repentance. To ignore this boundary is to assert that which is inconsistent with classic, consensual, ecumenical Christian teaching. In defining heresy as distinguished from orthodoxy, the struggle was about reality, about what is indeed true as divinely revealed, and as understood by the apostles—not about our opinions or hopes or intuitions or cultural analysis. Christian preaching tells the truth about the world, its beginning, its history, its sin, God's grace, and the future.

It is the Spirit who is attesting the truth of true belief in our hearts. That makes Christian belief entirely different from value-neutral dialogue. The valid quest for Christian *unity* has going for it only one thing, finally: *truth*. What the Holy Spirit insists upon is telling the truth, the whole truth, seen in the light of apostolic testimony. Oldline ecumenism had good intentions and personal skills and beliefs that many thought were true. But to start there is to start on the wrong foot.

What the relativists take to be arrogant, the faithful, who have inhabited the worshiping community for generations, hold as convictions with the certainty of faith. They have lived there long enough to understand the community of faith and its way of thinking about the Scripture as a whole single narrative of God's promise and its fulfillment. This certainty of faith is precisely what the secular worldliness wants to regard as exaggerated, arrogant, or thoughtless behavior. "How dare they assert the truth insensitively over and against what someone else thinks is the truth," they say. The deepest inner desire of absolute cultural relativism is never to say anything about the truth. But of course there is a deep internal contradiction in the desire itself.

Christians have a definite history of distinguishing between apostolic truth and untruth, hence *other than* (*haeresis*) Christian truth. The basic questions of faith have been worked through carefully so as to be long ago grounded in a consensual view of what Scripture teaches, by comparing Scripture with

Scripture, as viewed by its most widely trusted early interpreters. The conciliar view is imperfect but real. So the faithful know that Jesus died for our sins, that he suffered for us on the cross, that he was born incarnate God of a virgin, that he rose on the third day, that he is the only Son of the Father, and that his mission is now being completed by the Holy Spirit. This is the truth that absolute relativism cannot abide.

The Truth Is Revealed in God's Action in History

Christianity has a huge database of doctrinal cases debated and decided. The record is well reported. The reporting of these ecumenical resolutions of contested cases stretches over almost twenty centuries of debate over the written Word.

The fact that the ecumenical database is complex does not disqualify it. It means that this truth has gone through this rigorous, concrete, detailed, complex, deliberate form of challenge and resolution in history, and many phases of trial and error, and has indeed come up with consensual decisions that have a documented history.

There is indeed a deep center of Christianity that is profoundly simple. It is rehearsed in the creed, sung in hymns, and prayed in the Lord's Prayer. But the interpretative database that enables classical Christians to sing those hymns and trust that simplicity goes back to the history of the people of Israel and the emergence of the church around the world with a consistent confession of faith and a single canon of Holy Writ. That diversity of testimony is what ecumenical teaching brings into a cohesive focus and witness.

The Key to History

Only one key unlocks the truth of Christianity. It is the one key that opens the one door to the right understanding of Scripture and apostolic teaching. This key has been tested again and again. It is simply *the truth of Christianity as received by believers of all times and places by general consent.* This is ecumenical consent.

What is most trustable in surveying the diversity of Christian faith is the truth that God has spoken in the events surrounding the life, death, and resurrection of Jesus Christ. The faithful have the experience of generations of Christians who have tested this key against the written Word using reason and moral awareness. They know and repeatedly confirm its efficacy and its truthfulness. The key is orthodoxy, consensual Christian memory—ancient consensual teaching of Christian truth applied to ever-changing contemporary circumstances. All other keys are flawed. Those who try in other ways to force the lock jam it.

All other keys are different, and hence have some features of *haeresis* (other choices). They are in some way *different from* the particular quality, clarity, and simplicity of the faith of orthodoxy. They draw unsuspecting Christians into disastrous consequences: half-truths, faulty visions, injustice, blood, suffering, conflict. Those who say that what they individually believe overrides all of what Christians of all times and places have believed previously have not earned the right to speak for believing Christians.

When the Scriptures are opened up, the faithful understand that human history is a sad, sorry story of sin and self-assertiveness. It has required a great price for God to redeem. Who would have imagined that God would actually do what God has done? Who would ever have expected God's way of dealing with sin? That redemption was totally surprising—God coming to us as a human being to die for our sins, and to rise on the third day. These are the most unexpected events that did indeed, in God's own time and way, fulfill the expectation of the people of Israel concerning the Anointed One, the Christ.

The deepest human hunger is for a true vision of the meaning of human history. That is disclosed in the truth of the Christian faith. The body of reasoning, so enormously complex in its formation and historical outworking, is very simple in its confessional form. That simplicity is heard in its liturgy, hymns, confessions, and prayers, and is manifested in the Eucharist.

Admittedly much of what has been wrongly called Christian teaching has had terrible consequences (war, slavery, oppression) quite inconsistent with consensual Christian testimony. But the solution is not to do away with doctrinal reasoning grounded on classic Christian consent, but to do it better. That means more consistently, in greater harmony with the Scripture, and as a truer refraction of the cross-cultural wisdom of Christians of all times and places, languages and social locations, races and cultures.

Consensual ecumenical Christianity invites rigorous historical analysis. It is possible to ask objectively and historically: What have Christians of all times and places in fact believed? Such questions are amenable to impartial, even scientific, investigation.

The only unity that the faithful truly have in God's presence, the only unity that makes any difference, is the unity based on the truth of apostolic teaching—the truth as tested consensually by the Spirit in the church in all periods of its history, and daily attested personally in believers. To abandon that consensus is to create more division, even while pretending to overcome it. Confessing Christians intuitively understand that these pseudo-attempts at unity engender disunity among Christians.

The Tragedy of Putting Unity Before Truth: Why Ecumenical Arguments Fail

Oldline ecumenical debate and planning are prone to misfire through a fundamental misunderstanding of the relation of unity and truth: They do not seek *unity based on truth*.

Four modern ecumenical arguments in particular misfire, as shown by David Mills. They even make Christian disunity more likely. These four following arguments have prevailed in liberal ecumenism, each unintentionally eliciting disunity. Each is a mistaken "if-then" correlation:

1. If we can just get together on some common *ethical* standards, then we will therefore achieve the unity of believers.
2. If we could have the same open ecumenical *feelings* or experiences, then we would feel our unity.
3. If we could just be open to *dialogue*, then we would grow toward unity.
4. If we merge the separate *institutions* based on different memories created by the Spirit, then we would experience our unity through an institution, and thus we now must renew our commitment to the institutional vestiges of ecumenism.

All these attempts are alike in one way: they put *unity ahead of truth*. They squander the truth to achieve a superficial unity. All are mistaken. All spawn disillusionment with efforts at Christian unity. Together they have resulted in the ecumenical turbulence that now buffets us.

All misfire for the same reason: they base unity on something other than the truth, by avoiding the only basis from which Christian unity can emerge—that is the revealed Word whose hearing is enabled by the Holy Spirit and received through faith. Christian unity must be based on the truth of classical Christian teaching of holy writ concerning what has happened in Jesus Christ to transform the world. These four misplaced forms of ecumenism (ethical, experiential, conversational, and institutional) all tempt their adherents to forget the unique unity of believers created by the Holy Spirit—a unity which, like circumcision, is a matter of the heart. Together they have virtually buried prevailing ecumenism in our time in a way that will be difficult to reverse. I will examine these four lazy arguments for unity so common to modern liberal ecumenism: *a unity reduced* to a common ethical standard (not revelation); to religious feelings (not the Word of God in Scripture); to dialogue (detached from the truth question); and to institutional and sociological agreements (not the work of the Spirit in our hearts). I rely upon much of what Mills has written in his brilliant analysis.[1]

Each argument has appealed to the other argument's flawed reasoning to reinforce its own. Together they have rung the death knell of oldline ecumenism by systematically avoiding the truth question. They have sought desperately to find unity in something other than apostolic truth, as remembered consensually in the undivided early church and largely throughout the first millennium. They have conspired to reduce the unity of believers alternatively to ethics, experience, negotiation, or merger. Four idolatries lie hidden under these forms of reductionism. They need the critique of ancient classic ecumenism.

The Ethical Substitute for Witness to the Truth

The first wrong step is to assume that there is an *ethical* substitute for truth. This often springs out of a post-Kantian idolatry of moral reasoning—as if that were all that might be feasible in responding to God. It is the assumption that religious judgments can no longer be based on the revealed truth but only on our moral efforts and choices. Whether one is a defender of the free market or a controlled economy, whether one is for or against abortion, whether for or against military defense, the ecumenical arena is thought to be a table where the family essentially talks ethics, politics, social change, and moral judgments. This is not the Lord's Table. To base Christian unity on ethical agreement is to misunderstand the very unity that we already have in Jesus Christ. It is a unity that we discover by faith, by participating personally in Christ's body by faith, enabled and attested by the Spirit. It is *a unity created by truth*.

Liberal ecumenical leadership has repeatedly sought to bring the church organizations together on the moral basis of a common political commitment to the poor. However important the poor may be in the Christian life, it is not our sympathy for the poor that draws us together into one confession, one eucharistic unity. It is the atoning work of Christ on the cross. Meanwhile political strategies for government action on behalf of the poor continue to divide us, as they always will. The very premise that we are going to create our unity in Christ by our agreement on the Kyoto treaty, or equal pay for equal work, or military strategy, has deeply divided the body of Christ in our time.

Some think that if we could just agree on protecting the environment, for example, this would be the baseline moral issue upon which we can get general consent, and thus truly find unity as Christians. Whether the environment is to be protected by regulatory government policies or by the changing of the human heart, we do not agree; whether by private initiative or by central state planning, believers do not all agree. We differ on how jobs and families and mortgages are to be weighed in relation to spotted owls and redwoods. Differences of opinion exist at every point along the way about scientific evidence and legislative remedies and judicial actions. The attempt to bring Christians together on the basis of environmental policy is wrongly conceived, counterproductive, and in outcome intensely divisive.

Ethical conflicts do not unify Christian believers. Christians are brought together by God's suffering love for humanity in Jesus Christ, received in the heart by faith. Christians are brought together by a defining historical fact: incarnation. Yes, Christians believe that the incarnation is a fact, an actual event. That is the scandal. God has become human, and in doing so died for our sins, and is risen for us in order to demonstrate the truth of his earthly ministry. This alone brings us to unity in Christ. Christians are those who participate personally by faith in the truth of this revelation. This is not merely their own privately held belief, but a shared belief with all Christians of all times and places. Telling that good news is telling the truth, as attested by the Spirit, to each person willing to listen to Scripture.

The Psychological Substitute for Witness to the Truth

The second wrong step is to assume that there is a *psychological* or emotional or experiential substitute for truth. It sets aside questions of truth in order to deal with our feelings. This is a quick and sure way of diminishing the unity of the body of Christ: by basing that unity on passing feelings or experiences, telling one's story apart from God's story with humanity.

The idolatry of experience leads us astray. It says that in order to find our unity in Christ, we must look for some experience we all can share. So we listen to each other's experiences, and hope somehow that we can feel that others' experiences illuminate ours. But that says nothing about the truth of apostolic teaching, which is the only truth that matters if divine revelation is indeed made known in actual history. What Christian preaching has going for it is the truth indeed, the veritable truth of the apostolic teaching as attested by the Spirit as evidenced in classic Christian consensus. That is enough. Yet we persist in getting together to talk about our experiences, our "ultimate concerns," often focusing on our stories of oppression or being treated unjustly. This exaltation of my experience above truth detracts from the main business of listening to the apostolic testimony, by which we are freed in the Spirit to hear the truth of our own personal histories illumined by salvation history.

This sentimental idolatry substitutes our feelings for the truth of Christian teaching. This leads to the hubris that our experience ought to be decisive for someone else's experience, or theirs for us. The twisting routes of this maze are complicated by the fact that we all live out of a history of sin. We often hear the experience of others through the lens of sin, not grace, of guilt, not atonement.

The road of experience-oriented theology goes downhill on the slippery slope from Schliermacher to Spong. The result is absolute relativism, narcissism, and subjectivism. There is a direct line of succession from nineteenth-century German to twentieth-century American liberalism. In that tradition we have learned that what Christians have in common is no more than an experience, the experience of the transition from sin to grace. This transition implicitly, somehow, points us toward the "other"—God. But this other is never revealed. God is still hidden, buried in our perceptions and deceptions within a history of sin.

This way of reasoning is intrinsically divisive. It has led some to identify the highest spirituality with everything from oral sex to neopagan witchcraft. Yet still these views want to be legitimized as Christian—indeed most truly Christian. There is little that unites believers who take this way. It does not bring the body or family of Christ together, but breaks it up.

The Substitution of Dialogue for Witness to the Truth

The third idolatry elevates *dialogue* to the center of values. It is different from the experiential approach because one can have an experience without dialogue. Dialogue as such has become an "ecumenical strategy" focused on getting people together in a conversation not to be led to truth, but rather to talk. The ultimate goal is to open up to one another, to be vulnerable, self-disclosing, and nondefensive. By doing this it appears that conversationalists are talking their way into a deeper unity in Christ. But the fleeting glimpses of unity that this produces are not so much Christ as our momentary and variable interactions. It is a conversational substitute for truth.

The sexual analogue of this dialogue is the fantasy of open marriage, where it is not crucial whether or not partners covenant sexuality exclusively. That is not important at all. What is important is simply to be open about it. The absolute criterion of sexual integrity and legitimacy is disclosure, not covenant fidelity. The myth is that as long as they are entirely honest in dialogue, they are still one couple.

This is as far as much ecumenical dialogue goes. We talk with each other, and try to be open. This conversational idolatry is frustrating to a deeper ecumenism based on the truth of God's coming. What believers notice most in such dialogue is the avoidance of the apostolic testimony as consensually received. Self-disclosure as such does not always draw believers into the unity in Christ that the Spirit offers. It may fracture their union. Such conversation may teach baptized Christians how far apart they are from God's truth in Scripture.

Only when disciplined by the written Word is dialogue a healthy feature of Christian communication, but it can never be a substitute for apostolic teaching. How much more edifying it is to follow the way of truth made known in history in the chronicle of the great dialogue between God and humanity, which has received a conclusive verdict in the cross of Jesus Christ. There the truth is judge of dialogue, not dialogue of truth.

We see the thinness of this conversational idolatry everywhere in secular society. Any conversation that accidentally edges toward the assertion of truth makes us nervous. Such assertions may be regarded as dangerous in some places—political activity, psychology classes, literary theory, and psychotherapy.

The apostolic teaching calls us to be vulnerable not merely to each other, but more so to God's judgment and mercy. The Spirit is welcoming us to the mercy shown by God, not merely to the broken forms of mercy we may experience in interpersonal dialogue through talk or touch. This idolatry is counter-ecumenical. It may lead us from, not toward, the truth. Christian truth is not reducible to our dialogue.

The Institutional Substitution for Witness to the Truth

The fourth wrong step assumes that there is an *institutional* substitute for truth. This reveals a resilient counter-ecumenical idolatry: the worship of institutional continuity and maintenance. Institutional idolatry substituting for ecumenism is most evident in the hubris that attempts to build one institution that encompasses all other institutions. Even within this idolatry there may remain a fierce allegiance to one's own ethnic or national or denominational identity or organizational heritage, but these are proximately overshadowed by the larger "more inclusive institution" which becomes the arbiter of Christian truth and moral judgment. This view elevates institutional continuity above gospel truth. Pledging fealty to the institutional apparatus of international ecumenism may result in a diminution of faithfulness to the revealed truth.

Why is this so prevalent in modern ecumenical circles? Modern ecumenism has so focused on *visible* unity, which is itself often reduced to organic or institutional unity, that it has lost sight of the *hidden* unity of faith that Christ is creating through the Spirit. Church unity is reduced to organizational negotiations between complex institutions attempting to meld with each other. Each institutional church forming the ecumenical movement has its own vested institutional interest. As they try to salve their bad conscience because of their divisions and their failure to behold their unity in faith, they interpret the solution as an institutional merger. So they get together to feel guilty jointly and try by management and administration to surmount historic divisions. As they negotiate with other institutions, each tries to get their fair piece of the pie. So the most successful ecumenists become those who are most adept in organizational and negotiation skills. Some will find ways of stacking committees and controlling votes so that the outcome looks democratic and fair, but silent ideological premises lying far underneath the friendly surface control the outcome. This jockeying is not worthy of the name *oecumene*. This endless search for visible and organic unity has not been blessed by the Spirit.

It is especially anti-ecumenical when led by bishops and clergy whose ordination vows have promised to preserve the unity of the church in Jesus Christ. Institutional idolatry occurs in its most exaggerated form, sadly, in the vaulted principle of episcopal collegiality, which parades as an evidence of unity but then becomes a cover for corruption and deceit (sexual, political, or financial). The unity and convenience and jockeying of the bishops seem to trump the truth of Jesus Christ. In its worst form, the bishops, who are pledged to protect the laity from false teaching, descend to protecting each other from any charges of malpractice. They find clever ways to protect errant bishops from being discovered or challenged by faithful laity. The truth of Christian teaching is made relative to the absolute of institutional continuity. It thereby becomes anti-ecumenical precisely in its pretense to be ecumenical. The truth becomes relative to institutional needs, demands, assumptions, and sentiments.

The visible church is admittedly the bearer of revelation in history. But it is not one particular memory or polity or institution that the Spirit has chosen to bear the good news. Rather the one, holy, catholic, and apostolic church is the body of believers of all times and places who have remained humbly faithful to the apostolic testimony. This visible body in history cannot be sufficiently named either by terms like the World Council or the World Lutherans or the World Evangelical Alliance or the Moscow Patriarchate. However well intended, all these have proven less reliable than the ancient ecumenical consensus. All such historical structures are transcended by the living work of Christ as enabled by the Spirit in bringing the faithful to sing on the same key. The visibility of the church is like the circumcision of the heart, more a matter of faith than of physics.

Liberal ecumenism has withered into institutional idolatry. It has become a frantic quest for an explanation of itself, some *raison d'être* to justify its existence. So this despair dominates dialogue, earnest conversations, political rhetoric, and negotiation to obtain fleeting forms of institutional agreement, often pretending permanence.

Those of us who have spent decades being card-carrying liberal ecumenists have felt the burning desire to use the church as a vehicle for political change. We have yearned for institutional clout in lobbying. We seek affinities and collusions with other powerful bureaucrats and regulators. The goal is to acquire and possess the unity of the church under the heading of some institutional arrangement. In the mainline churches there is a particularly fierce form of this idolatry, most of all among Reformed and Methodist Christians. Reinforced by the fiction of nominal membership, it focuses on the pretense that if you nominally belong to a particular institution, you are a believer. Whether one is a truly faithful member or a nominal member becomes almost impossible to determine in liberal terms. The attempt to do so would be disruptive to institutional maintenance. So the first option rejected is the call to the holiness of the church. The aim is to keep institutional cohesion intact to support bureaucratic codependencies. Liberal ecclesiology works with that fiction by means of conversational, ethical, and dialogical strategies to get more paying clients into nominal membership. Meanwhile they vaguely hope that the cheerleaders and bill-payers will not become too distracted by the written Word or ancient ecumenical teaching.

This idolatry typically pretends to be inclusive. What inclusive means is functionally agnostic about truth claims. The face is pleasant, welcoming, and benign. But once a cabal of absolute tolerationists has gained control in legislative halls, they have time and again turned exclusive and restrictive, especially so against the orthodox and evangelicals whom they recognize intuitively as their most formidable challengers. This is the unfairness revolution claiming to be fairness within modern ecumenical elitism. After securing institutional hegemony, other voices are not really allowed into the process, except, of course, as a token. What is required is enough votes to purge anyone strongly committed to the deposit of faith and the truth of apostolic teaching. Better to have nominal accommodative members who will not make waves. But sharing in a pension plan is not the same as unity in Jesus Christ. Eternal meetings are not synonymous with eternal life.

An ancient enmity exists between institutional interests and gospel mission. Where there is diffuse talk of "mission" among institutionalists it often focuses on institutional goals that may prevent the specific mission assigned to Christians by the Great Commission: baptizing, teaching, and discipling all nations. The institutionalists do such things reluctantly, often only as they are useful for public relations. They are much more comfortable meeting together, enjoying their compatibility, dreaming, and strategizing. Under these conditions, nothing can get through as biblical faith except that which can get through the sieve of institutional idolatry.

The new ecumenism is less interested in institutional maintenance than in participation in life in Christ, sharing in Christ's own life, our lives being hid in his life, so the truth of his life may be refracted in our own lives. This is the premise of whatever continuing manifestations may emerge as a result of the confessing and renewing movements.

The church in history is not given endless time. It does not have time to be both in mission and at the same time steeped in institutional idolatries that stand in the way of its mission.

Fleeing Idolatry

All of these idolatries have failed us. We are now at the end of the modern ecumenical cycle. The way to unity in truth still lies ahead of us. God has not yet blessed these facile ecumenical ploys because of their idolatries. Their failure is not a failure of intentions or aspirations. Rather it is a failure to worship the true God. As long as they seek to negotiate unity on the basis of politics, feelings, dialogue, and institutional identity, they will fail. Yet this is the sad story of the familiar ecumenism of our time.

These four forms of idolatry (politics, experience, dialogue, and institutionalism) work together to reinforce each others' entitlements in modern ecumenism, colluding in the avoidance of truth claims. They need each other. The political idolaters need the experiential idolaters, and both of them need the process or conversational idolaters, because they are less seeking the truth than a feeling of inclusion. The basis of inclusion is now changed from apostolic truth to something else. In time it easily deteriorates to a series of fleeting fixations on shamanism, neopaganism, revolutionary fantasies, ecological salvation, and New Age fads.

This dismal diagnosis makes clearer what confessing movements and renewing movements in the mainline need to change, and especially not to allow another rerun. They must first pray for grace not to repeat these idolatries of politicization, sentiment, talk, or institutional maintenance. To worship the one true God is to give up these idolatries. Then it is on the firm basis of God's revelation in history that faith is awakened and sustained, and the unity of the faithful manifested.

The Transgenerational Community

The unity of believers is not limited to contemporary voices. In this *consensus fidelium* are voices from all cultural histories, all continents, and all languages, not just modern westerners north of the equator. Historic ecumenism was shaped centuries before the emergence of Europe. The record of ancient ecumenism is still available to study objectively and examine textually.

The confessing and renewing movements are being drawn back into this *consensus fidelium*, resurrected by the convicting power of the Spirit in the heart. This is what is enabling a new ecumenical configuration. These movements are being given life not for conquest or dialogue but for repentance and witness. They are privileged to share in the intergenerational and multicultural reality of the communion of saints. The church being created by the Spirit is not the manipulation or maintenance of a new institution, regardless of whatever alphabet soup (CUIC, NCC, NAE, WCC, WEA, etc.) by which it might be named.

Confessing Christians hold fast to the certainty that the Gospel narrative is indeed a true, not a false, report. Our assembling, our *ekklesia*, is a response to this enacted truth, not a substitute for it. If we lack this truth, we have no case to make, nothing whatever to celebrate, nothing to draw us into one body of faith. If we are only talking about improved institutional negotiations or better dialogue or a more inclusive process or more openness in dialogue, forget it. It is evident that these ploys are not being blessed. This is a history of failure that must now be overcome by ecumenical *irenics*—by seeking to make peace between differing ecclesial memories based on ancient ecumenical exegesis. The classic consensus of the faithful informs every angle of every vision of the truth. The failures must also be overcome by accurate, courageous, ecumenical *polemics*, which means drawing boundaries between true and false teaching. Not all views that claim to be of God are.

CORE TEACHINGS OF CONFESSING CHRISTIANS

The sole objective in this section of this study is to set forth the leading confessions or teaching texts of renewing and confessing movements.[1]

All are consensus statements. None of these confessional affirmations are purely private statements written by a single individual. They have been hammered out by confessing Christians who were seeking to state the heart of what they believe, especially in the face of current challenges. They have emerged out of corporate prayer and earnest discussion as a joint attempt to confess not private faith but the faith once delivered to the saints in a public way. All have arisen out of the living *koinonia* of worshiping and serving, confessing and renewing, communities of faith. None are motivated by schism, but by a desire to bring healing and renewal grounded in classic Christian teaching. All seek greater unity in the body of Christ.

These consensual statements are organized according to the major topics of classic Christian teaching. Thus they serve as a primary source for any who would seek to understand the commitment and reasoning of these burgeoning movements. Taken together they offer a theological compendium for confessing Christianity.

An important motivation for drawing together this collection is that it may serve as a resource for any persons or groups who are struggling to define the heart of Christian teaching. This compilation also has a strong ecumenical motive. For it brings together the disparate historic church traditions into a cohesive affirmation of classic Christian faith. It demonstrates a high degree of doctrinal consensus and spiritual affinity among traditional believers of the mainline. Their confessional positions are not split asunder by schismatic tendencies, as sometimes portrayed. Their biblical teaching stands in harmony with classical ecumenical teaching.

Contrary to the popular caricature that confessing Christians are fixated on sexuality issues, this presentation shows how extensively they have spoken publicly on numerous issues of broad relevance to both church and society. They have addressed passionate concerns for social justice, moral wisdom, and theological integrity, as well as issues of the value of marriage and family. These concerns must be seen in broader context of classic Christian teaching, and not simply as political ideology or power ploys.

10

On the Crisis of Integrity

To clarify the beliefs of renewing and confessing movements within mainline churches, one needs only to survey and compare what they have clearly been stating about what they confess. Since they are deliberately confessing movements, they all have statements of belief or confessional declarations or doctrinal affirmations.

All texts cited here (except the 1934 Barmen Declaration) come from consensual voices of believers within North American mainline churches of the last three decades. The reason the Barmen Declaration is included is that it has become a prevailing pattern of confessional declaration under conditions of a *status confessionis*, a state in which silence is no longer morally possible, when confession is required by conscience.

This collection for the first time brings together most of the major documents of the renewing and confessing movements within the mainline. The systematic, topic by topic presentation of these documents exhibits visually the emerging consensus among these movements, presented systematically, topic by topic. In *One Faith: The Evangelical Consensus*, Dr. J. I. Packer and I have brought together major confessional statements of the last fifty years of *global* evangelical Christianity. This collection is different in that it is limited to bringing together major confessional statements of renewing and confessing movements *within North American mainline Protestantism*.

Ordinarily in what follows, the generic term "confessing movements" refers to all the movements in the mainline that seek the recovery of classic Christian teaching, while the uppercase "Confessing Movement"

123

refers either to the Confessing Movement Within the United Methodist Church, or to the Confessing Churches Movement among Presbyterian Churches.

On the Present Crisis

The renewing and confessing movements have emerged as a result of an acute crisis of faith within the churches of the mainline. It is variously described as a membership hemorrhage, a failure of nerve, a crisis of theological integrity, a moral collapse, or a loss of mission. That the mainline is living from crisis to crisis is not disputed either by liberals or evangelicals. What is disputed is the connection of the crisis with the loss of theological bearings, biblical grounding, historic continuity with the apostolic teaching, and cultural wisdom.

Confessing Movements' Perspectives: On the Present Crisis

The DuPage Declaration (Association for Church Renewal)

A Call To Biblical Fidelity [Preamble]
We evangelical renewal leaders from North American mainline churches gathered at Wheaton in DuPage County, Illinois, March 19–20, 1990, express our concern for the Church of Jesus Christ in its drift away from the evangelical faith. What is needed, we believe, is a genuine revival rooted in the Word of God. We, therefore, present this declaration: *A Call to Biblical Fidelity*.

This declaration represents our understanding of theological and moral issues that are now in dispute in our churches. It is not intended to be an exhaustive list of church doctrines and concerns.

It is offered in the spirit of Christ, our Savior and Judge, who calls each of us to confess our complicity in private and public sin, "For it is time for judgment to begin with the family of God" (1 Peter 4:17, NIV; cf. 2 Timothy 4:1–5). We resolve to serve Him with total fidelity and obedience to His Word.

Confessing Movement within the United Methodist Church
An Invitation to the Church

I. The United Methodist Church is at a crossroads. We face either the peril of abandoning the Christian faith, thereby becoming unfaithful disciples of Jesus Christ, or embracing the promise of becoming God's instrument in a new awakening of vital Christianity. The causes of the crisis are complex and multiple. However we believe that the central reason is our abandonment of the truth of the gospel of Jesus Christ as revealed in Scripture and asserted in the classic Christian tradition and historic ecumenical creeds. Specifically we have equivocated regarding the person of Jesus Christ and his atoning work as the unique Savior of the world. We have been distracted by false gospels. We have compromised in our mission to declare the true gospel to all people and spread scriptural holiness. For the sake of the kingdom of God, it is now time for action.

Concerned Clergy and Laity of the Episcopal Church

... [is] a lay movement of concerned and faithful Episcopalians to renew and reform the Church. Today, there are two religions in the Episcopal Church. One remains faithful to the biblical truth and received teachings of the Church, while the other rejects them. ...

The majority of the court [of May 15, 1996] held that the Episcopal Church has no "Core Doctrine" in the area of human sexuality; therefore neither the doctrine nor the discipline of the Church has been violated [referring to the case of Bishop Righter].

Barmen Declaration (1934)

Church Unity and Renewal
I. An Appeal to the Evangelical Congregations and Christians in Germany
01 The Confessional Synod of the German Evangelical Church met in Barmen, May 29–31, 1934. Here representatives from all the German Confessional Churches met with one accord in a confession of the one Lord of the one, holy, apostolic Church. In fidelity to their Confession of Faith, members of Lutheran, Reformed, and United Churches sought a common message for the need and temptation of the Church in our day.

With gratitude to God they are convinced that they have been given a common word to utter. It was not their intention to found a new Church or to form a union. For nothing was farther from their minds than the abolition of the confessional status of our Churches. Their intention was, rather, to withstand in faith and unanimity the destruction of the Confession of Faith, and thus of the Evangelical Church in Germany. In opposition to attempts to establish the unity of the German Evangelical Church by means of false doctrine, by the use of force and insincere practices, the Confessional Synod insists that the unity of the Evangelical Churches in Germany can come only from the Word of God in faith through the Holy Spirit. Thus alone is the Church renewed.

United Church of Canada, 15 Affirmations[1]

We urgently call our Church to a more serious commitment to its theological foundations and to a more positive affirmation of Christian faith. What we affirm now is said out of a constraining concern for the integrity of the Gospel, for the well-being of the Church and for the salvation of the world. We are not attempting to re-write the Church's standards. We are re-affirming Christian faith in a situation of widespread confusion and uncertainty.

The Memphis Declaration (UMC 1992)

God's Revelation In Jesus Christ
Among the people called Christian—in many nations and among many peoples—including United Methodist, there has been a falling away from commitment to the basic truths and doctrines of the Christian faith.

Confessing Movement within the United Methodist Church, A Confessional Statement

[Preamble]
The crisis before us is this: Will The United Methodist Church confess, and be unified by, the apostolic faith in Jesus Christ; or will The United Methodist Church challenge the primacy of Scripture and justify the acceptance of beliefs incompatible with our Articles of Religion and Confession of Faith?

The United Methodist Church is now incapable of confessing with one voice the orthodox Trinitarian faith, particularly Jesus Christ as the Son of God, the Savior of the world, and the Lord of history and the Church. While giving assent to Jesus Christ as Lord, our denomination tolerates opinions that "strike at the root of Christianity" (John Wesley). Our Church suffers from private versions of the faith that do not find their root in Scripture.

On the Conditions Requiring an Act of Confessing Faith—*Status Confessionis*

Out of this crisis emerges the necessity to speak out. Traditionally the moment at which it is impossible to remain faithful without speaking out is called by its Latin name: *status confessionis*. To remain silent about these distortions is to repress the Word of God.

Confessing Movements' Perspectives: On the Conditions Requiring an Act of Confessing Faith—Status Confessionis

Concerned Clergy and Laity of the Episcopal Church

Radical activists seek to replace biblical truth and godly morality with secular humanism and moral relativism. We have become a church which contradicts our own teaching.

Despite this current sadness, there is a possibility of a new and hopeful day for the Episcopal Church. By acting ardently to support and encourage the presenting bishops who filed charges against one of their fellow bishops, we can assist them in their attempts to steer the Church clear of moral bankruptcy.

The Houston Declaration (UMC 1987)

Out of love and concern for the United Methodist Church, 48 pastors from 18 states, from Massachusetts to California, from Illinois to Florida, representing large churches and small, came together in Houston, Texas, December 14–15, 1987. We came as pastors who baptize and marry, confirm and bury and live among our people. We came to reaffirm and promote the central certainties of our faith. In the face of actions by some Boards and agencies and some caucus groups that tend to undermine these certainties, and in the fulfillment of our ordination vows, we feel compelled to speak to three crucial truths which are essential to the life, witness and scriptural integrity of the church: (1) the primacy of Scripture; (2) the nature and name of the one God, Father, Son and Holy Spirit; (3) the high and holy character of ordained ministry.

United Church of Canada, 15 Affirmations

We affirm that The United Church of Canada stands in the Reformed stream of the catholic faith.

As such the United Church is obligated to profess beliefs that are essential to this faith and to issue new statements of faith only after serious and prolonged examination of the Biblical witness.

We are therefore concerned that many pronouncements made in the name of The United Church of Canada—whether officially approved or not—have been giving the impression that our Church has compromised its theological integrity and casually ignored essential beliefs.

In the valid struggle to relate the Gospel to contemporary life, many have uncritically identified novelty with truth and have fallen prey to doctrinal distortion.

The Memphis Declaration (UMC, 1992)

In the tradition of THE HOUSTON DECLARATION, we come together to challenge United Methodists to live more faithfully as the body of Jesus Christ, under his lordship. This involves confessing, proclaiming and living the Apostolic faith. In light of the authority of Scripture, we affirm that:

1. God revealed himself in Jesus Christ, the only way of divine salvation.
2. Holy living is the way for Christians to live out the mandate of discipleship given by Jesus Christ.
3. The local congregation is the center for mission and ministry to the world.

Confessing Movement within the United Methodist Church, A Confessional Statement

During the First week of Easter, 1994, a group of 92 laity, clergy, bishops, and professors gathered to consult about the future of The United Methodist Church. We issued "An Invitation to the Church" for others to join us in exalting Jesus Christ as we confront the crisis of faith within The United Methodist Church. In love for the Church we [a gathering of over eight hundred United Methodists meeting in Atlanta, Ga. April 28–29, 1995] now present this Confessional Statement for the renewal and reform of The United Methodist Church.

On the Purpose of a Confessional Declaration

If confessing Christians have reached such a moment when confession is required, how and with what intent is this confession rightly to be made? What purpose is served by making a declaration or statement of faith amid crisis?

Confessing Movements' Perspectives: On the Purpose of a Confessional Declaration

Confessing Movement within the United Methodist Church, A Confessional Statement

The purpose of this Confessional Statement is to call The United Methodist Church, all laity and all clergy, to confess the person, work, and reign of Jesus Christ. This Statement confronts and repudiates teachings and practices in The United Methodist Church that currently challenge the truth of Jesus Christ—the Son of God, the Savior of the world, and the Lord of all. Aware of our own sinfulness, we who make this Confession submit our common witness and our lives to the judgment and mercy of God, as attested in Scripture, the written Word of God.

Barmen Declaration (1934)

09 In view of the errors of the "German Christians" of the present Reich Church government which are devastating the Church and also therefore breaking up the unity of the German Evangelical Church, we confess the following evangelical truths:...

United Church of Christ, Biblical Witness Fellowship

We perceive an erosion and denial of these truths in our church. Because of our concern for the people of our churches and the well-being of our denomination as a member of the body of Christ, we are called by God to make this confession.

On Scriptural Authority

To confess faith rightly in any generation is to return to the truth of the earliest apostolic testimony. Since Scripture has been so much abused in our time, taken captive by ideologues and reduced to mere historical debates, confessing Christians have found it necessary to state clearly the way they understand the authority of Scripture for the church today. The special attention given to this section is evidence of its central importance for confessing Christians.

Confessing Movements' Perspectives: On Scriptural Authority

American Anglican Council

Holy Scripture: We believe all Scriptures were "written for our learning" (Romans 15:4), that they are "God's Word written," and that we are to "hear, read, mark, learn, and inwardly digest them." We commit ourselves to regular Bible study and to preach and teach only that which is in accordance with Holy Scripture.

Confessing Churches Presbyterian Church USA

2. Holy Scripture is the triune God's revealed Word, the Church's only infallible rule of faith and practice.

Disciples of Christ, Disciples Heritage Fellowship

Our absolute and final authority in matters of faith and practice is Holy Scripture, the 66 books of the Old and New Testaments. We believe the Bible to be the divinely inspired Word of the Living God. Because the Bible is fully and verbally inspired by the Holy Spirit working in and through the human authors, it is without error, and thus stands alone as the supreme and final authority for the church and the individual Christian.

While we recognize the place that human reason, human experience, and church tradition play in our understanding of the Christian faith, we affirm that Scripture alone is God's divinely revealed word and that therefore reason, experience and tradition must bow to biblical authority. We reject the notion that reason, experience or tradition can be used to promote any teaching which is contrary to Scripture.

Presbyterians for Faith, Family, and Ministry

4. We believe the Scriptures of the Old and New Testaments to be, by the Holy Spirit, the inspired Word of God—the unique, reliable, and authoritative witness to Jesus Christ and his will for our lives.

United Church of Canada, 15 Affirmations

6. We believe that the Bible is the God-given basis and norm by which the Church's life, teaching and worship are nourished....

We recognize the value and need of critical scholarship. But the essential and vital need is the guidance of the Holy Spirit, without Whose inward illumination man cannot come to a saving understanding of divine revelation. Moreover in our struggle to grow in the knowledge and love of God, we should remember that now we know in part.

United Church of Christ, Biblical Witness Fellowship

3. We hold that the Bible is the written Word of God, the infallible rule of faith and practice for the church of Jesus Christ. The Scriptures have binding authority on all people. All other sources of knowing stand under the judgment of the Word of God.

United Church of Canada, A Covenant (1990)

BELIEFS: 2.1 belief in the Scriptures of the Old and New Testaments as the primary source and ultimate standard of Christian faith and life.

Evangelical Fellowship of Canada

The Holy Scriptures as originally given by God are divinely inspired, infallible, entirely trustworthy, and constitute the only supreme authority in all matters of faith and conduct.

United Church of Canada, Church Alive, 20 Articles

2.0 We, the representatives of the Presbyterian, Methodist, and Congregational branches of the Church of Christ in Canada, do hereby set forth the substance of the Christian faith, as commonly held among us. In doing so, we build upon the foundation laid by the apostles and prophets, Jesus Christ Himself being the chief cornerstone. We affirm our belief in the

Scriptures of the Old and New Testaments as the primary source and ultimate standard of Christian faith and life.

We acknowledge the teaching of the great creeds of the ancient Church. We further maintain our allegiance to the evangelical doctrines of the Reformation, as set forth in common in the doctrinal standards adopted by the Presbyterian Church in Canada, by the Congregational Union of Ontario and Quebec, and by the Methodist Church. We present the accompanying statement as a brief summary of our common faith and commend it to the studious attention of the members and adherents of the negotiating Churches, as in substance agreeable to the teaching of the Holy Scriptures.

Good News Junaluska Affirmation

The Holy Scriptures
Scriptural Christianity affirms as the only written Word of God the Old and New Testaments. These Holy Scriptures contain all that is necessary for our knowledge of God's holy and sovereign will, of Jesus Christ the only Redeemer, of our salvation, and of our growth in grace.

They are to be received through the Holy Spirit as the guide and final authority for the faith and conduct of individuals and the doctrines and life of the Church. Whatever is not clearly revealed in, or plainly established as truth by, the Holy Scriptures cannot be required as an article of faith nor be taught as essential to salvation. Anything contrary to the teachings of the Holy Scriptures is contrary to the purposes of God and must, therefore, be opposed. The authority of Scripture derives from the fact that God, through His Spirit, inspired the authors, causing them to perceive God's truth and record it with accuracy.

It is evident that the Holy Scriptures have been preserved during the long process of transmission through copyists and translators, and we attribute such accurate preservation to the work of the Holy Spirit. These Scriptures are supremely authoritative for the Church's teaching, preaching, witness, identifying error, correcting the erring, and training believers for ministry in and through the Church.

The DuPage Declaration

V. WE AFFIRM that Holy Scripture is the written Word of God, the uniquely inspired testimony to God's self-disclosure in the history of biblical Israel culminating in Jesus Christ. The Scriptures of the Old and New Testaments take precedence over experience, tradition and reason and are therefore our infallible standard for faith and practice.

WE DENY that Holy Scripture is a merely human document that records the religious experiences of a past people, that it is only an aid in understanding our experiences in the present rather than a rule that is used by the Spirit of God to direct the people of God in every age.

The Houston Declaration (UMC 1987)

I. The Primacy of Scriptures
We United Methodist pastors affirm the Wesleyan principle of the primacy of Scripture and recognize that we share a common heritage with Christians of every age and nation. We have witnessed the confusion and conflict resulting from the ambiguity of the present doctrinal statement as contained in Paragraph 69 of the 1984 *Discipline*.

We therefore endorse the following declaration regarding the primacy of Scripture, as included in the newly proposed doctrinal statement:

United Methodists share with other Christians the conviction that Scripture is the primary source and criterion for authentic Christian truth and witness. The Bible bears authoritative testimony to God's self-disclosure in the pilgrimage of Israel, in the life, death, and resurrection of Jesus Christ, and in the Holy Spirit's constant activity in human history, especially in the mission of early Christianity. As we open our minds and hearts to the Word of God through the words of human beings inspired by the Holy Spirit, faith is born and nourished, our understanding is deepened, and the possibilities for transforming the world become apparent to us.

We properly read Scripture within the believing community, informed by the tradition of that community. We interpret the individual texts in light of their place in the Bible as a whole. We are aided by scholarly inquiry and personal insight, under the guidance of the

Holy Spirit. Wesley's method of interpretation applied this rule: "The obscure text is to be interpreted by those which speak more plainly," and the more difficult passages understood in terms of the "analogy of faith," that is, "the whole scope and tenor of Scripture," the core witness of Scripture as a whole....The Bible serves both as a source of our faith and as the basic criterion by which the truth and fidelity of any interpretation of faith is measured.

Concerned Clergy and Laity of the Episcopal Church

As evangelicals and Episcopalians, we believe the Church's identity is founded on the proclamation of God's redeeming love through Jesus Christ.

Yet today we are witnessing the Episcopal Church embracing a secular humanism that refuses to acknowledge the meaning and authority of the Word of God as spoken through the person of Jesus Christ and revealed to us in Holy Scripture.

Recent events have forced us to a dismal realization—that we are a Church in disarray. We have become a Church which contradicts its own doctrine and teaching.

Great Commission Network (ELCA)

The Scriptures
We believe the canonical Scriptures of the Old and New Testaments are God's Word, divinely inspired and the authoritative source and norm for the Church in proclamation, faith, life, and witness (2 Tim 3:16).

The Houston Declaration (UMC 1987)

The Bible is sacred canon for Christian people, formally acknowledged as such by historic ecumenical councils of the church. Our doctrinal standards identify as canonical thirty-nine books of the Old Testament and the twenty-seven books of the New Testament. Our standards affirm the Bible as the source of all that is "necessary and sufficient unto salvation" (Articles of Religion) and "the true rule and guide for faith and practice" (Confession of Faith).

The most extensive statement of the authority of Scripture is provided by Canadian evangelicals, quoted here at greater length because it has proven useful to many other confessing Christians in North America.

National Alliance of Covenanting Congregations (United Church of Canada): Authority and Interpretation of Scripture

We affirm our belief in the Scriptures of the Old and New Testaments as the primary source and ultimate standard of Christian faith and life.... "We receive the Holy Scriptures of the Old and New Testaments, given by inspiration from God, as containing the only infallible rule of faith and life, a faithful record of God's gracious revelations, and as sure witness of Christ ..." (From the Manual of The United Church of Canada, 1995 edition).

We find the recent "Authority and Interpretation of Scripture" document produced by The United Church of Canada to be such that it undermines the faith upon which it was founded. It does this by describing Holy Scripture as a book among other books, commanding only the authority that any individual wishes to grant it. It reduces Christ from the Divine Son of God, to a caring and loving man who set an excellent example for us to follow. As such we find the document not only lacking but destructive in matters that are central to our faith.

All Scripture is given by inspiration of God, and is profitable for doctrine, for reproof, for correction, for instruction in righteousness, that the man of God may be complete, thoroughly equipped for every good work. (2 Timothy 3:16–17).

We support what the United Presbyterian Church in the United States has to say about the Authority of Scripture: "The one sufficient revelation of God is Jesus Christ, The Word of God incarnate, to whom the Holy Spirit bears unique and authoritative witness through the Holy Scriptures, which are received and observed as the Word of God written. The Scriptures are not a witness among others, but the witness without parallel. God's Word is spoken to His Church where Scriptures are faithfully preached and attentively read in dependence on the illumination of the Holy Spirit and with readiness to receive truth and direction."

We believe that the great moments of God's revelation and communication of Himself to us are recorded in the Scriptures of the Old and New Testaments. But the fullness of God's truth and grace were perfectly revealed in Jesus Christ.

We believe that, while God spoke His Word to people progressively in many portions, the whole is sufficient to declare God's mind and will for our salvation. The Writings were collected, preserved and shared by the Church.

We believe that the underlying theme of all Holy Scripture is the redeeming purpose of God for all His people, and that herein lies its unity.

We believe that in Holy Scripture, God claims the complete allegiance of our heart and mind; and that full understanding and acceptance of the authority and purpose of the Word of God contained in Scripture is the work of the Holy Spirit in our hearts; that, using the Holy Scripture, the Spirit opens the revelation and teachings of Jesus Christ for our spiritual nourishment and growth in grace.

So we acknowledge Holy Scripture to be the true witness to God's Word and the sure guide to Christian faith and conduct.

We are firm in our belief that the Holy Bible remains the greatest source of reforming power in our world. While we in the church may not reasonably expect either church or state to enforce all its spiritual and moral demands, neither ought we to expect that they will undermine them.

The Gospel

If Holy Writ is decisive for church reform and renewal, is it possible to state the core of that message, inasmuch as Scripture is a complex collection of books? Confessing Christians have not dodged the question of defining the heart of the story line of the centuries-long story the Bible tells.

Confessing Movements' Perspectives: The Gospel

United Church of Christ, Biblical Witness Fellowship

4. We affirm that the central content of the Scriptures is the gospel of reconciliation and redemption through the atoning sacrifice of Christ and His glorious resurrection from the grave. The good news is that we are saved by the grace of God alone, the grace revealed and fulfilled in the life and death of Jesus Christ, which is received only by faith. Yet this faith does not remain alone but gives rise to works of piety, mercy, and justice. The Holy Spirit, who spoke through the prophets and apostles, calls us today, as in the past, to seek justice and peace for all races, tongues and nations.

Confessing Movement within the United Methodist Church

The Confessing Movement is a witness by United Methodist lay men and women, clergy and congregations who pledge unequivocal allegiance to the Lord Jesus Christ. This faith centers on Jesus Christ, fully God and fully man; and on His life, death, resurrection, ascension, and promised return as attested in Holy Scripture.

Challenging "Another Gospel"

If the gospel speaks truthfully about the heart of the divine human relationship, what is to be done about views that directly deny or repudiate it? Is it possible or conscionable to say nothing at all about these false teachings?

Confessing Movements' Perspectives: Challenging "Another Gospel"

Confessing Movement within the United Methodist Church, A Confessional Statement

Any new teachings in the Church that seek to set aside the biblical witness cannot be established by votes, or appeals to personal experience, or by responding to contemporary social pressures. According to the apostolic faith, such teachings and practices are false and unfaithful to the Gospel.

Presbyterians for Faith, Family, and Ministry

We also reject the false ideology that teaches that the plain meaning of the Creeds and Confessions, understood in their historic context, are without authority in the church.

Presbyterian Action

Presbyterian Action believes that, in saying "yes" to the Gospel, the church must say "no" to any other ideology that would replace the Gospel or divert us from it.

Confessing Movement within the United Methodist Church, A Confessional Statement

We repudiate teachings that claim the person of Jesus Christ is not adequate to reveal the fullness of God (Heb. 1:1–3). We reject the claim that the maleness of Jesus disqualifies him as the true revelation of God. We reject the claim that God can be fully known apart from Jesus Christ. According to the apostolic faith, such teachings are false and unfaithful to the Gospel.

Concerned Clergy and Laity of the Episcopal Church

I believe our Lord Jesus Christ has given His Church an order which claims the loyalty of faithful Christians above and beyond any deviation sanctioned by any humanity-invented institution, whether secular or ecclesiastical.

On Creedal Tradition as Scriptural Summary

The effort to define the central story line of scriptural teaching has been attempted repeatedly in Christian history. The basis of Christian *catechesis* (basic teaching leading to Christian baptism and confirmation) is the transmission of this central story line. Confessing Christians today recognize the value of the attempts of previous generations of the faithful to state the apostolic testimony in a nutshell, to prepare persons for baptism, to serve as the core of Christian confession, and to be recalled regularly in services of worship as central points of scriptural teaching.

The teaching tradition among confessing Christians intends *never to be contrary to Scripture*. That would be a direct denial of the classic tradition itself. These attempts seek obedience to the address of God in the written Word. They never lord it over Scripture, but stand under Scripture.

The creedal tradition is a time-honored attempt to bring Scripture to a concise and memorable focus, from the Apostles' Creed and the Nicea-Constantinopolitan Creed, to the major Reformation confessions. This confessional tradition continues within confessing Christianity today amid the current waywardness of the mainline churches. Some congregational traditions, however, eschew talk of the historic creeds. Current confessions seek to stand accountably within the faith of the historic creeds insofar as they summarize scriptural teaching.

Confessing Movements' Perspectives: On Creedal Tradition as Scriptural Summary

Presbyterians for Faith, Family, and Ministry

We believe that the Creeds and Confessions of the church, while subordinate to Christ and the Scriptures, are nevertheless authoritative standards. Therefore, we reject the false ideology that declares that the Bible is an ancient document inapplicable to modern life, that God continues to give new revelation apart from Scripture, or that the meaning of Scripture is at variance with the plain meaning of its words understood in their historic context.

Concerned Clergy and Laity of the Episcopal Church

I accept the Apostles' Creed as the Batismal symbol, and the Nicene Creed as the sufficient statement of the Christian faith.

United Church of Canada, A Covenant (1990)

2. We affirm our roots in the Holy Catholic Church and the teaching of the Nicene and Apostles' Creeds. We value our Reformation, Methodist and Congregational heritages. We are in essential agreement with the Doctrine of the Basis of Union of The United Church of Canada.

Good News Junaluska Affirmation

Preamble

In a time of theological pluralism, Good News and other evangelicals within United Methodism have thought it necessary to reaffirm the historic faith of the Church. Our theological understanding of this faith has been expressed in the Apostles' Creed, Nicene Creed, and in John Wesley's standard Sermons and the Explanatory Notes upon the New Testament. We affirm in their entirety the validity and integrity of these expressions of Scriptural truth, and recognize them as the doctrinal standards of our denomination.

We also recognize that our situation calls for a contemporary restatement of these truths. The merging of two great traditions, the Evangelical United Brethren and the Methodist, with their two authentic witnesses to the historic faith, The Confession of Faith and The Articles of Religion, gives further occasion for such a statement. Moreover, we recognize the mandate which the doctrinal statement of the 1972 General Conference has placed upon "all its members to accept the challenge of responsible theological reflection." Consequently, we offer to the United Methodist Church this theological affirmation of Scriptural Christianity.

American Anglican Council

Historic Faith, Ecumenical Vision.

We affirm the Faith of the Church as it is set forth in the Nicene and Apostles' Creeds and in the classical Prayer Book tradition, including those documents contained in the "Historical Documents" section of the 1979 Book of Common Prayer (BCP p. 863). We further affirm the principles of the Chicago-Lambeth Quadrilateral (BCP p. 876) as an expression of the normative authority of Holy Scripture and as a basis for our present unity with brothers and sisters in the Anglican Communion and for the future reunion of all the divided branches of Christ's one holy, catholic and apostolic Church.

Confessing Movement within the United Methodist Church
An Invitation to the Church

II. The renewal, reform, and healing of our church can come only through the life-giving power of the Holy Spirit. We cannot yet see clearly how God will lead us along this path. However, with John Wesley we affirm both the apostolic faith of the universal Church and the Wesleyan distinctives which give form to our faith as articulated in the doctrinal standards of our own church (viz., the Articles and Confession of Faith, Wesley's Standard Sermons and Explanatory Notes). These constitute the essential, unchangeable truths of our tradition. We gladly own this anew for ourselves and seek to reclaim it for our whole church.

United Church of Christ, Biblical Witness Fellowship

5. We confess as our own the faith embodied in the great ecumenical and Reformation creeds and confessions, finding them in basic conformity with the teaching of the Holy Scriptures.

National Alliance of Covenanting Congregations (United Church of Canada)
Article I—On Faith

We believe that the twenty articles of faith, which are printed in the Manual of the United Church of Canada do set forth the substance of the Christian faith as commonly held among us. In doing so, we build upon the foundation laid by the apostles and prophets, Jesus Christ Himself being the chief cornerstone. We affirm our belief in the Scriptures of the Old and New Testaments as the primary source and ultimate standard of Christian faith in life. We acknowledge the teaching of the great creeds of the ancient Church. We further maintain our allegiance to the evangelical doctrines of the Reformation.

Concerned Clergy and Laity of the Episcopal Church

The presenter bishops have issued a statement that states that they "decry this Opinion as deeply flawed and erroneous. The Court's disclaimer not withstanding, its decision has swept away two millennia of Christian teaching regarding God's purposes in creation, the nature and meaning of Christian marriage and the family, the discipleship in relation to sexuality to which we are called as followers of Jesus, and the paradigm of the Church as Bride and Christ as Bridegroom. The distinction of "Core Doctrine" from other "doctrinal teaching" is without precedent or foundation in the Book of Common Prayer, the Resolutions of General Convention, or the Canons of the Church. The very term, "Core Doctrine," is a specious invention of the Court.

Concerned Clergy and Laity of the Episcopal Church
Declaration of Common Faith and Purpose

I do not consider the provinces of the Anglican Communion have authority to change the historic faith of the Church, and I will refrain from any and all actions which might signify acceptance of such purported change, and will resist all present and future attempts to compromise the integrity of the received Catholic Tradition of the Church.

Having discussed the *crisis* of the church, and the *basis* on which it must be met—the scriptural wisdom of two millennia of Christian teaching, the confessors turn to those major points of *substantive Christian teaching* required to meet the crisis. Since they are addressed to ordinary believers and worshipers (not professionals or clergy primarily), they do not contain technical language, but seek to set forth a concise, memorable, and reliable statement of faith that anyone can understand.

11

On God the Father
and God the Son

In response to the crisis of theological integrity in the churches, confessing Christians seek to make clear the basic teaching of faith that underlies all their efforts at reform. Anyone thirsting for something that is new, chic, and innovative will find this the wrong place to look. Confessing Christians are not presuming to create new doctrine but hold firmly to apostolic teaching in ways especially pertinent to current circumstances. The theology is orthodox, reliable, stable, beautiful, familiar, and glorious. By it the church has been blessed by God for two thousand years.

Those who are turning around the mainline here show how deeply they have reflected on the basic questions of the reality of God, language about God, the Triune God, the Father Almighty, Maker of heaven and earth, on creation and providence, and on the history of sin and its consequences for humanity. Not only have they restated these classic teachings in understandable contemporary terms, but have often shown just how the ancient teaching impinges upon the current crisis. They have also been forthright in identifying the falsehoods that negate the truth of classic Christianity.

On the Triune God

The biblical teaching of one God, God the Father, God the Son, and God the Spirit has been ridiculed and misunderstood in our time by faith's detractors. Confessing Christians have found it necessary to answer. This is especially needful in response to some egalitarian challenges to the classical language of God the Father and God the Son. What follows are some of the texts that express these efforts at theological recovery of the classic Christian doctrine of the Triune God, which has been such a defining doctrine for over two millennia of Christian worship.

Confessing Movements' Perspectives: On the Triune God

The DuPage Declaration

I. WE AFFIRM the Trinitarian name of God—Father, Son and Holy Spirit.
WE DENY that these designations are mere metaphors drawn from the cultural experience of the past and may therefore be replaced by new symbols reflecting the cultural ethos of today.

The Memphis Declaration (UMC 1992)

1. Biblical language and images . . . mandate the use of the name Father, Son, and Holy Spirit whenever we speak of the Trinity; [we] reject the replacement of Biblical language and images in the proposed *Book of Worship,* and in other church materials, with alternative language and images which alter the Apostolic faith.

Good News Junaluska Affirmation

The Holy Trinity
Scriptural Christianity affirms the existence of the one Eternal God who has revealed Himself as Father, Son and Holy Spirit, three equal but distinct Persons, mysteriously united in the Godhead which the Church historically has described as the Holy Trinity.

God the Father
Scriptural Christianity affirms that the first Person of the Holy Trinity, God the Father, is the Eternal One and reigns supremely. He has provided a covenant through which His creatures can be redeemed and through which His creation will be liberated from all evil and brought to final righteousness at the end of the age.

United Church of Canada, Church Alive, 20 Articles

2.1 Article I. *Of God.*
We believe in the one only living and true God, a Spirit, infinite, eternal, and unchangeable, in His being and perfections; the Lord Almighty, who is love, most just in all His ways, most glorious in holiness, unsearchable in wisdom, plenteous in mercy, full of compassion, and abundant in goodness and truth. We worship Him in the unity of the Godhead and the mystery of the Holy Trinity, the Father, the Son, and the Holy Spirit, three persons of the same substance, equal in power and glory.

Disciples of Christ, Disciples Heritage Fellowship

1. We believe that the God revealed in Scripture is the only God. We believe this God to be one in nature, yet existing in three persons—Father, Son, and Holy Spirit. We believe Scripture teaches clearly that God is eternal, unchanging, all powerful, all knowing, and everywhere present. We also find in Scripture such important attributes as love, mercy and justice. We believe that whatever we need to know about the nature and attributes of God can be found in Scripture. We reject any and all statements about God which cannot be supported by Scripture.
2. We believe the biblical God (Father, Son and Holy Spirit) created the heavens and the earth, and all things visible and invisible. Everything that exists owes its existence to God,

including those who rebel against the will of God. God is both the Creator and Sustainer of all reality.

Presbyterians for Faith, Family, and Ministry

1. We believe in the One living and true God who exists eternally in three persons—the Father, the Son and the Holy Spirit. We believe that "God is a Spirit, infinite, eternal, and unchangeable, in his being, wisdom, power, holiness, justice, goodness, and truth."

United Church of Christ, Biblical Witness Fellowship

1. We confess our faith in the triune God—Father, Son and Holy Spirit.

Great Commission Network (ELCA)

Statement of Faith
The Trinity
We believe in the Triune God, the one God who exists in three eternal persons: Father, Son and Holy Spirit.

Evangelical Fellowship of Canada

There is one God, eternally existent in three persons: Father, Son and Holy Spirit.

The Houston Declaration (UMC 1987)

II. The Trinity
We confess the historic Christian faith in the one God, Father, Son and Holy Spirit. In Jesus Christ, the divine Son, God has been definitively revealed to humankind, and the world graciously reconciled to God. At the exaltation of Jesus, the one whom he consistently called Father sent forth the Holy Spirit to declare the things of Christ, so that the good news of our redemption might be proclaimed to all people. At least since the gospel of St. Matthew, the church has consistently baptized "in the name of the Father, the Son, and the Holy Spirit" those who accept the message (Matthew 28:19–20).

We deplore the effort in baptism, ordination, and the total liturgy of the Church to re-symbolize the Faith by abandoning the name of God, Father, Son and Holy Spirit or adopting the inadequate substitutes. To do so is to deny the revelation attested in the Scriptures, transmitted by faithful men and women in the Christian tradition, and offered to the world for its salvation.

Formulas such as "Creator, Redeemer, Sustainer" or "Creator, Christ, Spirit" are inadequate substitutes. As to the first: God's richly personal being cannot be defined merely in functional terms. As to the second: Christ and the Spirit are not mere creatures.

We affirm equality and inclusive language in all human relationships.

On Revelation

God has freely made himself known to humanity in history. How do confessing Christians understand God's willingness to disclose his will in human history through historical events?

Confessing Movements' Perspectives: On Revelation

United Church of Canada, Church Alive, 20 Articles

2.2 Article II. *Of Revelation.*
We believe that God has revealed Himself in nature, in history, and in the heart of man; that He has been graciously pleased to make clearer revelation of Himself to men of God who spoke as they were moved by the Holy Spirit; and that in the fullness of time He has perfectly

revealed Himself in Jesus Christ, the Word made flesh, who is the brightness of the Father's glory and the express image of His person. We receive the Holy Scriptures of the Old and New Testaments, given by inspiration of God, as containing the only infallible rule of faith and life, a faithful record of God's gracious revelations, and as the sure witness of Christ.

2.3 Article III. *Of the Divine Purpose.*
We believe that the eternal, wise, holy, and loving purpose of God so embraces all events that, while the freedom of man is not taken away, nor is God the author of sin, yet in His providence He makes all things work together in the fulfillment of His sovereign design and the manifestation of His glory.

The DuPage Declaration
II. WE AFFIRM that God has revealed himself fully and decisively in Jesus Christ as attested in Holy Scripture.
WE DENY that there are other revelations in nature or history that fulfill or complete this one revelation of God.

Barmen Declaration
12 We reject the false doctrine, as though the church could and would have to acknowledge as a source of its proclamation, apart from and besides this one Word of God, still other events and powers, figures and truths, as God's revelation.

On Creation and Providence

How has God chosen to become revealed in creation and providence? Some forms of process theology and naturalism have come near erasing any distinction between Creator and creature. Some deny that almighty God has a hand in shaping history. Some exalt autonomous human freedom so as to deny any participation of God in history. The ancient heresies of Gnosticism (elitist, secret, knowledge of God), Marcionism (forget the Old Testament), and Manichaeanism (two gods in competition) have reappeared within the mainline churches under new guises.

These challenges require the reaffirmation of classic Christian teaching of creation and providence.

Confessing Movements' Perspectives: On Creation and Providence

United Church of Canada, Church Alive, 20 Articles
2.4 Article IV. *Of Creation and Providence.* We believe that God is the creator, upholder, and governor of all things; that He is above all His works and in them all; and that He made man in His own image, meet for fellowship with Him, free and able to choose between good and evil, and responsible to his Maker and Lord.

United Church of Canada, 15 Affirmations
A. *God and Man*
I. We believe that God created the world and has preserved it from falling into hopeless corruption and non-existence. The world is therefore God's world—an arena for the fulfillment of His sovereign purpose.

United Church of Canada, A Covenant (1990)

BELIEFS: 2.2 belief in the one only living and true God, the Father Almighty, the Creator who is above all his works and in them all, and out of whose great love for the world has given his only begotten son to be the Saviour of sinners.

Presbyterians for Faith, Family, and Ministry

We believe that God is our Creator, that he has revealed himself to us through the Scriptures of the Old and New Testaments, and that apart from this revelation we remain ignorant of his name, his nature, and his will.

Therefore, we reject the false ideology that asserts that the creature has the right to name and define the Creator, or to determine how God should act in any time and place.

On Human Existence under Sin and Grace

Some recent theologies and modern church leaders have in practice rejected the classic Christian doctrine of intergenerational sin. This has required the reaffirmation of classic Christian teaching on sin and grace. To speak rightly of creation, it is necessary to speak candidly about human creation as the great gift of God that has fallen into sin, yet is still hedged by grace. The story of creation is above all a story about humanity—its creation, fall, and redemption.

Confessing Movements' Perspectives: On Human Existence under Sin and Grace

United Church of Canada, 15 Affirmations

2. We believe that man and woman were created by God and endowed with freedom and dignity like His own. We are therefore not wholly determined by heredity or environment, but remain responsible moral agents. Moreover, we are not our own but God's. Our chief end is therefore to glorify Him and to find joy and fulfillment in His fellowship and service.

3. We believe that sin has mortally infected us all in our personal and social existence, showing itself in our alienation from God and our fellow man. But God's grace in Christ is sufficient to save us, and His mercy is ever extended to those who respond in repentance and faith.

Disciples of Christ, Disciples Heritage Fellowship

5. We believe human beings were created in the image of God, but fell from that lofty position by disobeying God. Humanity's fall into sin is taught in the book of Genesis and elsewhere in Scripture where we learn that sin has alienated us from God, placing us under divine condemnation. All humans need to trust in the sacrifice of Jesus for salvation, receiving also the regenerating and renewing work of the Holy Spirit. We believe the initial positive response to the gospel includes faith, repentance and baptism.

Good News Junaluska Affirmation

Humanity

Scriptural Christianity affirms that man and woman are fashioned in the image of God and are different from all of God's other creatures. God intends that we should glorify Him and enjoy Him forever. Since the Fall of Adam the corruption of sin has pervaded every person and extended into social relationships, societal systems, and all creation. This corruption is so pervasive that we are not capable of positive response to God's offer of redemption, except by the prevenient, or preparing, grace of God. Only through the justifying, regenerating and sanctifying work of the Triune God can we be saved from the corruption of sin, become increasingly conformed to the image of Christ, and restored to the relationships which God has intended for us.

United Church of Canada, Church Alive, 20 Articles

2.5 Article V. *Of the Sin of Man.* We believe that our first parents, being tempted, chose evil, and so fell away from God and came under the power of sin, the penalty of which is eternal death; and that, by reason of this disobedience, all men are born with a sinful nature, that we have broken God's law, and that no man can be saved but by His grace.

In these ways confessing Christians have come together to resist dilutions of classic ecumenical Christian teaching. The renewing movements in the mainline denominations, standing on the shoulders of ecumenical teaching, have reason to view themselves as the fit heirs of ecumenical truth. The classic Christian teaching of God is the proper basis upon which any new recovery of church life must be based, if blessed by the Spirit.

Having defined the basic teaching of God the creator that underlies confessing Christianity, the texts now ask how about the heart of Christian doctrine: Jesus Christ.

On Jesus Christ

This is the most contested arena of Christian doctrine: the church's teaching of the person and work of Jesus Christ, his incarnation, earthly life and teaching, death, resurrection, ascension, and promised return. Liberalizing theology has led the mainline church into many misunderstandings of Jesus Christ: that he is not truly God; not God incarnate in the flesh; not the Son of God; did not understand himself to be Messiah; did not perform miracles; was married or sexually active; he did die, but was not resurrected; he did not meet his disciples as risen Lord in a bodily resurrection; and did not ascend to heaven, nor will he return to judge the living and the dead on the last day. These are all ultramodern myths that must be demythologized.

The confusion of the liberalizing church is numbing. It has grown to tragic proportions. Worshipers have been violently torn away from classic Christian beliefs in the only Son of God, the Savior of the world, the Way, the Truth, and the Life. Those who have been taught by Scripture to believe that "no one comes to the Father except through the Son" have lived in a denominational setting where the incarnation, atonement, and resurrection have been grossly neglected.

If he is not all the expected One the church has held him truly to be for two thousand years, then what do we do with him? He must be desperately reinterpreted in a way that is acceptable to modern assumptions. The ensuing loss of all the major teachings of classical Christianity follow, leaving the mainline churches wondering whom they are worshiping, and to whom their prayers are addressed. This has required confessing Christians to state forthrightly the faith once for all delivered to the saints.

Confessing Christians have made clear how passionately they believe the straightforward testimony of the apostles as to Jesus's identity and mission. Rightly understanding God the Son shapes everything that follows in Christianity. These declarations make clear not only what confessing Christians believe, but also what false teachings these beliefs necessarily negate, and so must be forthrightly rejected.

Confessing Movements' Perspectives: On Jesus Christ

Barmen Declaration (1934)

10-1. "I am the way, and the truth, and the life; no one comes to the Father, but by me." (John 14:6). "Truly, truly, I say to you, he who does not enter the sheepfold by the door, but climbs in by another way, that man is a thief and a robber....I am the door; if anyone enters by me, he will be saved." (John 10:1, 9.)

11 Jesus Christ, as he is attested for us in Holy Scripture, is the one Word of God which we have to hear and which we have to trust and obey in life and in death.

American Anglican Council

We proclaim the Gospel of Jesus Christ, fully human and fully divine, who became incarnate from the Virgin Mary, lived a life of perfect obedience to his heavenly Father, died on the cross to atone for the sins of the world, and rose bodily in accordance with the Scriptures.

Evangelical Fellowship of Canada

Our Lord Jesus Christ is God manifest in the flesh; we affirm his virgin birth, sinless humanity, divine miracles, vicarious and atoning death, bodily resurrection, ascension, ongoing mediatorial work, and personal return in power and glory.

Confessing Churches Movement, Presbyterian Churches USA

1. That Jesus Christ alone is Lord of all and the way of salvation.

The DuPage Declaration

IV. WE AFFIRM that Jesus Christ is God incarnate in human flesh, fully human and fully divine, different from all other human beings in kind, not simply in degree.

WE DENY that Jesus Christ is essentially the flower of humanity, a spiritual master, a paradigm of what all human beings can become.

Disciples of Christ, Disciples Heritage Fellowship

3. Jesus is the Messiah, the Son of God, the Word who became flesh through His miraculous conception by the Holy Spirit and His virgin birth. He is God and man united in one person. We believe He lived His life without sinning, and freely and willingly went to the cross to atone for the sins of the world, thus satisfying divine justice and accomplishing salvation for all who trust in Him. While Jesus has many names and titles in Scripture, He is preeminently Lord and Savior. We believe He rose bodily from the grave, ascended into heaven and is now seated at the right hand of God the Father where He possesses all authority in heaven and on earth. We believe Him to be the only mediator between God and man, and that apart from Him there is no salvation. We believe in the literal return of

Jesus to the earth at the end of this age. He will come to bring salvation to His own people and judgment to His enemies.

Presbyterians for Faith, Family, and Ministry

2. We believe that Jesus Christ is God in human flesh. We believe that he was born of a virgin, lived a sinless life, performed miracles, suffered and died on the cross as an atoning sacrifice for our sins, rose again on the third day, ascended into heaven, is seated in glorious authority making intercession for his elect, and that he will return to judge sin and establish his eternal kingdom. Therefore, we reject the false ideology that denies either the human or divine natures of Christ, his atoning work, or his exalted Lordship.

3. "Jesus Christ, as he is attested for us in Holy Scripture, is the one Word of God which we have to hear and which we have to trust and obey in life and in death." Therefore, we reject the false ideology that asserts that there are other "lords" to whom we owe allegiance.

United Church of Canada, Church Alive, 20 Articles

2.6 Article VI. *Of the Grace of God.* We believe that God, out of His great love for the world, has given His only begotten Son to be the Saviour of sinners, and in the Gospel freely offers His all-sufficient salvation to all men. We believe also that God, in His own good pleasure, gave to His Son a people, an innumerable multitude, chosen in Christ unto holiness, service, and salvation.

United Church of Canada, A Covenant (1990)

BELIEFS: 2.3 belief in the Lord Jesus Christ, the Word made flesh, the only Mediator between God and humanity, the eternal Son of God, who was crucified for us, rose from the dead, and is with us by the power of the Holy Spirit; . . .

United Church of Canada, Church Alive, 20 Articles

2.7 Article VII. *Of the Lord Jesus Christ.* We believe in and confess the Lord Jesus Christ, the only Mediator between God and man, who, being the Eternal Son of God, for us men and for our salvation became truly man, being conceived of the Holy Spirit and born of the Virgin Mary, yet without sin. Unto us He has revealed the Father, by His word and Spirit, making known the perfect will of God. For our redemption, He fulfilled all righteousness, offered Himself a perfect sacrifice on the Cross, satisfied Divine justice, and made propitiation for the sins of the whole world. He rose from the dead and ascended into Heaven, where He ever intercedes for us. In the hearts of believers He abides forever as the indwelling Christ; above us and over us all He rules; wherefore, unto Him we render love, obedience, and adoration as our Prophet, Priest, and King.

United Church of Canada, 15 Affirmations

B. God's Word

4. We believe that Jesus Christ is more than the man for others. We believe that He is the Son of God made man and that He is the incarnation of God's Word of grace and truth. That is, in the life, death and resurrection of Jesus Christ, God was reconciling the world to Himself, teaching us the meaning of revelation, redeeming us from our sin, giving us sure hope of forgiveness and of eternal life, and providing the incentive and power for the life of faith, hope and love. To be more specific, we believe that the death of Jesus Christ on the cross was God's unique remedy for our sin, bringing life out of death; that the resurrection of Jesus Christ from the dead is both an historical fact and a spiritual truth; that the ascension of Jesus Christ assures us that our King is still with us by the power of the Holy Spirit; and that the coming again of Jesus Christ in glory will involve both the judgment of the world of space and time and also its transformation into the world of God's eternal kingdom.

Great Commission Network (ELCA)

Jesus Christ

We believe that Jesus Christ is God the Son who became human (Philippians 2:5–8) died for our sins and rose from the dead, and through repentance and faith in Him alone (Acts 4:12) one receives the forgiveness of sins and eternal life. We believe that faith in Christ is necessary for salvation and those without Christ will not be saved (John 14:6). We believe we are saved by the unmerited grace of God and not by our good deeds (Ephesians 2:8–10). We believe that good deeds are the fruits and evidence of our faith.

United Church of Christ, Biblical Witness Fellowship

2. We confess that Jesus Christ is truly God and truly man. Because of our sin and estrangement from God, at the Father's bidding the Son of God took on flesh. Conceived by the Holy Spirit and born of the Virgin Mary, He became like us in all things apart from sin. He died on the cross to atone for our sin and reconcile us to God and on the third day rose bodily from the dead. He is the sole head of the church, the Lord and Savior of us all, and will one day return in glory, power and judgment to usher in the kingdom of God in its fullness.

Good News Junaluska Affirmation

God the Son
Scriptural Christianity affirms that the second Person of the Holy Trinity, the Eternal Son, became incarnate as Mary's virgin-born Child, Jesus of Nazareth, the Christ. In His unique Person, He revealed to us both the fullness of deity and the fullness of humanity. By His life, suffering, death, resurrection and ascension He provided the only way of salvation. His sacrifice on the cross once and for all was to reconcile the Holy God and sinners, thus providing the only way of access to the Father. Now He intercedes as High Priest before the Father, awaiting the day when He will return to judge every person, living and dead, and to consummate His Kingdom.

Confessing Movement within the United Methodist Church, A Confessional Statement

We confess, in accordance with Holy Scripture and with the Holy Spirit's help, that Jesus Christ is the one and only Savior of the world. In him, we see not only the fullness and the glory of God, but also the model and power for our own freedom from the bondage of sin and death (Heb. 2:14–18). Through his obedient life, teaching, and ministry, his death on the cross for the sins of the world, and his bodily resurrection, he is the Savior of the world. God through Jesus Christ conquers sin and death, brings salvation to this rebellious world, and reconciles "the world to himself" (2 Cor. 5:18–21).

On the Uniqueness of the Person of Christ Viewed in Relation to the History of Religions

The most heavily contested point in the mainline debate today is whether Jesus Christ is the only way to God's justifying grace, or only one among many ways. Confessing Christians reject efforts to reduce the person of God the Son from being truly God and truly human to the idea of Sophia or to a political ethic or to the figurehead of a bureaucratic organization or to a civic club look-alike. Renewal movements have given specific and sustained attention to the question of Christ's uniqueness among world religions.

Confessing Movements' Perspectives: On the Uniqueness of the Person of Christ Viewed in Relation to the History of Religions

The DuPage Declaration

III. WE AFFIRM that there is only one way to salvation—God's way to us in Jesus Christ, which is apprehended by faith alone through God's grace.

WE DENY that other religions are pathways to salvation, or that one can be in a right relationship with God apart from repentance and faith in Jesus Christ.

United Church of Canada, A Covenant (1990)

4.1 Because Jesus said, "I am the way, and the truth, and the life. No one comes to the Father except through me" (John 14:6 NRSV), we affirm the uniqueness, indispensability and centrality of Jesus Christ. It is therefore a contravention of our faith to say that other religions and ideologies are equally valid ways to God, however ethical they may be.

4.2 Because Scripture says "the Word became flesh" about Jesus alone (John 1:14–18), we affirm that Jesus is God's only Son and that we are God's children by adoption (Rom. 8:15; Gal. 4:5; Eph. 1:4–5). It is therefore a contravention of our faith to speak of a repeatable and continuing incarnation of God in the world or in human beings or even in loving people.

American Anglican Council

The Uniqueness of Jesus Christ.

While religions and philosophies of the world are not without elements of truth, Jesus Christ alone is the full revelation of God. In and through the Gospel, Jesus judges and corrects all views and doctrines. All persons everywhere need to learn of him, come to know and believe in him, and receive forgiveness and new life in him, as there is no other name given under heaven by which we must be saved (Acts 4:12).

Confessing Movement within the United Methodist Church, A Confessional Statement

We confess, in accordance with Holy Scripture and with the Holy Spirit's help, that Jesus Christ is the one and only Lord of creation and history. In the midst of many competing voices, the Church seeks to hear, trust, and obey Jesus the Lord and his commandments (1 Cor. 8:5, 6).

The Memphis Declaration (UMC 1992)

If we are to be obedient to the teaching of Scripture and to our Wesleyan heritage, we must lift up Jesus Christ as God's gift of salvation offered to all humanity. There are doctrinal issues on which Christians may disagree. We dare not, however, deny our Lord in the name of a shallow pluralism or in a vain attempt to elevate tolerance above primary faith commitment to Jesus Christ. We must not surrender the uniqueness and centrality of Jesus Christ and our Christian heritage for the sake of an easy dialogue with those who are not yet Christian, or a false ecumenism with those who do not profess the fullness of the Christian faith.

The classic Christian teaching of God the Son is the foundation upon which any licit Christian doctrine of salvation depends. Only if the church teaches the truth about Jesus Christ will the church be blessed by God. Now the teaching proceeds to the more practical areas of the application of the work of God the Father through the Son, by rehearsing classic Christian teaching of the Holy Spirit, salvation, the church, and human destiny.

12

On the Holy Spirit
and the Church

Having reconnected with the classic Christian teaching of God the Father and God the Son, confessing Christians are able by grace to celebrate the continuing work of God the Spirit. The eternal Spirit is given by the eternal Father and the eternal Son to fulfill and bring to consummation the mission of the Son, both in our personal lives and in human history. By neglect of these tenets, the historic Protestant communions have fallen down many slippery slopes into the mire of deep moral confusion.

On the Holy Spirit

All previous points of classic Christian teaching come to bear in practice just at this point: the power of the Spirit to give new birth and growth to the life of the believer. This is why confessing Christians have given so much active attention to questions of the person and work of the Holy Spirit, the church and the worshiping community, the holy life, a life honoring to God, and to the end of history.

The popular press has often viewed evangelicals as fixated on the repression of sexuality. In truth the treatment of sexuality is always carefully set in the context of the biblical doctrines of creation, providence, and the work of the Spirit. These declarations make clear not only what confessing

Christians believe about the Spirit and the church, but the false teachings these beliefs necessarily reject.

Confessing Movements' Perspectives: On the Holy Spirit

United Church of Canada, 15 Affirmations

C. God's Spirit
7. We believe that God reveals Himself to the individual through the enlightening work of the Holy Spirit. We believe that the Holy Spirit creates true faith in the heart, assures the believer that he is a child of God through Christ and empowers the believer to bear witness, to do good and to love his neighbour as himself. We believe that the Holy Spirit moves within the Church to infuse life and meaning in its worship and witness. Moreover, we believe that the Holy Spirit continues to work in the world and in the life of mankind so that all things will eventually work to fulfill God's good purposes.

Disciples of Christ, Disciples Heritage Fellowship

4. We believe in the ministry of the Holy Spirit. We believe He works in the minds and hearts of persons when the Gospel is proclaimed and when biblical truth is taught. He draws unbelievers to faith in Jesus Christ, imparts new life to those who believe, and indwells every believer. He imparts to God's people both the fruits of the Spirit which enable us to grow in Christ-like character, and the gifts of the Spirit which empower God's people for Christian service. We admonish believers to expect the Holy Spirit to work in ways compatible with Scripture, and to beware of false spirits and teachings which cannot be biblically substantiated.

The Memphis Declaration (UMC 1992)

The power of Jesus Christ is at work in the person of the Holy Spirit and can transform every life and overcome every sin. He calls his Church to transform the current culture, not conform to it.

We urge all United Methodists, including ourselves, to turn away from a consumer mentality, greed, and moral disintegration. We are called to be servants and witnesses to our neighbors in word and deed, leading the world to repent and accept Jesus Christ as Savior and Lord.

Good News Junaluska Affirmation

God the Holy Spirit
Scriptural Christianity affirms that the third Person of the Holy Trinity, the Holy Spirit, was active from the beginning in creation, revelation and redemption. It was through His anointing that prophets received the Word of God, priests became intermediaries between God and His people, and kings were given ruling authority.

The Spirit's presence and power, measured in the Old Testament, were found without measure in Jesus of Nazareth, the Anointed. The Spirit convicts and woos the lost, gives new birth to the penitent, and abides in the believer, perfecting holiness and empowering the Church to carry out Christ's mission in the world. He came to indwell His Church at Pentecost, enabling believers to yield fruit and endowing them with spiritual gifts according to His will. He bears witness to Christ and guides God's people into His truth. He inspired the Holy Scriptures, God's written Word, and continues to illuminate His people concerning His will and truth. His guidance is always in harmony with Christ and the truth as given in the Holy Scriptures.

United Church of Canada, Church Alive, 20 Articles

2.8 Article VIII. *Of the Holy Spirit.* We believe in the Holy Spirit, the Lord and Giver of life, who proceeds from the Father and the Son, who moves upon the hearts of men to restrain them from evil and to incite them unto good, and whom the Father is ever willing to give unto all who ask Him. We believe that He has spoken by holy men of God in making known His truth to men for their salvation; that, through our exalted Saviour, He was sent forth in power to convict the world of sin, to enlighten men's minds in the knowledge of Christ, and to persuade and enable them to obey the call of the Gospel; and that He abides with the Church, dwelling in every believer as the spirit of truth, of power, of holiness, of comfort, and of love.

National Alliance of Covenanting Congregations (United Church of Canada)

We covenant:
   to foster a hunger and thirst to study the holy Scriptures; to profess and confess them by daily living and witness as containing the ultimate standard of Christian faith and life.
   to acknowledge and proclaim the presence of God's Holy Spirit among the faithful believers and congregations and to confess the Lordship of Jesus Christ as the supreme authority and head of the Christian Church.

On Salvation

If the Holy Spirit is truly God as Scripture attests, and if the mission of the Spirit is to bring into full actualization and consummation the work of the Son on the cross and in the resurrection, the next question is: how does the Spirit make God's saving act available to ordinary persons caught and bound in a history of sin? Confessing Christians view God's saving action as the premise of all that the church is called to be and do.

Confessing Movements' Perspectives: On Salvation

United Church of Canada, Church Alive, 20 Articles

2.9 Article IX. *Of Regeneration.* We believe in the necessity of regeneration, whereby we are made new creatures in Christ Jesus by the Spirit of God, who imparts spiritual life by the gracious and mysterious operation of His power, using as the ordinary means the truths of His word and the ordinances of divine appointment in ways agreeable to the nature of man.

2.10 Article X. *Of Faith and Repentance.* We believe that faith in Christ is a saving grace whereby we receive Him, trust in Him, and rest upon Him alone for salvation as He is offered to us in the Gospel, and that this saving faith is always accompanied by repentance, wherein we confess and forsake our sins with full purpose of and endeavour after a new obedience to God.

Disciples of Christ, Disciples Heritage Fellowship

6. We believe salvation to be wholly a work of God's grace. Salvation cannot be earned, merited or deserved, in whole or in part, through human good deeds or through religious ceremony. God credits His own righteousness to those who trust in Christ alone for salvation. We are justified by faith, apart from our own efforts to obey God.

7. We believe that the redeemed will live a new life of faithfulness and obedience to God, not to merit God's favor but because they have already received God's favor. True faith in Christ always leads to a new birth, and the mark of new birth is a new desire and ability to live according to the commands of Jesus. The redeemed love the Lord Jesus Christ and keep His commandments.

> **Presbyterians for Faith, Family, and Ministry**
>
> 5. We believe that from every generation and race, God has sovereignly called and redeemed a people for his own glory—"a royal priesthood, a holy nation, God's own people." We believe that Jesus Christ is alive and present with this people by the indwelling and empowering Holy Spirit, whose work it is to regenerate, give faith, justify, sanctify, and give assurance that we are, by grace, at the price of Christ's shed blood, the adopted sons and daughters of God. Therefore, we reject the false ideology that teaches that human beings have the capacity within themselves, by virtue of their humanity alone, and apart from redemption, to become the sons and daughters of God.

On Justification by Grace through Faith

The classical Christian teaching of salvation turns decisively on the doctrine of justification by grace through faith. Upon a clear understanding and upholding of this doctrine, the church stands or falls. This pivotal teaching of Reformation Christianity is conspicuously received and valued by confessing Christians today, as attested in these consensual declarations of confessing Christians, consistent with the official confessional statements of the historic Protestant communions. This is not a contested point among confessing Christians, but assumed to be at the heart of the classic Protestant confessions. Although all of the historic Protestant communions affirm justification teaching, it has been grossly neglected and profoundly misunderstood by recent mainline church innovators.

> ### Confessing Movements' Perspectives: On Justification by Grace through Faith
>
> **United Church of Canada, Church Alive, 20 Articles**
>
> 2.11 Article XI. *Of Justification and Sonship.* We believe that God, on the sole ground of the perfect obedience and sacrifice of Christ, pardons those who by faith receive Him as their Saviour and Lord, accepts them as righteous, and bestows upon them the adoption of sons, with a right to all privileges therein implied, including a conscious assurance of their sonship.
>
> **Good News Junaluska Affirmation**
>
> *Salvation*
> Scriptural Christianity affirms that God offers salvation to a sinful humanity and a lost world through Jesus Christ. By His death on the cross the sinless Son propitiated the holy wrath of the Father, a righteous anger occasioned by sin. By His resurrection from the dead, the glorified Son raises us to newness of life. When we appropriate by faith God's atoning work in Jesus Christ we are forgiven, justified, regenerated by His Holy Spirit, and adopted into the family of God. By His grace He sanctifies His children, purifying their hearts by faith, renewing them in the image of God, and enabling them to love God and neighbor with whole heart.
>
> **Barmen Declaration (1934)**
>
> 13-2. "Christ Jesus, whom God has made our wisdom, our righteousness and sanctification and redemption." (1 Cor. 1:30.)

14 As Jesus Christ is God's assurance of the forgiveness of all our sins, so, in the same way and with the same seriousness he is also God's mighty claim upon our whole life. Through him befalls us a joyful deliverance from the godless fetters of this world for a free, grateful service to his creatures.

Evangelical Fellowship of Canada

The salvation of lost and sinful humanity is possible only through the merits of the shed blood of the Lord Jesus Christ, received by faith apart from works, and is characterized by regeneration by the Holy Spirit.

On Sanctification

The scriptural teaching on God's justifying grace on the cross is intimately connected with the scriptural teaching of the call to the holy life. The justified life calls for a holy life. Justification thus is bound intrinsically with the teaching of the sanctifying grace of the Spirit that draws believers toward holy living. Confessing Christians understand the urgent need for the recovery of this teaching in their personal lives, worshiping communities, and society.

Confessing Movements' Perspectives: On Sanctification

United Church of Canada, Church Alive, 20 Articles

2.12 Article XII. *Of Sanctification.* We believe that those who are regenerated and justified grow in the likeness of Christ through fellowship with Him, the indwelling of the Holy Spirit, and obedience to the truth; that a holy life is the fruit and evidence of saving faith; and that the believer's hope of continuance in such a life is in the preserving grace of God. And we believe that in this growth in grace Christians may attain that maturity and full assurance of faith whereby the love of God is made perfect in us.

The Memphis Declaration (UMC 1992)

We affirm the call of Jesus Christ, the teaching of holy Scripture, and the faithful witness of John Wesley, that as Christians we are called to holy living. We cannot be self-righteous, because our own personal lives fall far short of his standard of holy living, but the standard must be upheld.

Evangelical Fellowship of Canada

The Holy Spirit enables believers to live a holy life, to witness and work for the Lord Jesus Christ.

Confessing Churches Presbyterian Church USA

3. That God's people are called to holiness in all aspects of life. This includes honoring the sanctity of marriage between a man and a woman, the only relationship within which sexual activity is appropriate.

Barmen Declaration (1934)

15 We reject the false doctrine, as though there were areas of our life in which we would not belong to Jesus Christ, but to other lords—areas in which we would not need justification and sanctification through him.

> **Great Commission Network (ELCA)**
>
> We view the body as sacred and to be used to honor God and to serve our neighbor. To destroy the body by misuse of chemical substances is against God's holy will.

On the Church

Out of God's justifying and sanctifying grace there necessarily follows the living community of faith and worship, which the Spirit is creating. It is in this community that these teachings are held, taught, and embodied and lived out. Confessing Christians ask: How is this saving grace transmitted in actual communities of worship and faith, living in time, and subject to the vicissitudes of changing history? Confessing Christians, who are sometimes thought to lack a positive ecclesiology, have given explicit attention in their consensual statements to the nature and mission of the church, as these extracts attest.

> ### Confessing Movements' Perspectives: On the Church
>
> **Good News Junaluska Affirmation**
>
> *The Church*
> Scriptural Christianity affirms that the Church of Jesus Christ is the community of all true believers under His sovereign Lordship. This Church, the Body of Christ, is one because it shares one Lord, one faith, one baptism. It is holy because it belongs to God and is set apart for His purposes in the world. It is apostolic because it partakes of the authority granted to the apostles by Christ Himself. It is universal because it includes all believers, both living and dead, in every nation, regardless of denominational affiliation. Its authenticity is to be found wherever the pure Word of God is preached and taught; wherever the Sacraments of Baptism and Holy Communion are celebrated in obedience to Christ's command; wherever the gifts of the Holy Spirit upbuild the body and bring spiritual growth; wherever the Spirit of God creates a loving, caring fellowship, and a faithfulness in witness and service to the world; and wherever discipline is administered with love under the guidance of the Word of God.
>
> **Presbyterians for Faith, Family, and Ministry**
>
> 6. We believe that as the people of God, we have been called and commanded to proclaim the good news of salvation through Jesus Christ, to call men and women, boys and girls, to the obedience of faith, and in every generation to reclaim and reform the purity of the Church's witness. Therefore, we reject the false ideology that denies the Church's call, in every generation, to challenge cultural distortions of the gospel and to witness to the uniqueness of our Lord and Savior Jesus Christ, the one mediator between God and human beings.
>
> **Disciples of Christ, Disciples Heritage Fellowship**
>
> 8. We believe Jesus Christ established His church on earth consisting of all persons who are joined to Him through saving faith. We believe God's people must assemble together regularly for worship, partaking of the Lord's Supper, edification from the Scriptures and for mutual support and encouragement.

United Church of Canada, 15 Affirmations

D. God's Church
8. We believe that God has called men, women and children into a sacramental community of faith, worship, fellowship, evangelism and service. This community is the Church, the Body of Christ, the household of faith, the people of God. The Church has never been perfect and at times has failed her Lord most scandalously. But God continues to work through fallible people who respond to His call and who seek to do His will.

Barmen Declaration (1934)

16-3. "Rather, speaking the truth in love, we are to grow up in every way into him who is the head, into Christ, from whom the whole body [is] joined and knit together." (Eph. 4:15, 16.)
17 The Christian Church is the congregation of the brethren in which Jesus Christ acts presently as the Lord in Word and sacrament through the Holy Spirit.

United Church of Canada, A Covenant (1990)

The Church, the body of Christ, consists of all true believers.

Great Commission Network (ELCA)

The Church
We believe the central mission of the Church is the Great Commission (Matthew 28:19–20), namely, to bring the knowledge of Christ to those who do not yet know Him as their Lord and Savior, and to disciple those who are already Christians to mature in their faith, love and service. We seek by the Holy Spirit's power to carry out the Great Commission through being a loving witness to the truth of Scripture within the Evangelical Lutheran Church in America (ELCA). We desire to support and encourage the ELCA and its leaders in upholding the authority of the Scripture, the confessions, and especially the centrality of evangelism and world missions.

United Church of Canada, Church Alive, 20 Articles

2.15 Article XV. *Of the Church.* We acknowledge one Holy Catholic Church, the innumerable company of saints of every age and nation, who being united by the Holy Spirit to Christ their Head are one body in Him and have communion with their Lord and with one another.

Confessing Movement within the United Methodist Church, A Confessional Statement

True authority in the Church derives from, and furthers obedience to this Lord. True authority in the Church holds the community accountable to this Lord, especially when teachings and practices arise that undermine or deny his Lordship.

On Confession and Unity

Is the church already one body in Jesus Christ? If one, according to Scripture, what is to become of our divisions, our denominationalism? How is the unity of the body of Christ held and argued among confessing Christians? Confessing Christians care about that Christian unity which is grounded in Christian truth. However much confessing movements may stress the recovery of their particular confessional tradition, that does not intend to neglect the unity of believing Christians of all times and places. Rather the recovery is based on the classic ecumenical consensus.

Confessing Movements' Perspectives: On Confession and Unity

United Church of Canada, A Covenant (1990)

BELIEFS: 7. And we covenant to pray Christ's prayer that all may be one, so that the world will believe (John 17:11, 20–23). We are here for the sake of the world which God so loved (John 3:16).

Barmen Declaration (1934)

06 We, the representatives of Lutheran, Reformed, and United Churches, of free synods, Church assemblies, and parish organizations united in the Confessional Synod of the German Evangelical Church, declare that we stand together on the ground of the German Evangelical Church as a federation of German Confessional Churches. We are bound together by the confession of the one Lord of the one, holy, catholic, and apostolic Church.

Disciples of Christ, Disciples Heritage Fellowship

We believe God intends for His church to be united through a common faith in Jesus and a common commitment to live under the authority of God's revealed Word.

On the Locality and Universality of the Body of Christ

The church that is joined to Christ, as branch with vine, and consists in the one body of Christ, unified in his headship, is both local and worldwide. Confessing Christians rejoice in both the locality of the church, and the historic, intergenerational, and crosscultural expressions of the reality of the church. The unity of the body of Christ is not inconsistent with the diversity of the body of Christ. The worldwide character of the body of Christ is present with and manifested in a local body of believers.

Confessing Movements' Perspectives: On the Locality and Universality of the Body of Christ

American Anglican Council

Congregational Life.
We hold corporate worship, discipleship, and mission to be interconnected and indispensable aspects of our response to God as he revealed himself to us in Jesus Christ. We are committed to being sacrificially involved in all three aspects of congregational life.

The Memphis Declaration (UMC 1992)

Local Congregation
The local church is the primary place where we encounter the risen Lord. It must again become, in doctrine and practice, the center of the mission and ministry of the Church. The purpose of the boards, agencies and seminaries must be focused on the equipping of the people of God to be in ministry where they worship and work.

United Church of Canada, A Covenant (1990)

1. We recognize as members of the church those who, by confession of faith, by example of life and by partaking the sacraments, profess the same God and Christ with us (Calvin).

> **United Church of Canada, Church Alive, 20 Articles**
>
> We acknowledge as a part, more or less pure, of this universal brotherhood, every particular church throughout the world which professes this faith in Jesus Christ and obedience to Him as divine Lord and Saviour.

On Prayer

Confessing Christians are praying Christians—praying for the church and the world, for the civil powers, and for the poor, for all conditions of humanity. The one body of Christ, which has both local and universal expressions, is characterized by its constant adoration of God, intercession for the world, and petition to the triune God for guidance.

> ## Confessing Movements' Perspectives: On Prayer
>
> ### United Church of Canada, Church Alive, 20 Articles
>
> 2.13 Article XIII. *Of Prayer.* We believe that we are encouraged to draw near to God, our heavenly Father, in the name of His Son, Jesus Christ, and on our own behalf and that of others to pour out our hearts humbly yet freely before Him, as becomes His beloved children, giving Him the honour and praise due His holy name, asking Him to glorify Himself on earth as in Heaven, confessing unto Him our sins, and seeking of Him every gift needful for this life and for our everlasting salvation. We believe also that, inasmuch as all true prayer is prompted by His Spirit, He will in response thereto grant us every blessing according to His unsearchable wisdom and the riches of His grace in Jesus Christ.
>
> ### United Church of Canada, 15 Affirmations
>
> 10. We believe that the ministry of worship, both private and corporate, is essential to the life and growth of the Church, as it was to the life of Jesus Christ. The Church's service to the world should never be divorced from Christian belief, worship and prayer.
>
> ### United Church of Canada, Church Alive, 20 Articles
>
> 2.15 Article XV. *Of the Church.* Further, we receive it as the will of Christ that His Church on earth should exist … for the public worship of God, for the administration of the sacraments, for the upbuilding of the saints, and for the universal propagation of the Gospel.

On Baptism and Eucharist

The ordering of the praying and worshiping community is centered in those acts of worship instituted by Jesus Christ himself. From the above affirmations on the church, the confessions move directly to baptism and Eucharist as instituted by the Lord according to Scripture. Under liberalizing church leadership, the mainline has tended to see the Lord's Supper as an occasional optional experience more than a gift of unmerited grace provided and commanded by God. To the extent that liberalism took the mystery of grace out of the Eucharist, and reduced baptism to a sentimental ceremony, it is necessary that confessing Christianity reassert the biblical understanding of the efficacy of divine grace in baptism and Eucharist.

Confessing Movements' Perspectives: On Baptism and Eucharist

United Church of Christ, Church Alive, 20 Articles

2.16 Article XVI. *Of the Sacraments.* We acknowledge two sacraments, Baptism and the Lord's Supper, which were instituted by Christ, to be of perpetual obligation as signs and seals of the covenant ratified in His precious blood, as a means of grace, by which, working in us, He doth not only quicken but also strengthen and comfort our faith in Him, and as ordinances through the observance of which His Church is to confess her Lord and be visibly distinguished from the rest of the world.

Concerned Clergy and Laity of the Episcopal Church

I accept the two Sacraments ordained by Christ Himself—Baptism and the Supper of the Lord—ministered with unfailing use of Christ's words of Institution, and of the elements ordained by Him. I accept the Historic Episcopate, locally adapted in the methods of its administration to the varying needs of the nations and peoples called of God into the Unity of His Church.

The Memphis Declaration (UMC 1992)

7. [We] affirm that baptism is a means of God's grace, but that a personal decision to accept Jesus Christ as Savior and Lord is essential for salvation and for full membership in the Church.

United Church of Christ, Church Alive, 20 Articles

2.16.1 Baptism with water into the name of the Father and of the Son and of the Holy Spirit is the sacrament by which are signified and sealed our union to Christ and participation in the blessings of the new covenant. The proper subjects of baptism are believers and infants presented by their parents or guardians in the Christian faith. In the latter case the parents or guardians should train up their children in the nurture and admonition of the Lord and should expect that their children will, by the operation of the Holy Spirit, receive the benefits which the sacrament is designed and fitted to convey. The Church is under the most solemn obligation to provide for their Christian instruction.

United Church of Christ, Church Alive, 20 Articles

2.16.2 The Lord's Supper is the sacrament of communion with Christ and with His people, in which bread and wine are given and received in thankful remembrance of Him and His sacrifice on the Cross; and they who in faith receive the same do, after a spiritual manner, partake of the body and blood of the Lord Jesus Christ to their comfort, nourishment, and growth in grace. All may be admitted to the Lord's Supper who make a credible profession of their faith in the Lord Jesus and of obedience to His law.

On Ministry and Church Order

Amid the deluge of secularization, the mainline leadership has reduced questions of calling to ministry to egalitarian issues of civil justice. Accordingly, the rite of ordination is viewed as a civil right, and the purpose of church legislation is no longer to provide for the sacred ministry of the proclamation of the Word and administration of the sacrament, but more obviously to provide funding for bureaucracies and social programs. To the extent that liberalism has reduced ministry to political organizational efforts, it becomes increasingly necessary for confessing Christianity to reassert the fundamental nature of the ministry and the missionary nature of the church.

We are proceeding step by step through a logical sequence of affirmations required by Scripture. Each step has profound relevance for the next step. All of the above points of teaching are now being brought to bear precisely on the *crisis of the church*. Not the least of these implications concerns ministry and church order where some of our most contested issues lie. How confessing Christians have sought consensus on these scriptural affirmations is seen in what follows. The way the church and its ministry are ordered under Scripture is an absolutely decisive issue for confessing Christianity.

Confessing Movements' Perspectives: On Ministry and Church Order

United Church of Christ, 15 Affirmations

9. We believe that every Christian is called to live his faith in all areas of life. But we believe also that some Christians are called, trained and ordained to a specialized ministry of preaching, teaching, sacramental ministration and pastoral oversight—in short, of equipping the Church to minister to God and the world. Within the New Testament and ever since, this ministry of the Word and Sacraments has been regarded—along with Scripture and Sacrament—as a precious gift to the Church from her risen and exalted Lord. We therefore affirm both the ministry of the laity and the ministry of the Word and Sacraments.

Barmen Declaration (1934)

As the Church of pardoned sinners, it has to testify in the midst of a sinful world, with its faith as with its obedience, with its message as with its order, that it is solely his property, and that it lives and wants to live solely from his comfort and from his direction in the expectation of his appearance.

United Church of Canada, 15 Affirmations

BELIEFS: 6. We covenant to support and counsel one another, remembering that if one suffers, all suffer, and if one rejoices, all rejoice (1 Cor. 12:26). We will do this through local congregations and by encouraging associations and fellowships among those of like mind and heart. Specifically we intend to hold periodic conferences and to facilitate communication of resources that will build up the Church.

United Church of Christ, Church Alive, 20 Articles

2.17 Article XVII. *Of the Ministry*. We believe that Jesus Christ, as the Supreme Head of the Church, has appointed therein an Ordained Ministry of Word, Sacrament, and Pastoral Care and a Diaconal Ministry of Education, Service, and Pastoral Care and calls men and women to these ministries; that the Church, under the guidance of the Holy Spirit, recognizes and chooses those whom He calls, and should thereupon duly ordain or commission them to the work of the ministry.

National Alliance of Covenanting Congregations (United Church of Canada)

Article II—On Ministry

It is expected that those called to the pastorate of associated congregations will strive to exemplify the highest ideals of faithful service in the exercise of their public ministry and will live in honesty, purity and charity with all people.

Barmen Declaration (1934)

19-4. "You know that the rulers of the Gentiles lord it over them, and their great men exercise authority over them. It shall not be so among you; but whoever would be great among you must be your servant." (Matt. 20:25, 26.)

20 The various offices in the Church do not establish a dominion of some over the others; on the contrary, they are for the exercise of the ministry entrusted to and enjoined upon the whole congregation.

21 We reject the false doctrine, as though the Church, apart from this ministry, could and were permitted to give itself, or allow to be given to it, special leaders vested with ruling powers.

The Memphis Declaration (UMC 1992)

We are concerned about ministerial leadership. We must be especially careful that a seminary education be consistent with our ... heritage and not dominated by a secular mind-set. Some of our seminaries are committed to both the teaching and modeling of our ... heritage, recognizing that seminaries are places where men and women are trained for Christian ministry. We celebrate their faithfulness to the Church and we pledge our loyalty and support to them.

Presbyterian Action

Presbyterian Action believes that the church must set an example of biblically based democratic practice in its own life. Debates should be open and orderly, information should be freely available, and power should be widely distributed.... When a political debate appears to have become slanted in one direction, Presbyterian Action points out alternative facts and arguments that ought to be heard.

United Church of Christ, Church Alive, 20 Articles

2.18 Article XVIII. *Of Church Order and Fellowship.* We believe that the Supreme and only Head of the Church is the Lord Jesus Christ; that its worship, teaching, discipline and government should be administered according to His will by persons chosen for their fitness and duly set apart to their office; and that although the visible Church may contain unworthy members and is liable to err, yet believers ought not lightly to separate themselves from its communion, but are to live in fellowship with their brethren, which fellowship is to be extended, as God gives opportunity, to all who in every place call upon the name of the Lord Jesus.

On the Future

The finishing and consummating work of the Holy Spirit leads directly into questions concerning the end of history, the future, and the Great Commission.

Confessing Movements' Perspectives: On the Future

Good News Junaluska Affirmation

The fullness of God's great salvation will come with the return of Christ. This cosmic event will signal the resurrection of the saved to eternal life and the lost to eternal damnation, the liberation of creation from the Adamic curse, God's final victory over every power and dominion, and the establishment of the new heaven and the new earth.

United Church of Canada, Church Alive, 20 Articles

We confidently believe that by His power and grace all His enemies shall finally be overcome, and the kingdoms of this world be made the Kingdom of our God and of His Christ.

Disciples of Christ, Disciples Heritage Fellowship

9. We believe that those who die in faith enter into God's presence, experiencing everlasting fellowship with our Lord and all the redeemed. Those who die in unbelief are forever separated from the Lord.

Good News Junaluska Affirmation

The Church, as the Bride of Christ, will ultimately be joined with her Lord in triumphant glory.

United Church of Canada, Church Alive, 20 Articles

2.19 Article XIX. *Of the Resurrection, the Last Judgment, and the Future Life.* We believe that there shall be a resurrection of the dead, both of the just and of the unjust, through the power of the Son of God, who shall come to judge the living and the dead; that the finally impenitent shall go away into eternal punishment and the righteous into life eternal.

United Church of Canada, A Covenant (1990)

Ultimately God will judge the living and the dead, those who are saved unto the resurrection of life, those who are lost unto the resurrection of damnation.

On Mission and the Great Commission

Under liberalizing mainline leadership, the mission of the church has tended to be interpreted as the expansion of the institutions, with its social projects coming under the umbrella of mission. A specific failure has been the absence or reduction of worldwide witnessing and preaching ministries. Confessing Christians today place strong emphasis upon the calling to preach the gospel to the whole world, according to Scripture, and according to the Lord's express command.

Confessing Movements' Perspectives: On Mission and the Great Commission

American Anglican Council

The mission of the Church is, according to Jesus' Great Commission, to "go and make disciples of all nations, baptizing them in the name of the Father and of the Son and of the

Holy Spirit, and teaching them to obey everything I have commanded you" (Matthew 28:19–20).

In a fresh commitment to that mission, we join together in common confession of the Gospel and in a radical commitment to support one another in accordance with classical Anglican orthodoxy.

Presbyterian Action

Presbyterian Action believes that the most powerful message the church can deliver to any society is simply the Gospel of Jesus Christ.

Disciples of Christ, Disciples Heritage Fellowship

10. Jesus Christ has commanded His church to proclaim the gospel throughout the world and to make disciples of all nations, baptizing believers and teaching them to observe all the commandments of Jesus. We believe the local church is mandated to evangelize in the local community and throughout the world.

United Church of Canada, Church Alive, 20 Articles

We joyfully receive the word of Christ, bidding His people go into all the world and make disciples of all nations, declaring unto them that God was in Christ reconciling the world unto Himself, and that He will have all men to be saved and come to the knowledge of the truth. We confidently believe that by His power and grace all His enemies shall finally be overcome, and the kingdoms of this world be made the Kingdom of our God and of His Christ.

The DuPage Declaration

VIII. WE AFFIRM that the mission of the church is to spread the good news of salvation by word and deed to a lost and despairing humanity. This mission to proclaim the atoning death and resurrection of Jesus Christ to all nations calls people of faith to discipleship and obedience in the pursuit of personal and social holiness. We further affirm that the fruit of the gospel proclamation is justice, mercy and peace.

WE DENY that the mission of the church is the self-development of exploited peoples or the political liberation of oppressed peoples.

American Anglican Council

Mission and Missions.

The Risen Lord commissioned his disciples to preach the gospel and to follow his commandments. The mission of the Church includes both evangelistic proclamation and deeds of love and service. We commit ourselves and our resources to this mission, both locally and to the uttermost parts of the earth. We affirm our particular responsibility to know, love, and serve the Lord in our local settings and contexts. Since the biblical pattern of witness moves from the local to the global, we will endeavor to be well-informed about our local communities and active in church planting, evangelism, service, social justice, and cross-cultural, international mission, with particular concern for the poor and the unreached peoples of the world.

The Memphis Declaration (UMC 1992)

[Proposals:]

1. Fiscal responsibility calls for the curtailment, reordering, and reduction of the bureaucracy of the Church so that more of our tithes and offerings will go directly into mission and ministry and *not* increasingly into general church staff and support for boards, agencies and study commissions.

2. Abolish the General Council on Ministries as an unnecessary and costly layer of bureaucracy. It is in direct conflict with the Constitution of the Church, which assigns to the Council of Bishops "the general oversight and promotion of the temporal and spiritual interest of the entire Church and for carrying into effect the rules, regulations, and responsibilities prescribed and enjoined by the General Conference." (Para. 50, Art. III, The Constitution).

3. Reduce the number, size, staff and costs of General Church boards and agencies.

4. Restore the Church's mission and evangelistic thrust. Establish a General Board of Evangelism, including the transfer of the section on church extension from the national division of the Board of Global Ministries, so that reaching the world for Christ will again be central to the purpose and mission of the Church.

United Church of Christ, Biblical Witness Fellowship

6. We confess that the mission of the church is to bear witness to God's law and gospel in our words and deeds. We are sent into the world as disciples of Christ to glorify God in every area of life and to bring all peoples into submission to the Lordship of Christ, baptizing them in the name of the Father and of the Son and of the Holy Spirit. We seek to obey this commission in the full assurance that our Lord and Savior is with us always, even to the end of the age.

13

On a Life Honoring
to God

In order to embody this mission appropriately, the confessing church prays that the Holy Spirit will inspire it to a life of holiness. Such a life would be honoring to God in all areas, especially those highly contested within contemporary culture: sexuality, family, and the value of human life.

On the Christian Life

Confessing Christians view justice issues within the frame of reference of God's justifying activity for sinners. Our good works are seen in relation to God's good work for us on the cross. The renewal movements have set forth strong statements on social, political, and economic justice. It is in the context of the gospel of salvation history that the motivation for social justice becomes transformed by grace.

Confessing Movements' Perspectives: On the Christian Life

United Church of Canada, 15 Affirmations

14. We believe that God wills reconciliation, healing and wholeness for His hurting world. This belief has practical implications for Christians, namely, that we must work for reconciliation in a hostile, divided world; and that we cannot do enough for the welfare of

the world. We believe that we must witness to God's love both in word and in acts of justice, mercy and compassion.

15. We believe that the Christian is called to be a leavening influence in life. In both his individual life and in his responsibility to the wider community, the Christian is called to be holy and to work for justice and mercy. In life and speech the Christian is called to proclaim the good news that God was in Christ reconciling the world to Himself.

Good News Junaluska Affirmation

Ethics

Scriptural Christianity affirms that we are God's workmanship, created in Christ Jesus for good works. These works are the loving expressions of gratitude by the believer for the new life received in Christ. They do not earn one's salvation nor are they a substitute for God's work of redemption. Rather, they are the result of regeneration and are manifest in the believer as evidence of a living faith.

United Church of Canada, 15 Affirmations

E. Life with God

11. We believe that God calls man to exercise his freedom responsibly, in accordance with His holy will. Although we recognize that moral decisions are made in the context of actual life, we affirm the basic moral standards of the Judaeo-Christian tradition as definitive guidelines for Christian living.

United Church of Canada, Church Alive, 20 Articles

2.20 Article XX. *Of Christian Service and the Final Triumph.* We believe that it is our duty, as disciples and servants of Christ, to further the extension of His Kingdom, to do good unto all men, to maintain the public and private worship of God, to hallow the Lord's Day, to preserve the inviolability of marriage and the sanctity of the family, to uphold the just authority of the State, and so to live in all honesty, purity, and charity, that our lives shall testify of Christ.

Good News Junaluska Affirmation

Our life in Christ includes an unstinting devotion to deeds of kindness and mercy and a wholehearted participation in collective efforts to alleviate need and suffering. The believer will work for honesty, justice and equity in human affairs; all of which witness to inherent rights and a basic dignity common to all persons created in the image of God. Such contemporary issues as racism, housing, welfare, education, Marxism, capitalism, hunger, crime, sexism, family relationships, aging, sexuality, drugs and alcohol, abortion, leisure, pornography, and related issues call for prayerful consideration, thoughtful analysis, and appropriate action from Christians, and must always be a matter of concern to the Church. Thus, we remember that faith without works is dead.

United Church of Canada, Church Alive, 20 Articles

2.14 Article XIV. *Of the Law of God.* We believe that the moral law of God, summarized in the Ten Commandments, testified to by the prophets, and unfolded in the life and teachings of Jesus Christ, stands forever in truth and equity, and is not made void by faith, but on the contrary is established thereby. We believe that God requires of every man to do justly, to love mercy, and to walk humbly with God; and that only through this harmony with the will of God shall be fulfilled that brotherhood of man wherein the Kingdom of God is to be made manifest.

United Church of Canada, A Covenant (1990)

2.5 and belief that the moral law of God, summarized in the Ten Commandments, testified to in the prophets and unfolded in the life and teachings of Jesus Christ, stands forever in truth and equity, and is established by faith.

Good News Junaluska Affirmation

God has called us to do justice, to love kindness, and to walk humbly with Him. In the Scriptures are found the standards and principles that guide the believer in this walk. These ethical imperatives, willingly accepted by the believer, enable us to be a part of God's purposes in the world. Moreover, in this we are called to an obedience that does not stop short of our willingness to suffer for righteousness' sake, even unto death.

On Christian Freedom and Religious Liberty

Global Christianity today lives under many different types of political regimes, some tyrannical and oppressive, some providing a greater measure of justice. The confessing church has been especially attentive to the urgent needs of those who live under dire conditions of persecution and oppression, aware that there has been more martyrdom of believers on behalf of testimony to Christ in the past hundred years than in all the previous centuries combined. There has been an unconscionable lack of interest among the liberal mainline leadership to see and respond to persecution of Christians in socialist and Marxist regimes. This neglect explains why ministries to persecuted Christians have become such a crucial element in the corrective offered by confessing Christianity.

Confessing Movements' Perspectives: On Christian Freedom and Religious Liberty

Presbyterian Action

Presbyterian Action believes that among the current issues on which the church should be able to speak most compellingly is the defense of fundamental human rights worldwide—including especially the freedom of religious belief and practice. The church should be the foremost voice on behalf of fellow Christians and others who are persecuted for their faith. Presbyterian Action supplies information and encouragement to Presbyterians seeking to highlight a concern for religious freedom worldwide.

Word Alone

We want the Evangelical Lutheran Church in America to manifest:
Freedom from sin, death and the devil through faith in Jesus alone
Freedom for representative governance throughout the church at all assemblies and councils with checks and balances on the authority of churchwide structures
Freedom in all rites and traditions that are neither commanded nor forbidden by Scripture
Freedom so that all baptized followers are empowered as members of the priesthood of all believers to proclaim the Gospel
Freedom to be and make disciples of Christ.

Barmen Declaration (1934)

25-6. "Lo, I am with you always, to the close of the age." (Matt. 28:20) "The word of God is not fettered." (2 Tim. 2:9)
26 The Church's commission, upon which its freedom is founded, consists in delivering the message of the free grace of God to all people in Christ's stead, and therefore in the ministry of his own Word and work through sermon and sacrament.

All the affirmations that follow on sexuality, the sanctity of life, inclusion and Christian social responsibility are firmly grounded in every confession preceding. It is not fitting to separate these ensuing contested issues apart from the previous biblical groundwork. To detach them or fixate upon them politically is to misunderstand the confessing movement.

On Human Sexuality, Marriage, and Family

Christian convictions on sexuality, marriage, and family emerge not out of partisan political ideologies or egalitarian metaphors, but out of the whole course of the previous confessional definitions on creation, providence, sin, salvation, and the holy life. On this basis, confessing Christians teach and speak actively of God's great concern for the continuity of the family, the sanctity of marriage, and the calling to sexual accountability. It is not evangelicals who first pressed, or stressed, or manufactured these issues; rather evangelicals have been forced to deal with them in light of attempts to substitute permissive sexuality for historic Christian sexual morality. Under these challenges, confessing Christians are unwilling to sit back and allow the destruction of marriage or the undermining of the family. All these arguments are biblical and theological, not primarily political or partisan. They need not be associated with any political party or effort. They are therefore neither left or right on the partisan political spectrum.

Confessing Movements' Perspectives: On Human Sexuality, Marriage, and Family

American Anglican Council

Human Sexuality.
Sexuality is inherent in God's creation of every human person in his image as male and female. All Christians are called to chastity: husbands and wives by exclusive sexual fidelity to one another and single persons by abstinence from sexual intercourse. God intends and enables all people to live within these boundaries, with the help and in the fellowship of the Church.

United Church of Canada, 15 Affirmations

12. We believe that God wills that marriage be a life-long union of faith, love and esteem between man and woman. Although we recognize that there are circumstances in which divorce can be justified, we affirm the sanctity of lifelong marriage.

Great Commission Network (ELCA)

Witness to Contemporary Culture
In response to various movements in our culture, we believe it is important to affirm the following based on the clear teaching of Scripture. Regarding sexual issues, we view sexual intercourse as designed by God for marriage alone, that life begins at conception and therefore must be fully protected at every stage, and that any sexual intercourse outside the heterosexual design of God is inconsistent with God's Word.

American Anglican Council

Marriage, Family, and the Single Life.
God has instituted marriage to be a life-long union of husband and wife, intended for their mutual joy, help, and comfort, and, when it is God's will, for the procreation and nurture of children.

Divorce is always contrary to God's original intention, though in a fallen world it is sometimes a tragic necessity. The roles of father and mother, exercised in a variety of ways, are God-given and profoundly important since they are the chief providers of moral instruction and godly living. The single life, either by call or by circumstance, is honored by God. It is therefore important for unmarried persons to embrace and be embraced by the Christian family.

The Memphis Declaration (UMC 1992)

The Church must reach out in a ministry of love, compassion, and healing to all persons—married, single, children, one-parent homes, and broken families. We affirm marriage as the God-ordained pattern of relationship between men and women. God created us male and female, and the natural order of creation and procreation is the union of male and female as husband and wife. The Christian Church has always held this to be in accordance with God's will. We challenge the Church to be unequivocal in support of the Christian family, the sanctity of human life, and Christian sexual morality: fidelity in marriage and celibacy in singleness.

The DuPage Declaration

VI. We affirm the biblical guidelines for human sexuality: chastity outside of marriage, lifelong fidelity and holiness in marriage, and celibacy for the sake of the kingdom.

National Alliance of Covenanting Congregations (United Church of Canada)

Fidelity in marriage and chastity in singleness, as defined by the 19th General Council, are among the standards of faithful conduct required of pastors of associated congregations.

On Same Sex Unions

One of the most pressing and divisive issues of contemporary church life has been the question of how Christians are to minister to persons with homosexual orientation without denying them their civil rights, yet calling them to the holy life intended by God in the crucial area of sexual accountability. This issue cannot to be taken out of context of the previous biblical mandates. It belongs as a necessary and urgent subpoint to the doctrines of creation and sanctification, but never separable from them. Confessing Christians insist that it not be taken out of this context. Those in the press who insist on separating this part from the whole are guilty of inaccurate reporting.

Confessing Movements' Perspectives: On Same Sex Unions

Concerned Clergy and Laity of the Episcopal Church

The presenter bishops have affirmed that it is not permissible, if it is even possible, in our polity for a bishop to teach or act on teaching which is neither supported by the Holy Scriptures, the Church acting corporately nor the Book of Common Prayer. They therefore have declared that bishops who knowingly ordain noncelibate homosexual persons or who permit or endorse the blessing of homosexual unions do so without the authority of the Scriptures, of the unbroken apostolic tradition, or of the Anglican Communion and are thereby threatening the unity and order of the Church. As a sign of the seriousness of this threat, they disassociate themselves from such "individually discerned teaching and preemptive action" by bishops, other clergy, or dioceses.

The Houston Declaration (UMC 1987)

III. The Ordained Ministry

The Church, on the authority of the Scriptures, has never viewed homosexuality as a part of God's diverse, good creation, but has always considered homosexual practices as a sin and a manifestation of the brokenness of God's fallen creation. Every scriptural reference to the practice of homosexuality is negative (Leviticus 18:22, 20:13; Romans 1:18–32; 1 Corinthians 6:9–10). Following the Old Testament prohibitions, the apostle Paul sees homosexual practices as the sign and consequence of a turning away from the Creator in order to worship the creature. Homosexual practices become an extreme expression of the turning in upon itself which is the essence of humankind's sin. We repudiate all irrational fear of and contempt for homosexual persons.

We affirm a ministry of Christian compassion, care and redirection for those who have engaged in homosexual practices as they seek help in overcoming temptation and changing their style of life. Persons may or may not be able to change their sexual orientation; persons can change their lifestyle. That possibility is the very essence of the gospel of Christ (1 Cor. 6).

It is not acceptable in the context of the Christian faith that persons engaging in homosexual practices should be ordained to the ministry or continue in representative positions within the Church.

United Church of Canada, A Covenant (1990)

4.3 Because Jesus recognized God's institution of marriage from the beginning (Matt. 19:4–6), because holiness and sexual self-control are linked (1 Thess. 4:3–8) and because there is healing through the Gospel (1 Cor. 6:11) and therapy, we affirm that God calls all people to loving faithfulness in marriage or loving chastity in singleness. It is therefore a contravention of our faith to solemnize same-gender unions ("marriages"), or to ordain, commission, settle or appoint self-declared, practising homosexuals, however admirable they may be.

The DuPage Declaration

WE DENY that premarital or extramarital relations, trial marriages, cohabitation outside of marriage, homosexual relations and so-called homosexual unions, can ever be in genuine accord with the will and purpose of God for his people.

The Memphis Declaration (UMC 1992)

6. Reaffirm Christian sexual morality and the current provisions of the United Methodist Discipline (Par. 71f, 402.2, 906.12). Homosexual persons are people of sacred worth to whom we are called to minister. Since the practice of homosexuality is, however, incompatible with Christian teaching, we call for the rejection of the report and recommendations of the Committee to Study Homosexuality, and oppose further official study. The Biblical witness and the unbroken tradition of the Church provide the foundation of our understanding.

Scripture plainly identifies adultery, fornication and homosexual practice as sins of the flesh (signs and consequences of the fallen condition of humankind that needs redemption). Let us cease to debate homosexual practice as if the witness of the Scripture and the tradition of the Church were not clear from the beginning. A militant minority must not be allowed to control the direction of the Church of Jesus Christ.

It is time for us to move on to the central purpose of the Church: to serve the world in Jesus Christ's name and win the world for Him.

On the Sanctity of Life

Confessing Christians today are profoundly concerned about the culture of death, the tendency within secularization to cheapen the value of life. This tendency has been blessed, and to some extent spawned, by liberal, secular, and humanistic forms of permissive individualism that have gained purchase in the mainline church bureaucracies. Nowhere is this more evident than in questions about the protection of life and resisting the culture of death. This is not an ancillary issue that is subject to compromise or negotiation or political juggling. It is a question of conscience before God.

Confessing Movements' Perspectives: On the Sanctity of Life

United Church of Canada, 15 Affirmations

13. We believe that God wills that every human life grow up into the maturity of Jesus Christ. Although we recognize that there may be exceptional circumstances in which human life must be taken in order to preserve other human life, we affirm the sanctity of human life before birth and afterward.

Moreover, we are not our own but God's. We therefore oppose abortion on demand, and we think that our Church's official position to remove abortion from the Criminal Code effectively puts the Church in the abortion-on-demand camp.

American Anglican Council

Sanctity of Life.

All human life is a sacred gift from God and is to be protected and defended from conception to natural death. We will uphold the sanctity of life and bring the grace and compassion of Christ to those who face the realities of previous abortion, unwanted pregnancy, and end-of-life illness.

The DuPage Declaration

VII. WE AFFIRM the sanctity of human life at every stage based on our creation in the image of God and our election by God for service in his kingdom.

WE DENY, for example, that the personal choice of either parent takes precedence over the right of the unborn child to life in the service of God's glory. We deplore the continuing traffic of abortion as the slaughter of innocents, which can only be an abomination in the sight of God.

On Equal Justice and Inclusion

Political correctness has gained temporary hegemony in many arenas of the mainline church agencies. Confessing Christians seek a greater inclusivity than that articulated by humanistic advocates of class warfare, arbitrary quotas, and manipulative limitations on democratic governance. They know that the ideology of so-called inclusivity has been extremely exclusive and dogmatic in blocking out orthodox believers from fair representation in church governance. In the name of inclusion, the liberal mainline has become adamant in excluding evangelical voices from its leadership.

Confessing Movements' Perspectives: On Equal Justice and Inclusion

American Anglican Council

True Inclusivity.
In grateful response to Christ Jesus, in whom there is neither Jew nor Greek, slave nor free, male nor female, we will extend the welcome of the Church to every person, regardless of race, sex, social or economic status, sexual orientation, or past behavior. We will oppose prejudice in ourselves and others and renounce any false notion of inclusivity that denies that all are sinners who need to repent.

Confessing Movement within the United Methodist Church, A Confessional Statement

We repudiate teachings and practices that misuse principles of inclusiveness and tolerance to distort the doctrine and discipline of the Church. We deny the claim that the individual is free to decide what is true and what is false, what is good and what is evil.

United Church of Canada, 15 Affirmations

We pray that all men may find their true unity and realize their true humanity by believing in the person and work of Jesus Christ, to Whom with the Father and the Holy Spirit, ever one God, be all glory and blessing. Amen.

Great Commission Network (ELCA)

We affirm the New Testament language of God as Father, Son and Holy Spirit and we reject attempts to eliminate masculine references for God when the original texts require them.

On Christian Social Responsibility

The liberal mainline core leadership has become so politicized in favor of partisan leftist politics that it often seems that these goals are their main concern. They sometimes view confessing Christians prejudicially as if they were advocating withdrawal or passivity or inactivity in relation to the social and political order. Confessing Christians have made it quite clear in their declarations that party politics of the far left or right must be avoided, especially by those who have representative clerical leadership roles, who preach and who offer Eucharist to all penitents of any party. Every believer, however, has deep social and political responsibilities, which challenge daily the conscience of confessing Christians. The gospel of Jesus Christ impinges upon democratic representation and governance, and fair decision-making. Confessing Christians are not going to yield to totalitarian, fascist, socialist, or thought-police views of Christian social responsibility. They have stated clear and passionately held views on the public responsibility of Christian believers, without appealing to pietism or quietism.

Confessing Movements' Perspectives: On Christian Social Responsibility

Presbyterian Action

Presbyterian Action believes that church pronouncements about partisan political issues should be made rarely, tentatively, and with full respect for others who reach different conclusions about the best means of pursuing the principles of the Gospel.

Presbyterian Action challenges church social witness statements and programs that seem to represent only the partisan political views of a narrow segment of the church.

Presbyterian Action suggests ways in which those statements and programs might more closely reflect the teachings of Scripture, the input of church members, and the outcome of a fair democratic process.

Barmen Declaration (1934)

18 We reject the false doctrine, as though the Church were permitted to abandon the form of its message and order to its own pleasure or to changes in prevailing ideological and political convictions.

Confessing Movement within the United Methodist Church, A Confessional Statement

We reject widespread and often unchallenged practices in and by the Church that rebel against the Lordship of Jesus Christ. For example: experimenting with pagan ritual and practice; consuming the world's goods without regard for the poor; accommodating the prevailing patterns of sexual promiscuity, serial marriage and divorce; resigning ourselves to the injustices of racial and gender prejudice; condoning homosexual practice; ignoring the Church's long-standing protection of the unborn and the mother.

American Anglican Council (Contemporary Implications of the Gospel)

Christian mission is rooted in unchanging biblical revelation. At particular times, however, specific challenges to authentic faith and holiness arise which require thoughtful and vigorous response. We therefore speak to the following issues of our time and culture.

United Church of Canada, A Covenant (1990)

BELIEFS: 3. We covenant to live in fellowship with our brothers and sisters in Christ and to seek to do justly, to love mercy, and to walk humbly with God (Micah 6:8). We affirm that we must demonstrate God's love visibly by caring for those who are deprived of justice, dignity, food and shelter. We affirm that the proclamation of God's kingdom of justice and peace demands the denunciation of all injustice and oppression, both personal and structural. We affirm that faithfulness to God as Creator includes serious commitment to environmental stewardship.

Great Commission Network (ELCA)

We affirm that all people stand equal before God and that racism is in violation of God's will.

On Church and State

The relation of church and state has been a perennial concern of orthodox and evangelical Christianity throughout recent years. Evangelical Christians had significant influence upon the writing of the U.S. Constitution and Bill of Rights. Confessing Christians today continue to speak out clearly on the responsibility of Christian believers amid the civil, economic, and political order.

Confessing Movements' Perspectives: On Church and State

Barmen Declaration (1934)

22-5. *"Fear God. Honor the emperor." (1 Peter 2:17.)*
Scripture tells us that, in the as yet unredeemed world in which the Church also exists, the State has by divine appointment the task of providing for justice and peace. [It fulfills this task] by means of the threat and exercise of force, according to the measure of human judgment and human ability. The Church acknowledges the benefit of this divine appointment in gratitude and reverence before him. It calls to mind the Kingdom of God, God's commandment and righteousness, and thereby the responsibility both of rulers and of the ruled. It trusts and obeys the power of the Word by which God upholds all things.

23 We reject the false doctrine, as though the State, over and beyond its special commission, should and could become the single and totalitarian order of human life, thus fulfilling the Church's vocation as well.

24 We reject the false doctrine, as though the Church, over and beyond its special commission, should and could appropriate the characteristics, the tasks, and the dignity of the State, thus itself becoming an organ of the state.

American Anglican Council

Church and State.
Biblical social commandments and Christian ethical principles are foundational to the well-being of every society. Recognizing the call of Christians to be faithful witnesses and a challenging presence in society, we are committed to seek ways to express these commandments and principles in all spheres of life, including the public life of the nation.

United Church of Canada, A Covenant (1990)

BELIEFS 4. We covenant to cooperate with the existing courts and human laws of the United Church as far as our confession of faith in Jesus Christ allows. Our prime loyalty is to Jesus Christ, the Head of the Church.

These affirmations lead not to withdrawal from political engagement, but to strong commitment and concerted action. Confessing Christians are called to covenant to seek reformation and renewal both personally and socially, in both church and culture.

The Covenant to Renew the Confessing Community

The heart of these confessions is a covenant to renew the church. Previous confessions of faith are fully adequate to give baptized believers guidance on essential Christian teaching. But the special need of our time that requires a stand-up confession of laity has its focus on the reform and renewal of the church by a thorough regrounding in classic Christian teaching.

Confessing Movements' Perspectives: The Covenant to Renew the Confessing Community

Confessing Movement within the United Methodist Church

An Invitation to the Church

III. Under God's judgment and by God's grace we covenant to participate in the Spirit's reconstruction of the church, which has been built upon the foundation of the faith once for all delivered to the saints. We covenant to engage in a revitalized mission which expresses our historic concern for social holiness and fidelity to the fulfillment of the Great Commission. To all United Methodists—regardless of race or gender—who desire to contend for this faith, we extend an invitation to join us in this endeavor.

The Houston Declaration (UMC 1987)

Conclusion

We covenant together to proclaim these central truths of the Christian Faith and to invest our lives and ministry in the continuing renewal of our beloved Church. We invite all laity and clergy of the United Methodist Church to join with us as persons who have been called to follow Christ and give our lives to advancing the gospel and the historic Christian Faith. The need is urgent—the time is now!

We stand as servants and disciples of Jesus Christ our Lord.

Confessing Movement within the United Methodist Church

An Invitation to the Church

We call upon all pastors, lay persons, and congregations to join with us in this Confessing Movement and to challenge and equip their people as agents of God's kingdom. We look to the Council of Bishops for doctrinal oversight according to paragraph 514.2 "to guard, transmit, teach and proclaim, corporately and individually, the apostolic faith as it is expressed in Scripture and Tradition, and, as they are led and endowed by the Spirit, to interpret that faith evangelically and prophetically." In particular, we ask the bishops to affirm their own teaching authority and to declare our church's commitment to Jesus Christ as the only Lord and Savior of the world.

We call upon the seminaries of our church to transmit the historic Christian faith. We call upon the boards and agencies of the church to fulfill their primary role of being servants of the local church.

United Church of Canada, A Covenant (1990)

5. We covenant to work for reform and renewal in the United Church and in the universal Church, praying that we may have the grace to love one another as Christ loved us.

Concerned Clergy and Laity of the Episcopal Church

Let us be resolved to:

Call upon the presenting bishops to take necessary steps to provide episcopal oversight functions to those faithful orthodox priests and parishes in revisionist dioceses;

Ensure financial contributions that are given by faithful Episcopalians—at parish, diocese and national levels—support only Christ-centered works and not programs that diminish biblical truth;

The hope for the future of our beloved Episcopal Church rests in our hands—the laity of the Church. If you share our concerns, join us in our efforts to reform and restructure our beloved church to be obedient to God's written word, the Bible.

There is Hope.

Word Alone

We believe in and value:

Seeking and following the guidance of the Holy Spirit
Practicing Jesus' love for each other
Hoping, working and praying for the renewal of the church
Living as the holy church Christ calls us to be

Discipline, Not Separation

These affirmations are in no way intended to be schismatic, but rather to bring greater unity to the body of Christ by adherence to scriptural teaching and church discipline. They are made on the assumption that the body of Christ is already one, and truly made one only in Jesus Christ. Despite the views of detractors, confessing Christians have a strong conscience about maintaining the unity of the body of Christ, and not splitting into a further schismatic denominationalism. Those who demean classic Christian teaching are the real schismatics, not the confessors of traditional faith in Jesus Christ. Repentance is the first task of the church in crisis. Humility is the first step toward repentance.

Confessing Movements' Perspectives: Discipline, Not Separation

American Anglican Council

Support of the Episcopal Church

We desire to be supportive of congregations, dioceses, provinces, and the national structures of the Episcopal Church and the worldwide Anglican Communion. However, when there arise within the Church at any level tendencies, pronouncements, and practices contrary to biblical, classical Anglican doctrinal and moral standards, we must not and will not support them. Councils can err and have erred, and the Church has no authority to ordain anything contrary to God's Word written (*Articles of Religion* XIX, XX—BCP p. 871). When teachings and practices contrary to Scripture and to this orthodox Anglican perspective are permitted within the Church—or even authorized by the General Convention ... we will disassociate ourselves from those specific teachings and practices and will resist them in every way possible.

Confessing Movement within the United Methodist Church

An Invitation to the Church

In order to enact the Discipline's call to "doctrinal reinvigoration" and to avoid schism and prevent mass exodus, we intend to form a Confessing Movement within the United Methodist Church. By this we mean people and congregations who exalt the Lordship of Jesus Christ alone and adhere to the doctrinal standards of our church.

United Church of Canada, 15 Affirmations

We make these affirmations of faith in humble awareness of our own inadequacies but in joyous faith in God's goodness, love and power. We are not committed to the exact wording of this document. Each one of us has a different emphasis and a different way of expressing the faith. But we are committed to the Lord Who is beyond our halting language. We are committed to His Gospel. And we are committed to His Church, particularly to our branch of the Church, The United Church of Canada.

United Church of Canada, A Covenant (1990)

BELIEFS 8. We urge all United Church congregations and courts, members and ministers, young people and friends, to consider this Covenant prayerfully. If it is contrary to Scripture, set it aside. But if you find that we are taking our stand upon Scripture, then let no fear or temptation keep you from walking with us on the path of faith and obedience to the Word of God. Make this covenant your own, for the sake of Jesus Christ, his Church and especially those who have not yet heard God's Word spoken in Christ.

9. Glory be to the Father, and to the Son, and to the Holy Spirit: as it was in the beginning, is now and will be for ever. Amen.

Confessing Movement within the United Methodist Church

Our purpose is to contend for the apostolic faith within the United Methodist Church and seek to reclaim and reaffirm the church's faith in Wesleyan terms. We are United Methodists within the United Methodist Church. We intend to stay within the United Methodist Church. The Confessing Movement is not asking for a new definition of faith, but for a new level of integrity in upholding our historic doctrinal standards in a thoughtful, serious and principled way.

Invitation and Appeal to Decision

All this leads to decision and action, not merely to further study or discussion. Confessing Christians characteristically have asked for a *decision* from believers to confess their faith and participate in God's work of renewing the church. The confessing movement is not another debate or discussion group. It is a call to decision, which often appears as the concluding appeal of the declaration.

Confessing Movements' Perspectives: Invitation and Appeal to Decision

Confessing Movement within the United Methodist Church

The Confessional Charge
This, then, is our confession: We confess that Jesus Christ is the Son, the Savior, and the Lord, according to the Scriptures. The United Methodist Church has never had an institutional guarantee of doctrinal diversity without boundaries. We implore other United Methodists, laity and clergy, to join us in this confession. Relying upon the power of the Holy Spirit, we vow to make this confession in the congregations, boards, divisions, agencies, seminaries, and conferences of our denomination. We will faithfully support United Methodist activities, groups, programs, and publications that further this confession, and we will vigorously challenge and hold accountable those that undermine this confession.

American Anglican Council

Invitation to Association
We invite all members of the Episcopal Church who concur in this classical Anglican perspective, to stand with us for mutual enlightenment, encouragement, mission, and ministry, and, where necessary, for protection of the right to live and minister in obedience to Scripture, Anglican tradition, and conscience. We further invite all persons who share this faith to stand with us.

Barmen Declaration (1934)

28 The Confessional Synod of the German Evangelical Church declares that it sees in the acknowledgment of these truths and in the rejection of these errors the indispensable theological basis of the German Evangelical Church as a federation of Confessional Churches. It invites all who are able to accept its declaration to be mindful of these theological principles in their decisions in Church politics. It entreats all whom it concerns to return to the unity of faith, love, and hope.

A Call to Ecumenical Action

In each denomination of the mainline there are important reasons for regrounding the denomination in its own specific historic church memory, without neglecting the need for concerted confession that is embraced by all confessing Christians in all denominations. Thus Anglican confessors seek deeper rootage in classic Anglican teaching, Reformed in Reformed teaching, and Methodists in Wesleyan teaching, but this does not imply that they are unaware of how those differing historical memories converge in classical ecumenical Christian teaching. So the decision and commitment required is not merely to be viewed within the constricted frame of a particular denomination, but in the ecumenical arena of the presence of true believers in all the denominations. Confessing Christians recognize that they often have more in common with confessing Christians of other denominations than with many in their own.

Confessing Movements' Perspectives: A Call to Ecumenical Action

Confessing Movement within the United Methodist Church

An Invitation to the Church

IV. The crisis we discern extends beyond our denomination. We witness similar strains and struggles among our sisters and brothers in all the churches of the West. Because we are baptized into the one universal Church, and because the problems we face will best be resolved by utilizing the gifts God gives to the whole community of faith, we rejoice in the stirrings for renewal that we see among other communions. We commit ourselves to praying with them for the coming of the kingdom in our midst . . .

All the while, readying for the coming of Jesus Christ in power and glory, we welcome ecumenical partnerships in the advancement of this confession.

Barmen Declaration (1934)

02 Therefore the Confessional Synod calls upon the congregations to range themselves behind it in prayer, and steadfastly to gather around those pastors and teachers who are loyal to the Confessions.

03 Be not deceived by loose talk, as if we meant to oppose the unity of the German nation! Do not listen to the seducers who pervert our intentions, as if we wanted to break up the unity of the German Evangelical Church or to forsake the Confessions of the Fathers!

04 Try the spirits whether they are of God! Prove also the words of the Confessional Synod of the German Evangelical Church to see whether they agree with Holy Scripture and with the Confessions of the Fathers. If you find that we are speaking contrary to Scripture, then do not listen to us!

But if you find that we are taking our stand upon Scripture, then let no fear or temptation keep you from treading with us the path of faith and obedience to the Word of God, in order that God's people be of one mind upon earth and that we in faith experience what he himself has said: "I will never leave you, nor forsake you." Therefore, "Fear not, little flock, for it is your Father's good pleasure to give you the kingdom."

United Church of Canada, 15 Affirmations

We invite United Church members who share our concern and who find themselves in general agreement with this affirmation to add their names to those below. Doing this will call the Church to a more serious commitment to its theological bases and to a more positive affirmation of Christian faith. Doing this will also show our brethren in other communions that we share with them the one faith of the Church Universal.

Confessing Christians in the mainline invite serious critics to offer specific proposed correctives to any or all of the above affirmations, rather than focus on single-issue politics. The future reconciliation of Christians in the mainline depends on the seriousness of the theological and exegetical discussion, rather than political posturing.

We invite liberal advocates to respond candidly to these affirmations. Among many of them we believe we could gain substantial consensus and agreement on many discrete points. This consensus between believing liberals and believing conservatives has not been sufficiently articulated, due to the polarization that has regrettably seized the day.

We now turn from the declarations of confessing Christians on their essential teachings to an examination of the very nature of confession itself. If confessing Christians are to confess rightly, they do well to study and know thoroughly what it is that constitutes confession of sin and confession of faith, and how to see their complementary relation.

PART 5

A PRIMER ON CONFESSION

14

The Biblical Teaching of Confession

The core issue of this modest study of mainline Protestantism is, how do we confess Christianity amid false teachings? Confessing Christians are relearning how the faithful have always rightly confessed their own sin while confessing the apostolic faith.

Learning to Confess

Confession (Greek, *exhomologesis*) is a standard topic of classic Christian teaching. It is a necessary subject area or point (*locus*) of systematic theology, a pivotal question in the doctrine of salvation.

If the subject should seem daunting, it is best to remember that life in God requires the believer to seek whatever depth of understanding of it that is understandable. Those who resist rigorous biblical study may feel that what follows is a distraction, but the faithful will understand that living with the Word is the heart of the matter of confessing Christianity.

The confessing movement has a responsibility to teach what confession means. Many young believers have not yet been blessed by the benefits of this teaching. They have not experienced the joy and power of confessing the faith *with* the whole intergenerational church over all times and places. It is moving for one to grasp that faith is confessed within the communion of saints. The irony is that a vast lay confessing movement has emerged without any deliberate attention to teaching the meaning of confession. This discussion seeks a remedy.

Two central questions must be first dealt with: Is it their *faith* or their own *sins* that they are confessing? Is it *to God* or *to other humans* that they confess?

Confessing Occurs within the Communion of Saints

In confession the faithful place themselves in harmony with others who make the same confession of truth. They are aligning themselves with the faith of the people of Israel and the apostles and believers throughout history.

This reality is implied in the prefix *con-* in the word confession. They make confession *with* (con) others, indeed all others of all times who believe that Jesus Christ is Lord. The Latin root (*con+fiteri*) reveals that confession means to speak *with*, not to speak alone. It is to join in the voices of those who respond in faith to gracious acts. No believer makes his confession alone. It is always *with* the *ecclesia* (the assembly), the *communion sanctorum* (the communion of saints), the *consensus fidelium* (the consensus of faith), and the *corpus Christi* (the body of Christ) of all times and places.

Confession occurs as a social reality, assenting in harmony with the faithful. Heaven is a choir. As baptism is not a private act, neither is confession. It is an act of common consent (*homologoumenos*, 1 Tim. 3:16). Confessing is an act of uniting together with a community of faith, confessing together with the whole church the lordship of Christ. Confession is the defining act of participation in the community of faith. To confess (*homologeo*) is to repeat with the congregation the truth of faith—it is to say the same (*homo*) word (*logia*) as the faithful everywhere always say together. It is to declare oneself as standing *within* the community of faith. This requires that one *stand necessarily against* whatever is opposed to this *standing within*. There is no confession without some presupposed understanding of the truth, and hence disavowal of contrary untruth.

The Greek word for confession (*homologia*) has the varied meanings of avowal, acknowledgement, and profession of faith. It implies a decisive conviction, a behavioral movement from an old life to a new life, from idolatry to the true God, from the passing age to the coming reign of God. The related verb, *exhomologeo*, deepens the metaphor by pointing to that which comes *from the heart*. It becomes public and hearable out of one's mouth but it comes *from* (*ex*) the deep inward core of the soul. It is an act of witness to who one is. To confess (*exhomologeo*) is to say the same as do the faithful from the heart, from one's inmost being, and from within the inmost center of the circle of faith. It means voluntarily agreeing with community of faith, confirming the faith of the worshiping community in the truth revealed.

Confession with the Lips and the Heart

Both lips and heart join in confession: "If you confess with your lips that Jesus is Lord and believe with your heart that God raised him from the dead, you will be saved. For man believes with his heart and so is justified. He confesses with his lips and so is saved" (Rom. 10:9 RSV).

Confession is not just words, but speaking from the heart, and not only believing from the heart but also confessing openly the lordship of Christ within the fellowship of the saints. His resurrection confirms the meaning of his coming in the flesh and suffering and dying for us (2 Cor. 4:13). All will be saved who confess and believe.

Confession is not intellectual assent alone, although it does not occur without intellectual assent. It is acknowledging the truth, not as if merely recognizing or knowing or conceptualizing true ideas, but an avowal of that which reaches into the depths of our being, of the event of the incarnate Word that intends to transform the whole of our behavior. When this happens, confession emerges with unqualified confidence in the only One who is worthy of worship, who is incomparably trustworthy: the one true God. It is a total surrender to his service, fully acknowledging his sovereignty, knowing that at the end of history all will recognize the truth of his lordship (Phil. 2:11).

The opposite of honest confession is hypocrisy, which only pretends to confess, or confesses only with the mouth, not the heart. Jesus said: "Not everyone who says to me 'Lord, Lord,' will enter the kingdom of heaven, but only he who does the will of my Father who is in heaven" (Matt. 7:21). If you say you know Christ but do not do as you say, the truth is not in you (1 John 2:4).

Confession of What to Whom?

To confess the faith rightly is to confess personal and corporate sins. Those who confess Christ as Lord remember who they are as sinners. The faithful confess the faith, their sins, and Christ all at once, knowing that each aspect resonates with the other. Believers do not rightly confess Christ as Lord without confessing their sins (1 John 1:9).

This confession is addressed first directly to God, while standing in the awesome presence of his holiness. The faithful say with the prodigal in Luke 15:18: "Father, I have sinned against heaven and against you." Sin offends

God. It shows contempt not only toward other human beings who suffer from its effects but also for the One who gives life. It lies unconfessed if not to God (Ps. 51:4), who gives human freedom. That freedom, when abused, hurts others. In that hurt those who sin lose the closeness they might have had with the holy God in a reconciled relationship.

Without ceasing to stand before God, the faithful confess to one another, and regularly do so in worship, and if necessary before the civil authorities. Paul was stern in his condemnation of one who had committed incest, and of those who had covered it up. The apostles called believers to sincere confession (1 John 1:9; cf. 2 Cor. 7:1). Acts 19:18 reports that Paul received many confessors publicly at Ephesus. Notorious offenses like murder, adultery, and idolatry have required public confession in past generations of Christians. If secret sins may be confessed secretly, public sins ought to be confessed publicly. The premise is that the locally gathered community church represents and embodies the whole church in that local place (1 Cor. 5:3; 2 Cor. 2:6),[1] extending the mercy of God to penitents.

Confession is intrinsically inward, before God, but looks for fitting ways of making itself an outward and open act. Confession of faith takes place most powerfully in the precise context where it is most unwelcome—when faith is being challenged. The confessor does not hesitate to speak the truth in the court, from the pulpit, on the job, or in the parental role. Whether public or private, confession must come from deeply within the inward citadel of the self, where the truth is recognized from the center out.

Confessing Our Sins to One Another

The faithful are also called to confess their sins quietly and personally to one another, to Christian brothers and sisters, or to a spiritual advisor or pastor or minister of the Word, or to a company of faithful believers (James 5:16). Just as they pray for one another, they confess with one another.

The early church continued the New Testament and earlier Jewish practice of confession to elders. As early as the letter of Clement of Rome to Christians in Corinth, believers were called to "Submit yourselves to presbyters, and receive chastisement unto repentance, bending the knees of your heart."[2] It is "good to make confession of trespasses rather than to harden the heart."[3] The Epistle of Barnabas, 19, urged believers to confess their sins, give spiritual counsel to one another, and thus to undermine hypocrisy. The Shepherd of Hermas urged the confession of doubts, dishonesty, neglect, and double-mindedness, all to be publicly confessed.[4]

Confession has special weight and depth when believers come to the Lord's Table.[5] Their confession in baptism and communion is a foretaste of their confession on the last day, when the confession of the faithful, of the whole body of Christ of all places and times, rightly and finally confess Jesus Christ as Lord (Phil. 2:9–11).

Grace Enables the Freedom to Confess Sin

Freedom in Christ imparts both the grace to confess sins and to confess faith. Confession of sin is a gift of freedom. But only when freedom is freed by grace is it able nondefensively to confess the power and subtlety of its collusions. Grace refers to God's enabling of what we normally cannot do under the power of the history of sin. Only one who is free can confess.

Only one who receives grace is sufficiently freed. Those who most truly confess are those most receptive to grace. Christian teaching views confession as a distinct gift of grace that opens up our human freedom, rather than binding it. The grace of confession is precisely "the freedom for which we are set free" (Gal. 5:1).

Believers are freed by the atoning work of God to confess not only their own individual sins, but to hold up humbly before God the sins of the nation, the family, and social systems that impinge on personal freedom. Whenever Christians meet for worship, they confess their own sins and the sins of the fallen world, the misguided state, the injustices present in economic life. They are freed by grace to confess the sins of the fractured and deficient community of faith, and their own personal collusions with those sins. Only those who have been freed by atoning grace are made truly free to confess sin and grace. The confession of Christ is intrinsically connected with the confession of sins (1 Tim. 6:13).

Since life is short, there is never unlimited time for repentance. Whatever time one has left is an unearned gift of grace. It is only the fleeting time between baptism and death.[6]

Repentance is a condition of receiving baptism once for all, and the Eucharist repeatedly. Confession is made first in baptism and confirmation, and thereafter at every opportunity to confirm baptism at the Lord's Table.

Confessing Sin in the Mainline: Why So Difficult?

Confession is made more difficult in the mainline insofar as it is considered unnecessary. If there is no serious sin, then Christian worship must have to do with something other than confessing sin. Mainline Christianity has been hard-pressed to think of what worship really is all about if there is no need for confession. The substitutes have been thin and disappointing. A major feature of the mainline church's blockage and malady is its inability to confess its sin humbly.

Before confessing Christians censure anyone else's misdeeds, it is fitting that they become completely honest before God about their own. They know their own misdeeds. They know themselves as believers who have inadvertently let the church over time slip into an ever-deepening crisis. They have failed to warn those on the brink of falling. They have stood around timidly while the church was withering. Especially those with leadership responsibilities have often passively watched their institutions being lost, sold out, or on the brink of apostasy, without protest or correction. The deposit of faith that should have been their highest guardianship responsibility has been left neglected, diluted, and symbolized to death. They have colluded in these sins.

The confessors are prodigals returning home. They are the wandering, forgetful sons and daughters of the church who have too long been silent. They have failed to admonish in a gentle, timely way those who distort faith.

Now through the grace of repentance they are being freed to confess their faith and their sins along with the whole historic church. This confession occurs precisely in the ashes and brokenness of contemporary church structures.

They do not come before God like the Pharisee who says, I am glad I am not like that man, that tax collector (Luke 18:10). They are indeed like the sinner who is unable to raise his eyes to God, aware of his deep complicity with social and intergenerational sin. The inheritors of classic Christianity have been nurtured by and benefited by the wealth of classic Christian teaching and its social products, only to abandon it and leave it to dust and worm. Now they are coming humbly to the Father as prodigals saying: "I am no longer worthy to be called your son" (Luke 15:19). The surviving faithful in the mainline are not worthy to be instruments of renewal: "Forgive us the wrong we have done, as we have forgiven those who have wronged us" (Matt. 6:12 NEB).

Confession Is Confirming Our Baptism Daily

The confession of our sins and our faith occurs prototypically in Christian baptism. All confession (of sin and of faith) is epitomized in baptism. What happens at one's baptism is not only that one is individually through faith cleansed by the water of the grace of God in baptism. But further one confesses that faith which with one voice the saints of all time confess, and disavows the demonic forces that have kept the human will captive. In repentance, faith, and baptism, the church teaches, our human wills are freed by the Spirit from the demonic powers that have bound us in sin, guilt, and death.

This confession is evident when we read the ancient texts of the baptismal confessions, where there is a disavowal of the devil and all his works, and a public confession of the lordship of Christ. In this rite, the whole self turns aside from all the works of darkness. Every subsequent confession of sin and faith is a recollection and confirmation of baptismal confession.

The early baptismal confession recalled in 1 Timothy 3:16 is still the heart of Christian confession, that the anointed One was manifested in the flesh, vindicated by the Spirit, seen by angels, preached among the nations, believed in the world, taken up in glory.

Paul called Timothy to keep the commandments undefiled, to hold fast to the confession made at his baptism. He reminded Timothy of the confession (Jesus Christ is Lord) that he made before many witnesses at his baptism (1 Tim. 6:12). This is what occurs at baptism: receiving the grace to confess sins, confess faith, die to the old, and live to the new.

On their day of baptism each one receives a Christian name. It is not the surname that comes by nature, but the Christian name that comes by grace. Those who do not live out the confession of sin and faith are choosing not to live out their own Christian name, choosing to be something other than they most truly are.

The choice is clear: either deny or confess (1 John 2:22) the Son who promised to confirm our witness before the Father. In the last judgment the faithful are clothed in the righteousness of Christ, who takes upon himself our sin.

The central intent of the confessing movement today is to encourage the recollection and reconfirmation of baptismal confession. This is the *confession* shared *with* all other Christian believers. The confessing movement today is reminding the whole church of its baptismal confession. The heart of its concern and theology is baptism. The essence of its active life is the confirmation of baptism.

Confessing Amid Opposing Voices When Clarity Is Required

Confession participates in the power of the cross most decisively when spoken openly in the presence of many contrary witnesses in a way that makes clear that one is willing to die for the truth, if dying for the truth is the direct consequence of speaking the truth (1 Tim. 6:12). Our confession is the renewal of our baptism, reappropriating and reliving our baptismal faith. This is especially so when that faith is challenged or defied or its truth put in doubt or covered under a cloud of distortion. Confession is most pertinent and inescapable when there is an open denial of the truth of Jesus

Christ, and especially when it involves taking risks that include suffering with Christ for the truth, or even one's own death as a participation in Christ's death and resurrection.

If we hold to our own private opinions, without making public our witness, our light does not shine on a hill, but is hidden under a bushel. This is especially so when the heart of faith is demeaned or challenged, or the gospel diluted. Then we *must* confess publicly if we are honest believers. Confessing both our sin and God's grace must become a public act recognizable to others when required by the circumstances. The confessing movement understands the present crisis to be such a time.

The Son Confesses for Us to the Father as Our High Priest

Jesus promised that "Whoever confesses me before men, him I will also confess before my Father" (Matt. 10:32 NKJV). Christ confesses our sins on the cross, as our intercessor and the High Priest of our confession (Heb. 3:1). Believers confess their sins in response to the cross.

Jesus is portrayed in the New Testament as our High Priest interceding for us, confessing for us before God, representing us before the Father. The Risen Lord has ascended to heaven to intercede with the Father for the faithful, making a good confession for us, so that he becomes our sponsor, our confessor, and an incomparable advocate on our behalf. Jesus stood with us in our sin. We are freed by him to stand up for the neighbor, and with the community of faith, even in its history of waywardness, to call it back to its mission.

Believers participate by faith in the relation between the Father and Son, by the power of the Spirit. Whoever confesses Jesus is the Son of God, God abides in him, and he in God (1 John 4:15). He dwells in God, participates in God's life by grace through faith, lives in God's household, and is heir to the family patrimony. The confession of his lordship today, even in the church, may take place among false witnesses ready to twist all that one intends to say.

The Model of the Good Confession: Jesus on Trial

Jesus's messianic mission remained unspoken and hidden during most of his earthly ministry, but at length the truth was fully told. It could not be understood without the resurrection. He confessed his identity by rising from the dead. His resurrection reveals the meaning and fulfillment of his incarnate coming, his birth as seed of David.

In standing up and speaking the truth, Jesus at his trial manifested the truth incarnate. Only he could do this because only he is the revelation of the true God in person, the expected One, the remnant of Israel, the only Son of God in the flesh, fully human. Because he was without sin, his confession was not of his own sin, but ours. He confessed the truth by embodying the truth.

Jesus himself made the good confession before Pilate, under conditions in which telling the truth was costly, even unto death. On trial he told the truth publicly even though it cost him his life.

As Jesus bore witness to his messianic vocation in the presence of the authorities amid false witnesses, so we are called to bear witness even when reviled by adversaries (Mark 14:60–63). Following in his way we are called to tell the truth even when it hurts. Even when our truth-telling will not be understood, we are being freed to confess our faith and our sins.

Biblical Models of Confession

In confessing today, believers are standing with Martha, who after Lazarus's resurrection made her confession: "I believe that you are the Christ, the Son of God" (John 11:27). The faithful are standing with Peter at Caesarea Philippi when asked by Jesus "Who do people say I am," and Peter answered as do all the baptized today: "You are the Christ, the Son of the living God" (Matt. 16:16).

Paul wrote to the Christians in Rome that he was "a servant of Christ Jesus, called to be an apostle, and set apart for the gospel of God—the gospel he promised beforehand through his prophets in the Holy Scriptures regarding his Son, who as to his human nature was a descendant of David, and who through the Spirit of holiness was declared with power to be the Son of God by his resurrection from the dead: Jesus Christ our Lord" (Rom. 1:1–4). Paul was sent to Rome on behalf of One who had risen from the dead who met him personally as living Lord.

In confessing today, believers hold fast to this same confession of One God the Father, who becomes flesh in one Lord Jesus Christ, who through the Spirit brings us to hearing the Word and responding in faith. All who respond in faith are unified in one body of Christ through one Lord, one faith, one baptism, one God and Father of us all (Eph. 4:4–6). They confess "one God, the Father from whom are all things and for whom we exist, and one Lord, Jesus Christ through whom are all things and through whom we exist" (1 Cor. 8:6).

Telling the Whole Truth

Telling the truth is costly. Telling the whole truth may cost everything in an earthly sense.

When Christians tell the whole truth, they always speak the name Jesus Christ. It is impossible for Christians to tell the whole truth about themselves or creation or history without ever mentioning his name. To hide his name is to hide the truth.

In court the witness is pledged to tell "the whole truth and nothing but the truth," praying for God's help that it may be told rightly. That means reporting accurately and completely what our eyes have seen. What the eyes of faith have seen is the revelation of God incarnate, dead and risen.

To tell only a piece of this truth is not to tell the whole truth. Christian confession wants the whole truth told. The church fathers knew that even the worst heretics always told some part of the truth, but never the whole. To hide some part is to hide the whole truth.

Each colored stone (tessera) of a mosaic was a simple cube of pigmented durable mineral. What is crucial to the beauty of the mosaic, and essential to its nature as art, is not the beauty of each tiny stone in isolation, but the part it plays in the whole configuration, the beauty of the whole. The moments of confession in time are like stones of a mosaic—they have no beauty or identity apart from the whole eternal picture to which they belong. Each stone is to be read as part of the truth of what God had made known to us—the full truth about him and ourselves. When believers confess the whole truth, they name the name of Jesus Christ.

Similarly, each discrete act of confession, however deepgoing, is to be viewed not as standing on its own, independently, but as an expression of the whole story we are living out—that God is alive in us through the atoning death of the risen Lord incarnate, and our lives are hid in him by faith.

Confession Is an Act, Not Just Speech

Confession is not just words spoken, but life lived. It is not a verbal formula primarily, but an enacted faith. Confession is not a formal statement of correct teaching as such. Rather it is actively trusting, so as to put one's life on the line, ready to risk whatever is necessary to speak the whole truth about ourselves and our world.

Confession is a lifelong commitment that arises out of the baptismal decision to confess Christ, to live out the new life of baptism, to participate in the death and resurrection of Christ, and to take whatever risks are involved in that commitment. This is what it means to con-fess (*con-fiteri*, to *declare* oneself *with* the believing community, to "acknowledge together"). It means to tell the truth about oneself as a sinner saved by faith within the community that acknowledges that Jesus is the Christ.

Not by water alone or bread or wine alone or words alone do we speak, but by our lively participation in the death and resurrection of Christ. This does not mean that words are unimportant. Timothy was instructed to search for the form of sound words ("wholesome instruction" Goodspeed), especially since he had voluntarily taken on the office of teacher, teaching as he had been taught (2 Tim. 1:13).

Confessing as Event, Not Idea

Confessing Christ requires remembering the historically eventful character of God's action in the incarnation and resurrection. We did not discover the mercy of God by contemplating the *idea* that God has come to us in the flesh. Rather we were found by it, as the shepherds were found by the star. The incarnation occurred as an observable *event* in actual history. Each one has to decide about its historical truthfulness, whether it did indeed happen that God became flesh and died for our sins. Those who confirm their baptism are clear about the answer.

Faith is our trusting response to the recognized event of God's own coming. The eventfulness of this death and resurrection is a reality in which we participate when we make the good confession when it is required, and indeed whenever it is fitting. Every time we receive Holy Communion, we renew this confession, and again participate in its reality *with* the community of faith. When we pray the Lord's Prayer, we confess our sins and ask for forgiveness for our sins, while at the same time confessing our faith in his power to forgive.

Philippians 2:5–11 was an early pre-Pauline hymn. Paul likely quoted it from an oral tradition as an already received form of the confession of faith. We still confess the same faith. We have not changed our confession. This is not a confession that Paul invented, but one that he doubtless had heard repeatedly in the church before he wrote his letter to Philippi.

First Corinthians 15 similarly offers a concise summary of the basic events in salvation history: the birth, life, death, resurrection, ascension, and expected return of the Son. This is the same confession that Christian believers in the Sudan and Cuba and Pakistan make daily under conditions of harassment. We freely choose to do the same. Daily we are called again and again to commit ourselves unambiguously and publicly to loyalty to Jesus Christ our Lord, Jesus as the Christ, as God's anointed one (see Matt. 10:32; Luke 2:8; Acts 23:6). This is a voluntary act of freedom. It is done fearlessly, resting on God's promises.

The Core of Christian Confession

These are the three key dimensions of confession: sin, grace, and faith. These constitute the core of a theology of confession. The confessing movements is called to understand this threefold confession.

The heart of the Christian service of worship is confessing our sin, proclaiming his Word, and dedicating ourselves in faithfulness and service. This threefold order of worship is reflected annually in the ordering of the Christian year, with two cycles of sin, grace, and obedience, totaling six liturgical seasons each year. We confess sin at Advent, grace at Christmas, and our faith in Epiphany. In the second cycle we confess sin at Lent, the resurrection at Easter, and in the season of Pentecost we confess the church's historic faith in responding to the grace of the Triune God. The central celebrations of Christmas and Easter form the center of the Christian year. In this way a theology of confession is deeply embedded in our entire annual and seasonal cycle of worship and prayer.

John's epistle notes that three witnesses attest in harmony: "There are three witnesses, the Spirit, the water, and the blood; and these three agree"(1 John 5:7–8 RSV). Leo the Great (fifth century) commented: "This means the Spirit of sanctification, the blood of redemption, and the water of baptism, which three are one."[7] All three witnesses are present in our good confession when we bear witness to the truth.

Central to all Christian confession is the confession of the person and work of Christ. We confess our trust not in an idea but in a person, unique by being truly human and truly God. He is the object of our confession. We confess Christ in the church, in its hymns, creeds, sermons, Eucharist, and acts of mercy. We confess Christ amid the civic order, primarily through our behavior, but whenever idolatry is coerced, through overt confession of his sole lordship. We confess Christ not just as individuals but in community, the community of faith, and as families. We confess God the Son in the presence of God the Father by the power of God the Spirit. We confess that Jesus Christ is Lord. We cannot make that confession from the heart except by the power of the Holy Spirit (1 Cor. 12:3). Jesus is truly God, the same incomparable Lord who has met us in the history of Israel and who meets us now.

Confessing Sin, Grace, and Faith

The term "confessing movement" embraces three interrelated levels of living out truth both speaking and acting:

confession of sin,
confession of grace, and
confession of the church's historic faith.

All are aspects of a single integral act of confession. Simultaneously the faithful are confessing their faults, God's grace, and historic Christian belief. They are invoking divine mercy, and remembering their baptism within the community of faith. They are confessing inwardly in the presence of God and outwardly in the presence of the worshiping community. Where necessary they must also be ready to confess before the earthly powers and authorities. As they confess their sins and God's grace and the faith of the church, confessors are keenly aware of God's final judgment that impinges on their here-and-now judgments. They cannot be dishonest with God. He sees through their hearts. They stand exposed before God.

Confession binds the speaker to his word in the presence of a company of witnesses who also bear witness to the same truth. As God discloses his grace to them, they disclose God's grace to the world. They make known God's deeds among people (Isa. 12:4). The disciples reported "all that God had done" (Acts 14:27). As they are witnessing openly in confession, the Spirit is witnessing within them inwardly (Rom. 8:16; cf. Acts 5:32). God has not left himself without witness in world (Acts 14:17). When believers come to the Lord's Table, they are surrounded by this great cloud of witnesses (Heb. 12:1).

The apostles called all hearers simply to repent, believe, and be baptized. Ongoing confession rehearses the prototypical act of baptism. Conversion requires both repentance and faith. Together they draw the penitent toward reconciliation with God. Together in the Eucharist they constitute the central act of Christian worship. Every Lord's Day, Christians celebrate his resurrection by making this confession.

Much of what remains to be said in this chapter is mainly for young people who have grasped what has been said above. Younger confessors are often given the grace of greater courage.

Suffering for Confession: Martyrs and Confessors

In a relatively safe democratic society with constitutional guarantees of freedom of speech, the freedom to confess is protected by law. Acts of confession hardly ever require any discomfort, or risk greater than psychological uneasiness or occasional minor forms of social ostracism. Seldom do they require risk of life or limb. These freedoms are valued historical achievements, but they present a temptation to the faithful to take them for granted. Those who neglect the freedom to confess are vulnerable politically to losing the precious freedom to confess.

Genuine believers living even within the soft comfort zone of such political guarantees are nonetheless *in principle willing to die for the truth if required*. The true confessor is ready to give all if need be to tell the whole truth. Confessing Christians today are, thank God, shielded and eased by the guarantees of civil liberty. These liberties are in part the social product of a long history of legal guarantees shaped by classical Christian teaching. They rest on the shoulders of two millennia of costly Christian witnesses. They were not bought without a price. The freedom to confess sin and grace in relation to the political order is hard won. Meanwhile there remain large areas in which harassed believers do not have these guarantees, places such as North Korea, northern Nigeria, Armenian Nagorno Karabahk, and Iran. Every day they may be called to be ready to lay their lives on the line. They confess Christ with the risk of their blood. Believers at ease in Zion must not forget them, must pray for them, and act on their behalf.

Those unwilling to die for the truth have not understood their baptism. The very meaning of baptism is that one has died, renounced the old life, and come into the new age of the kingdom. This is the new birth. The Spirit may give youth who are reborn to this grace greater power to risk than their elders who seemingly have more to lose.

To say "ready to die in principle" is loosely put. The real condition of confessors is that they are ready to die in fact. But that readiness awaits conditions in which such a sacrificial witness is actually required or necessary or in extreme cases unavoidable.

The Holy Spirit has not greatly blessed any movement of Christian confession that was not willing to die for the truth. The most persuasive form of witness in this century, as in previous centuries, has been the witness of those who gave their very life blood unsparingly.

Witnessing through One's Life

All baptized believers, young and old, male and female, are called to witness. If loss of life is the necessary consequence of the witness, that loss is rendered as a sacrifice on behalf of testimony to the truth. It is willingly offered up with the awareness of the great privilege of sharing in the fellowship of suffering in Christ (Heb. 2:9–10; 2 Tim. 2:3–9; 1 John 1:3–7).

In ancient Christianity this was not a grudging act, but a joyful and expectant act. The martyrs, both male and female, again and again attested that their life in Christ was enhanced, and made more, not less, valuable than physical life itself, however incomparably valuable physical life is known to be, especially as it is known among the faithful. The Christian confessor remains steadfast through whatever suffering might have to be faced on behalf of the whole truth, whether torture, imprisonment, or death. That is what witness (*marturia*) means in the ancient church.

No century has had more Christian martyrs than the twentieth. This twenty-first century is well on its way to exceed that. There may be much more martyrdom in our future than in the past, God help us. But the faithful are promised that God will not tempt them beyond what they can bear, and will find a way out, fitting to God's purposes.

Remembering the Martyrs

Following the Acts of the Apostles, the earliest form of church history was a record of the acts of the martyrs. Long before Eusebius came the acts of the martyrs of North Africa.

The martyrs who died for their testimony to the truth very early in church history were solemnly remembered and revered for their acts. Eucharistic feasts were often held annually in a celebration at the tomb of a martyr, or where his or her death occurred or physical remains were resting. No doubt there were abuses in remembering the saints and martyrs, but it is important to keep in mind why they were venerated: they gave witness through offering their lives. The historical discipline called hagiography is a literary genre that has sought to establish an accurate remembrance of the acts of these saints, confessors, and martyrs, and observe their calendar days for remembrance.

The term confession is also used for a place, the location of a *marturium*, the particular site where a martyr died or is remembered. The martyr's death day was regarded as a birth-day for eternal life, and the place of death memorialized as a holy place, recollected annually. The location of a *marturium* often became the site of pilgrimage, signs and wonders, a shrine, church, crypt, or a cathedral. This is a tradition seen from the beginning with the remembered martyrdom of Peter and Paul in Rome, James in Jerusalem, and Mark in Alexandria.

The Martyr and the Confessor

There is a profound connection between confession and martyrdom. Not every confessor is required to be a martyr. Circumstances most often do not call for physical martyrdom. But every genuine confessor is willing if necessary to offer up his life for the truth if circumstances require.

A confessor is one who endures suffering due to the confession of faith in Christ, yet not the full sacrifice of martyrdom. In the context of the early persecutions, prisoners were often tortured precisely in order to obtain a confession. Some died as martyrs. Others lived through the ordeal. The martyr died; the confessor survived to witness again, but would have been ready to die for the whole truth if required. The forms of torture applied in a modern democratic society are, of course, less physical than social and psychological, but still they may involve suffering and anguish.

At the time of writing of the Letter to the Hebrews, many were in chains precisely because of their confession. The worshiping community is still called to *remember prisoners as if chained with them* (Heb. 13:3), since the faithful in prison were viewed as here and now participating in the same body as those not in prison. Together the imprisoned confessor and the confessing community confess the truth of God's coming. Intercession for the faithful who are currently suffering for the faith is an ordinary act of traditional Christian worship. It is an act of joint confession. It happens in every worship service, every season of the Christian year.

Witnessing by Life Choice

The baptized magnify God's name by making this good confession publicly and boldly where necessary, despite the risks. Christians of the first century were typically expelled from synagogue if they confessed Jesus as Messiah. Stephen was the first martyr to follow Jesus to death. When hunting down Christians, the prosecutor Saul was driving them out of synagogues because of their confession of Jesus as Lord following the dictum reported clearly in John 9:22, that the authorities "had already agreed that if anyone should confess him to be Christ, he was to be put out of the synagogue." The martyrdom of Stephen (Acts 22:20) occurred when Saul was busy killing and hunting down Christians. Shortly thereafter he encountered the risen Lord on the road to Damascus. The converted Paul then repeatedly faced imprisonment, torture, and death, right from the outset of his first missionary journey.

The third century Roman imperial cult at times required public confession that the emperor was god or that the gods of Roman civic religion were truly gods. This is what one had to say publicly in order to remain alive. Such an act of idolatry was unthinkable to Jews and Christians. They could not say that. The only alternative was confession. Christians knew that there could only be one Lord, and that one is revealed in Jesus the Christ.

So they in fact gladly gave up their lives for this testimony. Their witness was not their words, but deeds, and eventually their last deed, the giving of their lives. The Holy Spirit worked mightily through these living witnesses. Far more persuasive than their brilliance or rhetoric or argument, they spoke by living and dying. They were heard not because of what they said but because of their voluntary willingness to die, their readiness to speak the truth in love, gently and humbly, even when it required their death.

It did not take long for secular beholders to grasp the powerful center of Christian testimony: the willingness to die for the truth. Persecution occurred not just in the amphitheaters of Rome, but from the very first week of Christian testimony—in Jerusalem, then in Samaria, Antioch, and on to Ephesus and Alexandria, and everywhere, in present-day Algeria, Turkey, and China.

The risk of death accompanied early Christian confession every step along the way. And so today confessors are willing to die for the truth. This is so even if the political conditions that once required death have largely disappeared for us.

The good confession, such as that which Stephen, Peter, and Paul made in following Jesus, was required under the conditions of the rejection of the truth. These conditions required either a confession of idolatry or death. After the apostles, the followers of the apostles were required similarly to respond to the idolatries of civil power with the whole truth of the gospel, and so are believers today.

The confessing movement does not apologize for putting confessors under situations of risk. It rather warns any inattentive person in advance that risk and struggle are likely.

Rot from Within

Virtually everyone in the confessing movement has had to face not just benign ostracism, but at times harsh vilification and retribution because of his or her confession of faith. For years the hegemony of elite liberalism had blocked off from voice or representative office anyone who has had orthodox identifications or even evangelical friendships. Students were excluded from the seminaries. Faculty faced subtle but real litmus tests—from abortion to homosexuality to pacifism. Seminarians were forced to run the gauntlet of experimental, rapidly secularizing, liberal theological education if they were to be ordained. The faithful have wept to see their suffering. Many came to seminary not knowing that it would be the supreme test of their faith. Others became confessors precisely in the seminary. Many have not been intimidated. More and more are faithfully surviving and confessing as each year goes by.

Confessing Christians are troubled not simply by challenges coming from outside the church, but more so from the rottenness of heresy coming from within the leadership of the church. This requires careful discernment. Under these circumstances, it becomes necessary to make the good confession clear precisely *within* the church, its legislative halls, its ordinal committees, its conferences, and its schools, so as to proclaim and guard the deposit of faith.

False teachers emerged very early in New Testament times. They have continued until today, preying upon the unsuspecting baptized. Many of Paul's greatest struggles at Corinth, Galatia, and Ephesus were with these false teachers who thought of themselves as Christians, yet who taught "an entirely different gospel" (Gal. 1:6). That is the root meaning of the Greek word *haeresis*, from which we get our word heresy (from *hairein*, to choose independently for oneself). The false teachers appear to confess Christ, but their works deny his lordship (Titus 1:16).

Confession as Decision

John's epistle drew this sharp dividing line: "Every spirit that confesses that Jesus Christ has come in the flesh is of God, every spirit that does not confess Jesus is not of God." A basic decision is required today for the faithful, just as it was required of the apostles, as they risked announcing the coming kingdom: if someone claims in Christian worship that Christ has not come in the flesh, then witness (*marturia*) is mandatory and must be made in some way appropriate to the context. The faithful cannot remain silent. Those who say from the heart that Jesus is the Christ, the Son of God, always find that God lives in them, and that they live in God (1 John 4:15).

Jesus confronted his hearers with the necessity of a here-and-now decision about the future. In meeting him they could not avoid making a choice: either yes or no. Today Jesus calls every hearer to live for or against the coming kingdom of God. One who is still attached to the world, who wants to go back and plow the field before taking any decisive step to affirm his lordship, or bury his relative first before hearing the Lord, is not ready to make a confession of Jesus as true Lord, only Son of God, over against all other gods.

15

....

The Confessing Movement

I f the description in chapter 14 is what constitutes confession, then what constitutes a confessing movement?

When Confessing Becomes a Movement

Confession, which belongs to the very nature of the church, becomes a *movement within* the church only when the church lacks confessional discipline, or defaults conspicuously on truly confessing the faith.

Where there is no admonition of sin, and where there is the pretense of forgiveness without repentance, the church prays for the renewing movement of the Spirit. The faithful pray that the Spirit will move within the morose church to make it alive again. If that discipline were already in place within the church, there would be no need for a confessing movement within the church.

Confession becomes a movement within the church only when there is no other option for the faithful than obedience to the Spirit. Evasions are no longer possible. A movement is not an institution or organization but a response to the moving of the Spirit.

This is a movement *within* the church, not as if external to the church, but from its deepest center, calling the church to its mission, its grounding in reality. It is a penitent act of a desperately sick church praying for recovery. Whether mainline worshipers are actually involved or not in a confessing church movement, those whose hearts are ready for it are those who are confessors of their sins, confessors of God's grace, and confessors of the church's faith.

The confessing movement does not need a new formal confession, for it has available to it already the Scripture, the same ancient ecumenical tradition interpreting Scripture, and liturgy and hymns that have accompanied the witnessing community through extended time. It confesses the same God the Father, Son, and Holy Spirit who were first confessed by the apostles. This same apostolic confession is made in each act of baptism. It confesses the Son who manifests the will of the Father, and the Spirit who continues to encourage and fulfill and enable the work of the Son unfolding in history, in accordance with Scripture.

The Confessing Churches of the 1930s: The Model of the Barmen Declaration for Confessing Faith Today

Many have asked how the confessing movement in North American churches relates to the Confessing Church (*Bekennende Kirche*) in the 1930s. That confessing movement (*Bekenntnisbewegung*) grew out of Martin Niemoller's Pastors' Emergency League in protest to German Christians who were willing to let Hitler's policies prevail in the church. The Nazis were actively attempting to take over the church, its congregations, its schools, its libraries, its agencies, its property, and make them engines of Nazi ideology.

What happened in Barmen, Germany, in May 28–30, 1934? A synod of confessors unequivocally declared the ancient faith of the church in the face of the emerging Nazi political captivity of the church.

Many today in the North American confessing movements feel their deep affinity with those confessors at Barmen. They too know that many in the church have sold out to the ideological biases of the times: hedonism, naturalism, narcissism, dependency politics, and nihilism. Confessing Christians today have watched their pulpits and church institutions betray classic Christian teaching and fold to even the flimsiest modern ideologies. They know the present situation is not so different from that faced by Niemoller, Barth, and Bonhoeffer.

The threat today is not fascist power, but an even more subtle ideological conceit. Confessors today face the threat of a massive secular cultural totalitarianism that intends to engulf all believers, all the vestiges of classical Christianity, and especially the church's institutions, schools, and mission endowments. The analogies with Barmen should not be exaggerated, nor should they be ignored. In Germany the Confessing Church found it necessary to set up its own alternative synods, seminaries, and communities of worship. They were forced underground. Many died.

Sixty Years after Barmen

When the North American mainline Confessing Movement was born on April 5, 1994, sixty years after Barmen, the participants sought to discern whether there were any historical models that provided specific instruction for their confession of faith in their time. Many agreed that the primary model available to them for what they were attempting was the confessing church that stood firmly against the Nazi Christians.

It was a powerful model from which to draw both analogies and lessons, as well as to acknowledge differences. Barmen showed steadfastness, courage, and scriptural fidelity in the midst of serious challenges to the integrity of the church during the Hitler malignancy. Beleaguered Christians stood squarely against Hitler's racial policies at great risk by confessing Jesus Christ as only Lord. North American confessors have listened closely to their antecedents who resisted Hitler. They have learned from them.

Barmen was the concrete moment of decision and declaration for the confessing churches in Europe in the 1930s. It represented what the tradition has called a *status confessionis*, a moment in which *a confession of faith is absolutely and unequivocally required* by the idolatries of the present order. Signers of the Barmen Declaration recognized that it was a costly, distinctive moment in which they did not have the choice to sit back and do nothing. They were compelled by faith to speak out clearly and unambiguously in their culture on behalf of the true God. They held fast to classic Christian teaching under conditions of great risk and demonic distortion.

The North American Confessing Movement is in some ways in a similar situation six decades after Barmen. There are no pretenses that any of the North American confessors have the courage and determination of the confessors of Barmen. But it is a decisive paradigm for their worship, teaching, and decision. Confessors today are faced not with the coercive power of the Nazis, but with a more subtly intimidating established network of seemingly benign leaders drifting toward apostasy, with some insisting that the church itself become apostate.

The debate ensued in 1994 as to whether North American Christians had a right to the term confessing movement, since it seemed to be a response to a much more dangerous and dramatic set of conditions than they were facing. At first it seemed too complex to try to explain how they were both like and unlike the struggle of the Confessing Church in Germany. The outcome: most felt that "Confessing Movement" came closer to describing who they were than any alternative term. Once adopted, they knew intuitively that it was right, and that they had a lofty model to live up to.

How is the confessing movement in North America analogous to Barmen? Both have maintained the unity and accountability of the body of Christ precisely in the presence of radical distortions of faith, boldly confessing Christ under conditions of denial, deception, heresy, alienation, and persecution.

Post-Implosion Renewal

In the wake of the mainline implosion, we are witnessing the reemergence of a Barmen-like confessing church movement within North American Christianity. There can be no doubt that there exists a growing phenomenon on this continent, roughly called the confessing movement, seeking to reground in classical Christian teaching the troubled denominations of the mainline churches, where blatant challenges to classical teaching have become ever more common, acute, and chronic.

This implosion has been gradually occurring for over fifty years. We are only now able to rightly name the movement in response to it as a confessing movement. How did this movement emerge? When, where, and how did it begin? These are historical questions immediately ahead of us.

The Rebirth of Confessional Christianity in North America

When the Confessing Movement within the North American mainline churches was born on April 5, 1994, it was the first time, according to most observers, that the term *confessing movement* was explicitly applied to name a specific movement within the North American mainline crisis. This happened without planning in an urgent conference called in Atlanta to assess the future of the troubled mainline. In this case it was mostly Methodists, but it could just as easily have been mostly Presbyterians or Episcopalians or Lutherans. In the course of that constitution of ninety-two orthodox and evangelical leaders, a movement was born which on the third day was named as the Confessing Movement Within the United Methodist Church. From there on, a series of initiatives began which have continued to grow exponentially to this day. This term came closer to describing what this movement was than any other.

There already existed among the Methodists significant efforts and organizations for the renewal of missions (Mission Society for United Methodists), for the renewal of Scriptural Christianity (*Good News* magazine), for charismatic renewal (Aldersgate Fellowship), for social witness (Institute for Religion and Democracy Methodist Initiative) and for spiritual formation (Walk to Emmaus), and others. But it was widely felt that however well intended all of these might be, none of these efforts had sufficient theological depth or a broad enough base to give clear voice to firm believers, both lay and clergy, who were variously described as orthodox or traditionalist or liturgically conservative or evangelical, but not yet identifiable as a viable and unified voice.

The Confessing Movement was intended to gather all of these who confessed classic Christian faith into a broad coalition to call the church back to its senses. Its intention was to encompass many who did not deliberately identify themselves as evangelicals but were committed to classic Christian teaching, moral theology, mission engagement, and orthodox Christology, and bring them into effective connection with other existing renewing movements.

In the preceding years in the liberal mainline the very word *evangelical* was a term of bitter controversy, and in fact a pariah word applied by the leadership elites to those they thought to be backward and obstreperous. It conveyed the nuance of narrowness and naïveté. As a card-carrying movement theologian for many years, I myself have many times used the word *evangelical* as a term of reproach with these shades of meanings.

In time it became clear that this was a rhetorical strategy of the left to exclude and isolate classical Christian believers. The Confessing Movement was too liturgically grounded and doctrinally orthodox to want to be pigeonholed as strictly a restatement of charismatic Christianity or evangelicalism alone, although from the outset it was clear that many evangelicals and charismatics were energetic and valued partners. This movement was a new union of evangelicals and Catholics and Orthodox and traditionalists and mission-serious believers who wanted to get beyond the press's fixation on sexuality issues to deeper issues of theological integrity and biblical authority. They sought to draw into their coalitional orbit many uncommitted institutional centrists who were having ambivalent responses to the experimental madness, and were praying to restore mainline institutions to classic Christianity, but saw no viable way. There was in 1994 much talk of an "exit strategy."

Interlude: A Personal Note

For me 1994 was an important year of fruitfulness and new beginnings. In that same year I was involved in launching three major efforts that would preoccupy the rest of my life: the Ancient Christian Commentary on Scripture, *the writing of* Requiem, *and the Confessing Movement. These three efforts were completely harmonious in my mind, although they seemed disparate to some of my academic colleagues who viewed them as totally separable arenas of discourse: one of patristic exegesis, the second, a critique of theological education, and the third, ecclesial reform and church renewal. But in my view I was working as a scholar to recover classic ecumenical exegesis, and at the same time working to see if anything might be salvageable from the devastations of the decades of liberal elitism (of which I as a Bultmannian had been a collusive partner, but later had disavowed).*

The church in which I was baptized and ordained was for two centuries (mid-eighteenth to mid-twentieth) a major prototype of evangelical revivalism, but the prototype had by that time been taken over by liberal activist leadership more interested in experience than truth, sentiment than Scripture, permissiveness than apostolic faith, and political posturing than confessing Christ. Wesley would have been horrified to see the abyss into which his children have fallen.

The genesis of the Confessing Movement in Atlanta 1994 was a previous discussion in Christmas of 1993 where I met with the John Wesley fellows, the intellectual vortex of Methodist renewal, in a former Shaker settlement in Kentucky. There on a Sunday afternoon I had a block of time free to talk with the staff from the Good News *magazine: James V. Heidinger, Steve Beard, and Robert Rempfer. We there first fantasized about the development of what we then were calling a "think tank" for church renewal leadership, especially in the service of our own communion, now mired in a membership hemorrhage and a secularization crisis. The metaphor of a "think tank" seemed more fitting then than now. We were focused on bringing together biblically and historically grounded intellectual leadership to the service of church reform. My main recollection of that conversation was how funny it was, how hilarious to think of the absurdities prevailing within our church, and how ripe for comedy. Everyone watching the parade was saying "how elegant" except the outspoken child who said the obvious: "The Emperor has no clothes."*

It was in this conversation that I laid out before colleagues my hope for a deeper and broader movement of believers committed to classic Christian teaching: deeper biblically than egalitarian politics; broader than the established frame of reference of evangelicals, charismatics, and discontents, who though well-intentioned were tainted with the charge of narrowness and somewhat lacking in a catholic sense. It was out of that conversation there emerged a preliminary envisioning of how this movement might develop. The first task was to bring together the brightest and most faithful intellectual leadership within our church to consider what we might be able to do about this church in its particular crisis of wandering and loss of identity, We wondered: What could be possibly salvaged? The seminaries? That's a laugh. The mission boards that have so much money? Too deep in bureaucratic self-interest. The council of bishops? Entirely too cautious. Out of ensuing conversations between Bishop William R. Cannon, Maxie Dunnam, and myself, the three of us were asked to write the call to the gathering in Atlanta 1994 that became the beginning of the Confessing Movement. The concern was to engender a new constellation of intellectual leadership devoted to biblical grounding, liturgical wisdom, mission commitment, and theological criticism. It sought to bring together the most articulate advocates of classic ecumenical teaching whether from evangelical or charismatic or liturgical or pietistic or postmodern orthodox frames of reference. It was from this invitation that ninety-two leaders were brought together with no fanfare, eschewing press coverage, for prayer, study, and candid communication. It was out of this wrenching first discussion that the idea of the confessing movement unexpectedly emerged. We began to describe to each other who we were and what we hoped to do. Though no one had planned or pre-envisioned the outcome as a major grassroots effort, and no one could have named the ongoing partnership beforehand, virtually all agreed that we were in fact the Confessing Movement Within the United Methodist Church. The twenty-six theses upon which I proposed that the new alliance be based, or should at least be taken into account in its formation, were contained in my address at Atlanta the day before the Confessing Movement was formed. These theses appeared with minor editing under the title "Reclaiming Stolen Property" (in God and Man: Perspectives on Christianity in the 20th Century, ed. Michael Bauman, Hillsdale, Michigan: Hillsdale College Press, 1995, some portions of which appear in edited form in chapter 1 of this book, "The Emergence of Confessing Christians in the Mainline").

The core group that later became the Association for Church Renewal was formed by executive officers of renewing movements within the mainline: David Bareford Runnion, Parker Williamson, and Allan Churchill being among its key motivators. They constituted the remnant, the chief thread of connectivity, that the Holy Spirit provided in making the confessing movement an ecumenical reality. Out of their partnership came the DuPage Declaration, the first Barmen-like ecumenical statement that anticipated the coming confessing movements in the mainline, a wake-up call for the modern ecumenical movement. The leading figures at this stage in the writing of the Declaration were Presbyterians Donald Bloesch and Richard Lovelace, Methodist James Heidinger, and Episcopalian Todd Wetzel. Some of the text of the DuPage Declaration is found in various extracts in Part Four. The leaders of these spirited renewing movements were all faced with much the same dilemmas. They had long recognized the similarities between their efforts, but were struggling to bring them into a viable cohesion. Their earlier conversations had focused on personal narrative, mutual pastoral care, and strategic consultation. They sought to support each other in their various communions' renewal efforts. Meanwhile the focus remained on their own separate denominational renewal, not necessarily yoked with other denominations of the mainline. The move toward a unified effort at mainline renewal would flow eventually into a coordinated renewing effort that would trend ever more toward grounding in classic Christian teaching and historic orthodoxy. It was not until the formation of the Confessing Movement in 1994 that this writer became an active agent in evangelical ecumenism, serving as a theological consultant from the Confessing Movement to the Association for Church Renewal, and an active participant in the World Evangelical Alliance. These initiatives were growing toward unity in truth, theological depth, and multi-movement coordination. This is the new configuration that has only recently been taking shape. In my book The Rebirth of Orthodoxy there is a description of the embryonic shape of the movement that has sometimes been called the "new ecumenism."

Staying Within

The assumption of being and staying "within" the mainline was a crucial indicator of the movement's identity. Although they thought of their mission and identity as located first of all within a particular church tradition, their intention and outlook was deeply ecumenical from the outset. It was the very opposite of their being either schismatics or denominational partisans. They were committed to recovering their own confessional teaching within their own communion as an expression of classic ecumenical Christianity.

Parallel movements of recovery were simultaneously emerging among the Reformed, Anglican, Wesleyan, and Congregational traditions. But each one was at that early stage preoccupied with its own particular troubled corner of the ecumenical neighborhood. During the 1980s many renewing Christians had been working together within each communion to recover their own doctrinal standards and liturgical integrity, whether Lutheran, Congregationalist, or Episcopalian. They understood their own communions to be alienated from their own confessional tradition. They viewed the recovery of their own tradition as the best route to becoming truly catholic and truly evangelical. So to bring their own confession back into their communion was at the same time to bring their communion back toward ancient ecumenical teaching. This is an easily misunderstood premise, but very important. Hence from day one they were intuitively aware of the need to relate their intradenominational reforms to analogous interdenominational confessional movements. This was underscored in the Atlanta document. But each renewal movement had enough fires to put out and problems at hand within their own wandering fold before attempting a serious ecumenical correlation.

The feasibility of a viable ecumenical coalition between confessing and renewing movements across the mainline would emerge only gradually as each became more deeply acquainted with what other movements were doing in their separate vineyards. In the early years of the confessing movement, all parties had to work hard to overcome the verbal obstacles between traditionalists, orthodox, evangelicals, charismatics, and institutional moderates. For there had been previously some subtle conflicts between these tendencies. All these eventually came into a workable consensus.

All recognized that they were much closer to each other than any were to their delinquent liberal establishments. They did not want to settle for an oversimplified choice between being either ecumenical or evangelical. They were exasperated over the flawed public perception that orthodoxy and evangelicalism were recalcitrant, dated, old-fashioned, right wing, or extremist. It was with the consent of the evangelical leadership that all concurred that it would be better for the whole movement if the most conspicuous evangelicals were not playing the most vocal and public roles in this new coalition. They took a backseat voluntarily. It was an important and generous act of self-constraint. From the outset they were a major part of the stream but not the whole stream of classic Christianity within the mainline. Meanwhile the confessing movement relied heavily on their journalistic acumen, as well as charismatic dynamism. Accordingly it was evident that this new effort should not be called together by the evangelical leadership alone, but by this new coalition of classical centrists that included evangelicals and those committed to liturgical renewal. In due time they all acknowledged their orthodox and evangelical center, but at this early stage, the term *evangelical* was not a word that brought people together. Rather it tended to be somewhat divisive, or was perceived as such. That is not so true now, but was then.

Three Phases of Growth of the Confessing Movement

The brief history of the Confessing Movement can be summarized in three exponentially growing phases: First, 1994–1998, it was a movement of highly articulate and committed leaders, largely clergy. Second, 1999–2000, it shifted from clergy leadership to a broad grassroots lay movement (among the Methodists the appointment of Senator Pat Miller as executive director of the Confessing Movement Within the UMC as their first full-time executive marked the beginning of this phase). The third phase came only after the Cleveland 2000 AD General Conference of the UMC, and the Presbyterian Church USA General Assembly, where the movement began to have significant legislative victories on accountability, fiscal, representational, and sexuality issues. The present stage is the attempt to conceive and embody an ecumenical form of the confessing movement.

The church leaders watched warily from a great distance as this movement was forming. It arose with only minimal assistance and considerable resistance from them, but with the election of new church leaders and bishops in this millennium, and with the increased strength of orthodox and evangelical leadership, the future of the confessing movement became much brighter. Talk of "amiable separation" refers to the willingness of the orthodox to allow those who have a wrenched conscience in following the discipline of the church to leave amiably with pensions and property, not the departing of the orthodox from the existing denominations.

The core of the younger theological leaders who have conceptually formed and guided the confessing movement have been Ephraim Radner and Philip Turner (ECUSA); Bruce McCormack, Robert Gagnon and Mark Achtemeier (PCUSA); David Bareford-Runnion (UCC); Walter Sundberg and Christopher Hirschman (ELCA); Donna Hailson (American Baptists); Victor Shepherd (United Church of Canada) and the late Diane Knippers. Among Methodists the major voices have been William Abraham, Leicester

Longden, and Scott Jones, who shaped the core reasoning of the 1994 Atlanta statement, "An Invitation to the Churches." Subsequent documents of the Confessing Movement have been extensions and developments of that Invitation, which has been referenced frequently in part 4 of this study.

The aim in this chapter is a description of the *uniting* of the renewing and confessing movements within the whole mainline, not with their work in the several denominations (already reviewed in chapter 7). The outcome is less a defined organization than an emerging spirit, less a structure than a new convergence. Evangelicals are growing more aware of ancient ecumenical history. Ecumenists are becoming more than before familiar with evangelical commitments, vocabulary, and values. Put simply: *The orthodox are reviving, while the revivalists are becoming more orthodox*. The national gathering called Confessing the Faith, held in Indianapolis, October 2002, represents an early expression of this new ecumenical convergence. It was a "sound of coming rain" (1 Kings 18:41). These ecumenical renewing and confessing movements of the mainline are already curbing the momentum of permissive deterioration. They are rebuilding on a firmer foundation.

The Streams Flow Together

How were these two streams brought together? At first it did not seem evident that they even could be. But the looming force driving them together was the specter of unrelenting liberal domination throughout the mainline. The more these communities of discourse talked with each other, the more they knew they belonged together and needed each other, and did not have the luxury of allowing themselves to remain in a distanced relation. It was similar to the gradual recognition that was taking place between Orthodox and Evangelical delegates to the Canberra World Council of Churches Assembly and within the World Evangelical Alliance. All of these streams were valiantly struggling against much of the same permissive, naturalistic ideologies that tended to be neglectful of Scripture, tradition, mission, and sexual accountability. These streams together were Spirit-led to tackle the difficulties strewn about following fifty years of latitudinarianism. The same energies were rising simultaneously among the Anglican, Presbyterian, American Baptist, Lutheran, and United Church of Canada faithful. But how could they persuade those who grasped only one aspect of that historical memory that the other aspects were crucial to their interests?

Some of these persons, including Philip Turner, Richard John Neuhaus,[1] Carl Braaten, and this writer, were more identified with the orthodox-ecumenical than with the revivalist-evangelical stream. None of these had sustained identification with renewing movements such as Good News or the Presbyterian Lay Committee or the World Evangelical Alliance. Others, such as Edmund Robb, Jr., Victor Shepherd, and James V. Heidinger, were leading evangelicals but not strongly identified with patristic or liturgical studies or ecumenical orthodoxy. Others, like Robert Webber, Donald Bloesch, and Parker Williamson were from the outset bridge-builders between the orthodox and evangelical forms of leadership. Among Methodists, the leading evangelical elder statesman models were Harry Denman, Ed Robb, and Maxie Dunnam, whereas the primary models for the classical ecumenical Methodists were Albert C. Outler, John Deschner, Bishop William Cannon, and Geoffrey Wainwright. It was heartening to watch the emergence of two generations of theological leadership willing to take risks, stand up and be counted, and not intimidated by the loss of upward mobility in the establishment. Before Atlanta 1994, however, many had virtually given up on the viability of a cohesive movement for renewal and confession.

The "deep ecumenists" are those who, having *once* looked to the *modern* ecumenical movement for an expression of unity in the body of Christ, at length having been disillusioned from those illusions, are *now* looking toward *ancient* ecumenism for contemporary wisdom. They see key figures of the Reformation tradition, such as Luther, Calvin, Cranmer, and Wesley, as expressions of this deeper classic confessional, pan-Protestant and patristic (Trinitarian and Christological) consensus.

Antecedents to Mainline and Evangelical Confessional-Ecumenical Movements

The World Council of Churches (WCC) was constituted in 1948. The confessing movements in the mainline today stand in unrecognized continuity with pre-WCC evangelical efforts aimed at manifesting the unity of the body of Christ among the inheritors of revivalism and pietism. The modern use of the term *ecumenical* came out of evangelical and missionary circles, long before the social gospel. Notable ecumenical statements among the nineteenth century evangelicals were the 1846 Doctrinal Basis of Faith of the World's Evangelical Alliance, the Report of the Eleventh International Conference of the Evangelical Alliance, 1907, the Lausanne Covenant, and the DuPage Declaration. Five to ten decades before modern ecumenism, the Evangelical Alliance's confessional statements were refined in the period following 1846.

Confessing movements in each of the contemporary mainline churches owe a great debt to those pre-WCC evangelical confessors who have paved the way for current confessional and evangelical ecumenism. Efforts today stand on the shoulders of these predecessors. It is a little-known story, however, as to how the current ecumenical movement is indebted to its nineteenth-century predecessors. Necessary reading for anyone who wants to understand this is

One Body in Christ: The History and Significance of the Evangelical Alliance, by Ian Randall and David Hilborn.[2]

Long before the ecumenical conferences from Edinburgh (1910) to Amsterdam (1948), there were active efforts to bring Christians together, not under a latitudinarian premise, but under a deliberate confessional-evangelical commitment. The eighteenth-century antecedents of the evangelical ecumenists were George Whitefield, Jonathan Edwards, Nicholas von Zinzendorf, Philip Doddridge, and John and Charles Wesley. In the nineteenth century, among the great evangelical ecumenists were Charles Finney, Lord Shaftesbury, William Wilberforce, John Newton, F. D. Maurice, Charles Simeon, and Henry Martyn Gooch. Key evangelical ecumenists prior to the formation of the World Council (1948) were Abraham Kuyper, Dwight Moody, John R. Mott, and Phillip Schaff. Recent evangelical ecumenists like Stephen Niell, John Stott, Billy Graham, Clive Calver, J. I. Packer, and Vinay Samuel stand on their shoulders. Preceding confessors have blazed the path. The promise of evangelical unity is being fulfilled less in modern ecumenical organizations than in the new ecumenism of orthodox Christian teaching after the collapse of modernity.

The confessing movement today is not to be regarded as discontinuous with these evangelically shaped ecumenical and renewal movements that preceded it. They are continuous. They belong together.

The vital energy of the confessing movement has stunned all beholders with its promise and possibility. The closer one comes to grasping this vitality, the more likely they are to feel that this movement could not have occurred without God's own blessing and empowerment and providential guidance. The Spirit has hedged and emboldened this confessing movement mightily by shepherding it through these hazardous transitions in the mainline with few resources.

The confessing movement has come out of a perspective largely rooted in nineteenth- and twentieth-century evangelical revivalism, and has moved to a perspective formed by the best energies of that tradition combined with classical ecumenical teaching. The confessing movement today has shifted the focus of renewal more firmly upon classical ecumenical teaching, and in doing so it has broadened and deepened the evangelical-ecumenical coalition.

16

How the United Church of Canada Lost Its Confessional Identity

The United Church of Canada (UCCanada) provides a case study of the dynamics of implosion and renewal. In the view of many observers, the UCCanada has voluntarily elected to disavow its ecumenical identity and leave entirely behind its ecumenical legacy. What follows is a comment on how this has come about and what it means for historic ecumenism.

The Voluntary Forfeiture of Ecumenical Identity

The UCCanada has repeatedly made a free decision to abandon crucial aspects of historic ecumenical teaching on creation, sin, and the blessings of marriage. It no longer speaks with one voice for believers in Canada. Even less can it speak for believers of all times and places—the church catholic. In its present form it can no longer claim to stand in full communion with classical ecumenical Christianity. Hence many believers no longer regard the UCCanada as properly to be called an ecumenical communion because of its own testy choices. It has of its own will elected to divest its own Basis of Union. This forfeit of ecumenical identity has been its own voluntary decision.

Elsewhere one can find chronicled the UCCanada's practical abandonment of classical Christian teaching on how the faithful are called to honor God through their sexuality. But this much is crystal clear: what has always and everywhere been believed by Christians about covenant sexual fidelity is no longer respected or affirmed by the UCCanada leadership.

The irony: it is not by some external verdict that the UCCanada has become in this sense "de-ecumenized." Rather, the leaders themselves have chosen by their own willful action to abjure, dissociate, and abandon the ecumenical commitments that brought them together, and the historic ecumenical reality and consensus.

This by no means implies that the laity or the general church membership of the UCCanada has consented to this leadership. Far from it. It only means that the leadership appears determined to lead the church in a counter-ecumenical direction.

Due Process Aborted

Many lay believers within the UCCanada have sadly concluded that the leadership manipulated the outcome of the legislative acts that took these divisive actions presumably on behalf of the whole UCCanada laity. The defensive leadership ensured that the omnibus report of Commission C could not be changed by the governing Council, which would have been due democratic procedure. The result is that "The 37th General Council has put an unbridgeable gulf between those of us who affirm the Bible's teaching on sexuality and those who don't."[1] The question remains as to whether this method of decision making by Commission C on behalf of the whole Council is a legal act according to its Basis of Union which requires a remit (or referendum) to all Presbyteries and pastoral charges before any change in government can become law. This question has not yet been fully adjudicated.

The issue is not whether churches will engage in empathic, caring ministries to homoerotic parishioners. Most classic Christian believers support such ministries. Rather it is whether the denomination can disavow its own ecumenical Basis of Union and still legitimize the pretense that it remains truly ecumenical.

Liberal ecumenists need to understand how their decisions are being read and interpreted by laity standing within the *consensus fidelium*, and by all who appeal to the ancient ecumenical consensus. If there is no willingness to honor the voices of the faithful, the claim of inclusivity so frequently heard from them becomes pathetic.

In 1960 the General Council voted a general approval of a sixty six-page report of its Commission on Christian Marriage and Divorce, which (among many other subjects) stood firm on the covenant of marriage, against proposals to legitimize same-sex behavior as a fulfillment of the divine will. In August 2000, the General Council officially disavowed the crucial affirmations of that statement, and adopted a new statement crafted by activists in close collusion with the Council leadership. So the UCCanada has now acted decisively. The signal has been indelibly sent.

This shows that the leadership elites no longer care about and no longer even recognize the intergenerational, cross-cultural precedent of universal church teaching. Hence they no longer receive the faith of the *oikoumene* as historically received and most widely held. Historic voices mean nothing to narrow political revisionists. What they care about is conforming to a politically correct ideology of absolute toleration. Those who for reason of conscience cannot consent to the permissiveness of absolute toleration have been treated as if full of hatred, and not allowed due democratic process. This in effect abandons any effort to seek to define the truth of male-female complementarity and durable covenant in God-given sexuality.

In officially renouncing classic teaching, they took the further step of calling upon both civil and church legislative and judicial processes to become politically active in making up for "the damage inadvertently caused by the historic stance of our church." They urged laity to affirm—even if by ignoring conscience and due process—that almost all conceivable human sexual "orientations," whether "Lesbian, Gay, Bisexual, Transgendered, or Heterosexual" are equally a "gift from God." They went on officially to "affirm lesbian and gay partnerships, recognize them in church documentation and services of blessing, and actively work for their civil recognition."[2] Civil recognition means that these unions would be assumed (and compelled by law) to have the same validity and legitimacy as sacred marriage, that the special legal protections surrounding marriage in western history are to be abandoned, and that UCCanada laity are now all supposed to be working actively for these political objectives.

This is occurring at the very time when the recovery of the blessing and importance and cohesion of marriage is being so widely affirmed by Christian believers the world over, and by many in Canada.

Free Fall

No wonder many laity feel that now "the church is in free fall." No wonder that "Statistically speaking the future of the [United Church of Canada] is grim."[3] Yet the leadership has remained silent about the UCCanada's decline in numbers, influence, credibility, and finances.

But this statistical decline is not the main point here. The more decisive verdict, now unambiguous, is that the United Church leadership has disavowed historic ecumenical teaching, and hence can no longer honestly call itself ecumenical. Those who are sentimentally attached to the term *ecumenical* are compelled entirely to redefine *oikoumene* by radical dilution of its historic meaning.

Moreover, the actions of general North American legislative bodies of the Presbyterian and Methodist traditions (primary founding members of the UCCanada) have taken the opposite direction by holding firmly and with ever-widening majorities to the historic Christian understanding of marriage as a God-blessed union of a man and a woman that can within covenant love engender, protect, and nurture children.

This action does not imply that UCCanada's decision is irreversible. That is a matter to be determined in future legislative processes, whether constitutional or extraconstitutional. But for now it is clear. Its ecumenical status has been substantially forfeited and delegitimized. The United Church of Canada has lost its ecumenical virginity. It will be as hard to recover as it was easy to lose.

Actions of the General Council of the United Church, according to its Basis of Union (8.6.2) are subject to "the approval of a majority of the Presbyteries, and, if advisable, Pastoral Charges also." Articles vii, xiv, and xx are contravened by these illicit actions of the General Council. Each act calls for a remit, where the question is sent to Presbyteries to see whether they agree with a change in the Basis of Union or in an official church doctrine or policy. The doctrinal changes in question concern the classic Christian doctrines of creation, sin, holy living, and marriage. These doctrines are treated in The Basis of Union (cf. Section 2.14). That marriage is exclusively between a man and a woman is evident not only from Jesus's own words ("For this reason a man shall leave his father and mother and be joined to his wife, and the two shall become one flesh"), but also from the United Church's own 1950 Book of Common Order,[4] and its 1969 Service Book.[5]

The leadership cannot justly declare the church's mind on subjects that have caused heated and divisive debate over the course of decades without raising questions about arrogance and manipulation. A change of doctrines so fundamental as those of creation, sin, and marriage, especially under conditions of dubious due democratic process, requires a confirmation by the Presbyteries and also by the pastoral charges, where the services of marriage are performed. But the defensive and ill-tempered leadership is afraid for the issue to be referred for vote by the Presbyteries or pastoral charges.

USA-Canadian Mainline Mutual Interests

What is the standing of observers in the United States of America in speaking of Canadian matters? They are not speaking of Canadian matters, but of ecumenical matters, of what permits one honestly to use the term *ecumenical*, of what qualifies as consistent with classical Christian teaching, and of defiant abuses that cannot qualify as such. The issue here is the definition of the *oikoumene* (the general and universal teaching of the intergenerational, multicultural Christian community), in this case in the sphere of sexuality.

For whom am I speaking? One does not need special credentials or a Canadian passport to enter this debate. It is about the definition of the church as one, holy, catholic, and apostolic. Any faithful Christian layperson is eligible to enter this discussion, and may be called to do so when Christian teaching is distorted. This is not a matter of counting votes but of fidelity to Christian teaching. That fidelity cannot be assessed apart from the teaching that is ecumenically received, in this case particularly on sexuality, which one may see by examining the history of commentary on Romans 1:22–28.[6] Many lay members and clergy in Canada are urgently concerned about the tragic misjudgment of dismissive and overconfident church leaders. The many renewing and confessing Christians in the North American mainline commonly feel a sense of pathos and sadness regarding the UCCanada.

This is pertinent because these are historic sister churches of the UCCanada, where several renewing and confessing movements remain valiantly within the UCCanada. They have struggled unavailingly for basic justice in their church, and for fair voice within its legislative processes. Many feel the tragic consequences of this abandonment.

What remains at issue is historic ecumenical legitimacy. What bizarre view has the right legitimately to call itself ecumenical? The fitting answer: only that is honestly ecumenical which is informed and confirmed by the historic teachings of ecumenical Christianity. The UCCanada has a long and honorable history of ecumenical life. That is precisely what it has voluntarily renounced, discontinued, abdicated, and forsaken.

Since the UCCanada brought the Methodist Church of Canada under its ecumenical umbrella from the outset in 1925, Methodists worldwide have more than an incidental interest in their Canadian partner's actions. North American Methodists are in good standing to enter an amicus brief on behalf of many of the voiceless faithful former Methodist families and congregations in Canada. They are determined not to allow the language and legitimacy of ecumenism to be taken captive by counter-ecumenical forces that spend away the heritage of classic Christianity.

The Boundary

The distinguished ecumenical theologian, Wolfhart Pannenberg, has wisely written: "Here lies the boundary of a Christian church that knows itself to be bound by the authority of Scripture. *Those who urge the church to change the norm of its teaching on this matter must know that they are promoting schism.* If a church were to let itself be pushed to the point where it ceased to treat homosexual activity as a departure from the biblical norm, and recognized homosexual unions as a personal partnership of love equivalent to marriage, such a church would stand no longer on biblical ground but against the unequivocal witness of Scripture. A church that took this step would cease to be the one, holy, catholic, and apostolic church."[7]

Believers in sister churches that have remained faithful to historic Christian teaching pray for their Canadian brothers and sisters in their trauma.

. . . .

WHO OWNS LOCAL CHURCH PROPERTY?

A Case Study

The issue of local church property rights is an active question for many believers in Presbyterian, Episcopal, Methodist, and United Church of Canada traditions. Town by town, the question of who owns local church property is emerging as a painful, volatile dilemma. There is only one reason why it is a dilemma: the mainline leadership has refused to listen to its own laity. The remainder of this inquiry takes one case study of the history of a single tradition (Methodist in this instance) of understanding the relation of local property rights to judicatory responsibilities. Many analogies are easily drawn with other communions.

17

Property Deeds
and Established Doctrines

This is a "time bomb" issue for many local churches whose governance is both connected with and disaffected by denominational commitments. This issue is arising with particular poignancy and passion among the rising voices of confessing Christians. It is intensified by the "stay or leave" dilemma. It remains highly contested and confusing, especially to lay leaders within major mainline denominations.

This is an issue in which many laypersons, pastors, boards of trustees, judicatories, local church study groups, and church councils will have to face, like it or not, and about which they will necessarily have to be informed.

Multi-denominational Analogies

This argument is pertinent not for one denomination only, but by analogy for property issues in all the mainline traditions. Further, the interested parties in this dispute are not only those of the "mainline," but rather are generic, since the dilemma is felt in every quarter of North American Protestantism—whether evangelical or liberal or liturgical. The struggles and agonies in the mainline are bound to have a ripple effect upon nonmainline congregations that struggle with similar issues, especially in long-established denominations.

Settlement of local church property conflict differs widely among denominations, depending upon whether they are *congregationally* governed, as distinguished from what the law calls *hierarchically* governed, where the trusteeship of the local church property is entrusted by law to the denominational discipline or to some nonlocal legal entity.

Congregationally governed congregations own their own church property. Denominationally governed congregations operate under a church law or discipline or constitution that defines the terms of local ownership and trusteeship. Those in the former category will not be so directly affected by the ownership dilemma. Those in the latter category will be greatly affected by legal determinations of who owns the local church property, and to whom is it legally entrusted.

Although many details of what follows are relatively denomination-specific, the same generic issue persists in all church traditions. This chapter leaves it to others to grasp and reflect upon analogies with the history and polity of the diverse church bodies.

Why the Special Focus on the United Methodist Property Issue?

Since it is too much to try to deal with all the traditions of the mainline, we focus on only one in particular, in this case the Methodists, although it equally could have been Episcopalian or Presbyterian.

It is fitting to focus on trusteeship of local church property in the largest of the mainline Protestant denominations: the United Methodist Church. The choice to limit the discussion in this way does not make any assumption that the decisions made in Methodist circles will be valid for other denominations, but it does assume that there will be analogies in other denominations who will face the same urgent dilemma.

It is hoped that the argument could be examined without prejudice and fairly as an historical, legal, and constitutional argument, and analogous reasoning applied to other similar situations. What follows is arguably a turnaround line of reasoning in the property-use arena. It could change the way of framing the question of church property by focusing on the constitutional history of local church deeds.

Regrettably, this sort of research has not been generally available. This argument and documentation could mean thousands of dollars of savings for local church boards of trustees for legal fees and opinions, and can be ignored only at their peril.

If the following argument seems complicated, it is necessary to spell it out accurately, and remember how important it is for thousands of local congregations. If not spelled out with precision, it might appear cavalier or tendentious.

Narrowing the Question

The question must first be narrowed to ask: What does the legal history of deed making (i.e., uniform deeds of trust of all local churches) in American Methodism clearly establish that impinges upon contemporary disputes over who owns the right to occupy and use United Methodist church property today? And how does this history correlate with other Protestant traditions?

The constitutional and disciplinary standards of this church tradition have been respected by the courts for over two centuries. Most observers remain confident that they will continue to respect them. It is on the basis of these constitutionally grounded doctrinal and disciplinary standards that the courts have reserved a generous and deferential space of freedom for church law. It is to be administered within church judicatories by due processes governed by the conferences of the denomination under their Book of Discipline.

The issue: Who owns title to local church property when that property has been long connected with a denomination that has become wayward in the doctrinal commitments that stand permanently at the legal authority of the denomination? Put simply, the legal problem is: Who owns title to local United Methodist Church property—those who follow United Methodist doctrine and discipline or those who do not? Do those who defy these standards have equal status with those who remain faithful?

The Model trust deed of 1773 formed the pattern for all American Methodist deeds of trust of local church property, and its relevance remains indisputably pertinent to contemporary church property issues.

Why Now?

In July 2002 a District Superintendent under the direction of her bishop changed the keys on the locks of a local United Methodist Church without notice and without due process. This local board was seeking scrupulously to follow United Methodist doctrine and discipline. Within the last two years several congregations seeking to defend United Methodist polity have been similarly harassed or even expelled from their church property and required to rent space from a local school.

It is no longer possible to avoid asking: does the conference or judicatory have the right to use or administer or direct conditions for use of local United Methodist Church property if such actions run counter to the authorizing *trust clause under which properties are legally chartered*?

Put differently: how do established doctrinal and disciplinary standards impinge upon the use of local property according to the trust clause embedded in the deeds of every local church of the communion?

What follows is an advisory opinion based upon many years of study of constitutional church law. The argument welcomes critical responses from all who care about the unity of the church and the integrity of Christian teaching.

The issue is not primarily about freedom of the pulpit or criteria for judging what can be licitly preached in local churches. These are long-settled questions: preachers remain free to preach the Word of God. Rather it centers on what happens when a broader judicatory or Conference defies its own established church doctrine.

When local church boards and pastors who are faithful to doctrinal and disciplinary standards are thwarted by those who teach contrary to the communion's disciplinary standards, where is the remedy to be found? This is not a purely theoretical question. The faithful are subject to being deprived of their local church property, their locks changed, and their property confiscated by those who themselves are not following disciplinary standards.

Thesis

Although not widely recognized, there already exists a legitimate recourse under church law—the model trust deed in the American Methodist tradition, which for over 200 years has impinged upon civil court judgments on how the property of the local church is rightly to be governed and used. But its implications have not been adequately studied, understood, tested, or applied.

The doctrinal and disciplinary standards embedded in these local deeds are unmistakably clear. They are stated in every Book of Discipline and have been substantially and repeatedly stated since founding constitutional conferences in 1784 and 1808 without change, and without diminution.

When the guardianship trust vested in judicatory officials (whether ordained pastors, superintendents, conferences, or boards of trustees) has been neglected or abandoned or disavowed, those parties do not have a self-evident clear or legitimate claim to the use of church property. Rather those who support the doctrine and discipline of the United Methodist Church have reasonable legitimate recourse to the courts that they be allowed not only to use church facilities, but that they be protected from being denied access to these facilities.

Here the inquiry necessarily becomes historical in nature. The argument that follows will show textually that the doctrinal standards remain clear and binding.

Titles in Trust in Church Property—a Legal Duty within the Secular Order

First, it is widely conceded in church law that the church "exists in the secular world and that civil authorities may seek legal definition predicated on the nature of the United Methodist Church" (Book of Discipline, 2004, para. 139, 94, hereafter noted as Disc., 2004, para. 139, 94).

While the church is of God, it lives within the context of a civil society, and hence must duly account for its property as a matter of secular and civil accountability. The church's doctrine is protected from infringement by civil authorities, but the church's business practices and legal obligations cannot be exempt from civil responsibilities.

The Trust Clause Embedded in Every Local Church Property Deed

Every local United Methodist church must have a property deed that places it under the authority of the historic *trust clause*. The title requirement is clearly stated in all Methodist Disciplines: "Titles to all real and personal, tangible and intangible property held at jurisdictional, annual, or district conference levels, or by a local church or charge, or by an agency or institution of the Church, shall be held in trust for The United Methodist Church and *subject to the provisions of its Discipline*" (Disc., 2004, para. 2501, 671, italics added).

The Discipline itself places clear constraints on what legislators and administrators can do. The provisions of the Discipline begin with a Constitution that enumerates the specific texts of the established standards of doctrine and discipline and their central importance for the use of property.

Every Trust Clause Embedded in Every Local Church Deed Is Subject to the United Methodist Constitution and Discipline

Local church properties cannot be held legally without reference to the Book of Discipline which states: "All written instruments of conveyance by which premises are held or hereafter acquired for use as a place of divine worship or other activities for members of The United Methodist Church shall contain the following *trust clause*: In trust, that said premises shall be used, kept, and maintained as a place of divine worship of the United Methodist ministry and members of The United Methodist Church, *subject to the Discipline*, usage, and ministerial appointments of said Church as from time to time authorized and declared by the General Conference" (Disc., 2004, para. 2503.1, 671–72, italics added). This is the starting point for understanding property usage according to United Methodist doctrinal standards.

There Are Four Specified Historical and Contemporary United Methodist Doctrinal Standards

The Plan of Union accepted by the Evangelical United Brethren and Methodist traditions in 1968 takes great pains to specify that the phrase "our present existing and established standards of doctrine," includes "as a minimum John Wesley's forty-four *Sermons on Several Occasions* and his *Explanatory Notes upon the New Testament*. Their function as 'standards' had already been defined by the 'Large Minutes' of 1763, which in turn had been approved by the American Methodists in 1773 and 1785. To these *Sermons* and *Notes* the Conference of 1808 added The Articles of Religion" (Disc., 1968, Preface, Part II, 35, and continuously sustained in subsequent editions). After 1968 "The Confession" was also included in protected doctrinal standards, in reference to the Evangelical United Brethren Confession of Faith. So there are four texts of doctrinal definition: three from The Methodist Church doctrinal tradition (Articles, Sermons, and Notes) and one added to these from the EUB doctrinal tradition (the Confession).

Even without an Explicit Local Trust Clause, the Duty to Guard and Maintain These Four Doctrinal Standards Remains in Effect "Subject to the Provisions of the Discipline"

Suppose, however, someone objects: "We have examined our local church deed, and we do not see any explicit reference to the Sermons, Notes, Articles, or Confession. How could a trust clause be enforceable in doctrinal matters if there is no explicit reference to the texts of the doctrinal standards?" The Discipline's answer is explicit and unambiguous. The trust deed functions precisely under accountability to the Discipline, which compacts into legislative and administrative language the cohesive and continuous historical correlation of doctrine and deed making. This history is a consistent and unabrogated tradition, as will be demonstrated. The Discipline specifies these doctrinal standards that are the very reason for writing the trust clause.

The absence of explicit reference does not legitimate ignoring the Constitution which requires the doctrinal standards in the Book of Discipline. Thus the lack of a trust clause with cited texts does not "absolve a local church or church agency or the board of trustees of either, of its responsibility and accountability to The United Methodist Church" (Disc., 2004, para. 2503.6, 673), which stands under the specific constraint of its established doctrinal standards.

If local trustees examine their local church deed, they will not see the trust clause appearing directly. But the Discipline explicitly states that this in no way excludes "a local church or church agency, or the board of trustees of either, from or relieves it of its connectional responsibilities to The United Methodist Church," which under its constitution is legally bound to guard and respect its own doctrinal standards embodied in the Sermons, Notes, Articles, and Confession.

The Purpose of the Deed Is Not to Protect the Judicatory but the Doctrinal Standards

But why do Methodists have a doctrinal trust clause written into all their deeds? *The very reason for the trust clause in deeds is to protect the doctrinal standards, not the Conference. The Conference is legitimized only insofar as it protects the doctrinal standards. The Restrictive Rules as interpreted by the Plan of Union and subsequent Disciplines textually specify the documents of the doctrinal standards* (Disc., 2004, para. 103, 59–74). Only on this basis can the local church be required to revert its property.

Much of the remainder of this argument focuses on the next point, which will be meticulously documented textually.

Use of Property under the Trust Clause Is Subject to the Discipline's Doctrinal Standards

Title to all United Methodist church property, whether it is "taken in the name of the local church trustees, or charge trustees" is "held subject to the provisions of the Discipline" (Disc., 2004, para. 2504, 673), hence the doctrinal standards that the Discipline holds inviolable.

Title to real property is held in the name of the local church in trust for the benefit of the United Methodist Church *but always subject to its doctrinal and disciplinary standards.* To be "subject to the usages and the Discipline of The United Methodist Church" (Disc., 2004, para. 2503.5, 672) requires first of all to be subject to its Constitution, hence subject to the Restrictions on the General Conference in the Constitution, which limits the General

Conference or any Conference from amending or negating the doctrinal standards found in the Sermons, Notes, Articles, and Confession.

Since church property "shall be held, kept, maintained, and disposed of for the benefit of The United Methodist Church and subject to the usages and the Discipline of the United Methodist Church," (Disc., 2004, para. 2503.5, 672) there can be *no licit uses of the property that are not subject to the Discipline, and therefore the doctrinal standards.* "This provision [the trust clause] is solely for the benefit of the grantee" (Disc., 2004, para. 2503.1, 672). Who is the grantee? Precisely the United Methodist Church that is pledged to remain "subject to the Discipline," which itself is pledged to guarantee the doctrinal standards.

Hence no local or conference Board of Trustees that holds property in trust for the United Methodist Church can function legally apart from the constitutional guarantees of the Restrictive Rules which limit the General Conference and Annual Conferences concerning doctrinal standards. No property can be duly used apart from its being "authorized and declared by the General Conference," which stands under the constraints of these Restrictive Rules, which requires use of property to be restricted to responsible accountability to "our doctrinal standards"—namely: the Standard Sermons, Notes, Articles, and Confession.

No use of property is licit "that violates the right of the Church to maintain connectional structure." This recalls that the notion of connection for two and a half centuries has specifically meant *connection with Mr. Wesley,* as defined in his writings, and notably in his Standard Sermons and Notes (Disc., 2004, para. 2506, 674).

How the Plan of Union Keeps the Trust Clause in Constant Application, Even When Not Explicit in the Local Church Deed

The Plan of Union (1968) is a legal instrument that defines the lawful status of the trust clause in property deeds of the successor organizations of the former Methodist Episcopal Church, Methodist Episcopal Church South, the Methodist Church, and the Evangelical United Brethren Church. All formerly devised deeds are legally folded into the Plan of Union, as specified in all subsequent Books of Discipline.

The Plan of Union maintains the manner and conditions of deeds without reference to "lapse of time or usage." A central feature of the Plan of Union is the provision stated explicitly in every United Methodist Discipline: "Nothing in the Plan of Union at any time after the union is to be construed so as to require any existing local church of any predecessor denomination to The United Methodist Church to alienate or in any way *to change the title to property contained in its deed or deeds at the time of union, and lapse of time or usage shall not affect said title or control."* (Disc., 2004, para. 2504, 673, italics added; also protected in Section VIII of the Local Church on Protection of Rights of Congregations, Disc., 2004, para. 261, 182). This binds all conferences to follow the doctrinal standards, most of all on property issues.

The stated purpose of this paragraph (2504) was to show the *continuity between the trust clauses before the Plan of Union and after,* and to make it easier under the conditions of proposed mergers to properly maintain and examine and prove merchantable titles after the Plan of Union in all jurisdictions.

The "time of union" was 1968. No trust clause written after that time can fail to be legally bound to the Restrictive Rule established in 1808 and confirmed in 1968, in reference to our doctrinal standards—the Sermons, Notes, and Articles, and after 1968, the Confession.

Crucial to the argument is the next step.

The Plan of Union Confirms That the Four Doctrinal Standards Are Textually Specific

The Plan of Union (between Methodists and the EUB) of 1968 clearly specifies that the phrase "our present existing and established standards of doctrine," includes "as a minimum John Wesley's forty-four *Sermons on Several Occasions* and his *Explanatory Notes upon the New Testament*" (Disc., 1968, Preface, Part II, 35). "In the present plan of Union ... the Confession, the Articles of Religion and the Wesleyan 'standards' are thus deemed congruent if not identical in their doctrinal perspectives and not in conflict" (ibid., 36). These four documentary standards are protected by Restrictive Rules from revision or abrogation by any General Conference acting on its own authority or without amending the Exception of 1832. Title deeds from the beginning have been written in order to protect these doctrinal standards. This will be demonstrated textually in what follows.

The record of the General Conference of 1972 makes this continuity clear: *"We have tried to clarify the contextual relationships between the Articles, the Confession, and Wesley's Sermons and Notes and Rules in order to clarify the reference in the First Restrictive Rule about 'our present and existing and established standards of doctrine'. We have not altered these standards"* (1972 DCA, 291, italics added).

By 1980 this rule was further underscored and reinforced: "The Discipline seems to assume that for the determination of otherwise irreconcilable doctrinal disputes, the Annual and General Conferences are the appropriate courts of appeal, *under the guidance of the first two Restrictive Rules (which is to say, the Articles and Confession, the Sermons and the Notes)"* (Disc., 1980, para. 67, 49, italics added).

Binding Standards That Affect the Writing of Church Property Deeds and Mortgages

The Plan of Union cannot be circumvented licitly by any Conference, bishop, Committee of Investigation, or Judicial Council. It is intrinsic to the Constitution. If the right of a local church or pastor to teach according to United Methodist doctrinal standards is tested in any court, church or civil, the Plan of Union must be quoted directly as a legal instrument binding on all subsequent United Methodist polity and all subsequent General Conferences, since it belongs permanently and intrinsically to the Plan of Union: "Wesley's Sermons and Notes were specifically included in our present existing and established standards of doctrine by plain historical inference" (Disc., 1984, 49). The current Discipline states even more tersely that "Wesley's *Sermons and Notes* were *understood specifically to be included* in our present existing and established standards of doctrine" (Disc., 2004, para. 102, 58, italics added), hence not just inferentially.

The once contested debate leading up to the General Conference of 1988 about the strength and purport of "plain historical inference" was settled by the 1988 General Conference, and remains textually embedded in all subsequent disciplines to date as Articles, Confession, Sermons, and Notes (Disc., 2004, para. 102, 58).

It is too late to revisit or revise the legally binding constitutional decisions made in the Plan of Union. Even if the terms of the Plan of Union do not appear in detail in a local church deed, that does not abrogate the terms of Union, as the Discipline makes clear. These were settled in 1968 as an act of civil law. A complex series of judicial challenges would follow from any attempt to revise the Plan of Union.

This legal clause constitutes a remarkable guarantee from the 1968 Plan of Union that the trust clause in deeds cannot be circumvented or changed from the conditions legally established in the Constitution (i.e., established in the 1808 General Conference with its Restrictive Rules for all future Conferences).

This means: any future local title deeds that are legally written for any future local United Methodist Church stand accountable to the doctrinal standards of the Sermons, Notes, Articles, and Confession. Any future merger must respect the trust clause that limits the ability of any future General Conference to emend or revamp any of the established doctrinal standards. The Plan is clear and specific: "Title to all property of a local church, or charge, or agency of the Church shall be held subject to the provisions of the Discipline" (Disc., 2004, para. 2504, 673), hence subject to the Restrictive Rules whose very purpose is to guard these doctrinal standards set forth in specific texts.

What If the Trust Clause Is Violated?

The naked title for *ownership* of local Methodist Church property normally lies in the hands of the local church board of trustees. Their *use* of the property is conditioned upon the trust clause.

First, if the trust clause is violated by the local church, the property can, through due process, revert to the Annual Conference Board of Trustees or an agency vested with accountability under the trust clause.

When asked to decide whether "the voluntary placement of a 'Trust Clause' on the title deed of real property" when discontinued or abandoned allows funds to be used "in another location," the Judicial Council held that they can, provided they are administered "through the Annual Conference Board of Trustees" (Judicial Council Decisions, hereafter noted as JCD 688, 1993).

Second, if the trust clause is violated by the conference or agency or judicatory itself, the judicatory officials could be liable to the charge of teaching contrary to doctrinal standards and discipline. Bishops and ordained conference members, who are all solemnly and voluntarily pledged to defend these doctrinal standards, are subject to charges if they inveigh against these doctrines. The tide is now shifting in the direction of more attention to this second point, without diminishing the first.

There are ample precedents for the title of local church property to revert to the conference when the local church violates doctrine or discipline (the first point made above). But we still have ahead of us the challenge of argument for cases (on the second point), where the conference itself violates its own constitutional doctrine or discipline. There is nothing in historic or contemporary United Methodist Discipline to protect the Conferences or bishops from full accountability to the trust clause.

The consequences of these legal instruments have not yet been tested in detail in either church law or civil law, but to the extent that challenges occur, they will likely be tested in the light of more historical information than has usually been considered. All the documentary evidence is now, at long last, in place for a defense of constitutional standards of doctrine.

Suppose a judicatory, bishop, or Annual Conference publicly, flagrantly, and repeatedly is determined to defy and resist official United Methodist doctrine and discipline. The local church laity, remaining *faithful to the connection*, have a right to be protected from flagrant doctrinal and disciplinary abuses and evasions, even and especially when done by a judicatory official.

This brings us to distinguish between two different types of connectionalism, faithful and unfaithful.

"Faithfulness to the Connection" Means "According to Established Doctrinal Standards"

What does it mean to be faithful to the connection? *"The connection"* is a crucial concept characteristic of Methodist history, doctrine, and polity, and has been pivotal since the earliest Conference of 1744, where the ministers *"in connection with Mr. Wesley"* were brought together under his leadership to confer on doctrine and discipline. Although Wesley made the decisions on what would be entered into the Minutes, he listened carefully to the advice of preachers.

Faithfulness to the connection in the early Methodist tradition meant faithfulness to the teaching and direct pastoral care of Mr. Wesley, always under the authority of Scripture. Faithfulness to the connection in the present Methodist tradition still means faithfulness to the teaching and patterns of pastoral care established by Wesley under scriptural authority, but for some it has become so thinly diluted that it points merely to simple loyalty to the present institution and management. In either sense faithfulness to the connection rightly understood means *faithfulness to the doctrinal and disciplinary standards* that were constitutionally defined first by Wesley, then refined and amended by the early American Methodists, and now are mandated for all who follow this Discipline. These are the doctrinal standards that are necessitated, taken for granted, meant, predicated, expected, entailed, and required in every title deed. This is a duty for anyone who administers United Methodist church property.

Unfaithfulness to the connection would therefore imply any form of teaching contrary to these doctrinal standards protected in every trust clause. This is a *chargeable offense* for anyone who has become ordained to sacred ministry (Disc., 2004, para. 2702.3.C and 2702.3.D), a binding, solemn, and voluntary act.

The Difference between Being Faithful and Unfaithful to the Connection

The issue here is not between *congregational* governance (which would make the local congregation the sole authority for local policy) versus *connectional* or denominational governance (which would make the constituted Book of Discipline the authority for local church policy).

All parties in Methodist conflicts must follow the rules of connectional polity. Most who wish to enter the arena of this discussion view themselves as already dedicated to connectional governance by virtue of their confirmation of their baptism.

This is an important point: the confessing movement is speaking from within the frame of reference of a faithful connectionalism, and *in opposition to an unfaithful abuse of connectionalism*. Readers who think exclusively in terms of congregational governance may stumble over this point. The confessing movement is not proposing to revert to congregational governance, but rather to protect the innocent from those who abuse connectional governance.

Hence there is no question whether a local church that is *disobedient* to doctrinal and disciplinary standards has a right to challenge the use of connectional church property apart from established church law. That is not a presumption here, nor is it even a contested question. The question rather is, *what happens when judicatory officials who have been authorized to guard the Discipline default on that guardianship, or when they take measures against precisely those who faithfully uphold the doctrine and Discipline?*

It may seem an anomaly that most voices in conflicted property situations consider themselves to be intensely faithful to the connection. Few voices among Methodists are arguing specifically for a purely congregational polity or against connectional polity. The issue is rather what constitutes doctrinal responsibility to the connection, and how is that related to the connection with Mr. Wesley and the authorized texts of his writings. The key question is: what right do denominational or judicatory officials have to act against established church law and doctrine? This is a question of *unfaithful abuse of the connection* in which unfaithful precisely means unfaithful to doctrinal standards.

So the Methodist debate is occurring primarily *within* the arena of Methodist connectional polity, not *outside* it, and not on the premise of an alleged autonomous or congregational local authority. No traditional or orthodox or evangelical Methodist who knows Methodist history and polity could plausibly argue that the local congregation as such is the final legitimate source for determining Methodist doctrine. The reason for that is that each local church is an expression of the whole body of Christ in that locale. Baptism is not baptism into a local church, but into the church of Jesus Christ, into the one, holy, universal, and apostolic church. So the form of polity under which the Methodist issue emerges is not congregational or synodal or charismatic, but Methodist and Wesleyan in its connectionalism, which means a direct relation to Mr. Wesley and his teaching. Although this distinction may seem like a parochial issue only for Methodists, there remain broad analogies with other forms of polity.

The Connectional Anomaly

Those who are *unfaithful to the connection* and its doctrine have shown signs of being at times ready to disavow those standards of doctrine and discipline and yet still attempt to hold on to the property, and to administer its use against disciplinary standards. This is now being challenged as illicit.

Those who remain most *faithful to the connection* and its doctrine, and who seek to guard, protect, defend, and embody the connectionally established doctrinal standards, have previously been forced into having to defend their faithfulness to the connection. That defensiveness has come to an end. They are now asking the courts of church law, and if necessary civil law, strictly to respect the repeatedly upheld constitutional history and the right to teach United Methodist doctrine. They are becoming more free to ask the courts to understand and respect the legal trust clause, and factor in its bearing upon the present use and administration of local church property.

This, as will be shown, is a continuing tradition with substantive continuity and cohesion and legal standing. But is it a binding requirement for pastors? This is our next subject.

What the Pastor Is Required by Church Law to Know about Doctrinal Standards

This is a crucial piece of the puzzle: is the pastor as local administrator of church property responsible for knowing the standards?

Every ordained elder must answer this question: "Have you studied the doctrines of the United Methodist Church? After full examination do you believe that our doctrines are in harmony with the Holy Scriptures? . . . Will you support and maintain them?" (Disc., 2004, para. 331.d.8–12). Failure to answer yes from the heart, *ex animo*, with sincerity, may call into question or jeopardize one's ministerial credentials and accountability. What is included in "the doctrines of the United Methodist Church"? It is clear: Sermons, Notes, and Articles (and after 1968 the Confession).

Are the Doctrinal Standards Settled Church Law?

The core of the doctrinal standards of the United Methodist Church have been clearly agreed to and established since the earliest deeds in 1773 and the founding Christmas Conference of 1784 and the constitutional Conference of 1808 (as further strengthened by the Exception of 1832). Since 1988 there has been no doubt about the meaning of "our doctrinal standards," textually defined and repeatedly reconfirmed. A leading constitutional expert, Bishop Holland N. McTyeire, summarized the standards this way: "American Methodists (1781) vowed to 'preach the old Methodist doctrine' of Wesley's 'Notes and Sermons.' May, 1784, 'the doctrine taught in the four volumes of the Sermons and the Notes on the New Testament' was reaffirmed. The Deed of Declaration (February, 1784) legally established these standards in the present body. The Rule (1808) guards them equally with the Articles" (*Manual of the Discipline*, Nashville: Southern Methodist Publishing House, 1870, 20th edition, 1931, 131).

The question of "theological pluralism" (referred to in the Discipline of 1980, para. 69 p. 72) has been subsequently placed under strict limitation since 1988, when The General Conference voted to view theological pluralism as standing "*under the guidance of our doctrinal standards*" (Disc., 1984, para. 69, 72)—the Sermons, Notes, Articles, and Confession, along with the General Rules. This core is a standard that stands as an immovable dictum in the Constitution, unamendable according to the Restrictive Rules.

Since we are here discussing only the core documents of doctrinal standards protected by the constitution and pertinent to the trust clause, we are not entering here into speculations about other documents that may lie beyond the penumbra of this core. These have been thoroughly discussed in my documentary history of *Doctrinal Standards in the Wesleyan Tradition* (Grand Rapids: Zondervan, 1988, hereafter DSWT). There one can find a more explicit discussion of ancillary issues on the penumbra: the number of sermons in the standard sermons, occasional pamphlets, the General Rules, the "Binding Minute," the Ward Motion, and other issues.

The Purpose of the Doctrinal Standards

The doctrinal standards of the Methodist tradition are designed to serve as: (a) a summative guide for Christian teaching concerning the central truth of Scripture; (b) an authoritative source to define the official teaching of the church textually; (c) a means of protecting against the abuse of church property by dissemination of contrary doctrines; (d) an authoritative constitutional standard to which one may appeal in matters under controversy; and (e) a criterion for monitoring and regulating the teaching office of the church, its leaders, pastors and conferences, to defend against abuses, and to unite a diverse church.

The doctrinal standards fulfill three complementary purposes, according to one of the leading Methodist constitutional historians: "*The standard of preaching*—the fifty two sermons embraced in the four volumes; *the standard of interpretation*—the notes on the New Testament; and *the standard of unity* with the sister churches of the Reformation—the Twenty-five Articles" (N. Burwash, *Wesley's Doctrinal Standards*, hereafter WDS, Toronto: Wm. Briggs, 1881, preface, x, italics added).

To recapitulate the cohesion of the historic textual core: (a) the four volumes of Sermons on Several Occasions (first volume published in 1746) place church teaching under the authority of *Scripture* and serve as doctrinal standards for preaching, (b) the Notes Upon the New Testament (1755) link our standards with the *exegesis* of the original apostolic witness, under whose authority they stand, (c) the Articles (1784) state "our common *heritage* from the great principles of the Protestant Reformation, and from the still more ancient conflicts with error in the days of Augustine and Athanasius" (Burwash, WDS, preface, x, italics added), and (d) the Confession was added in 1968.

Needed: Reliable Historical and Constitutional Counsel

Laypersons increasingly will want to understand their rights to their local church property under valid church law as specified above. At times they may feel that they are having to work extremely hard to possess and enjoy these rights. The documentation here shows how firmly grounded are the doctrinal standards and how well guaranteed they are by the Constitution, the Discipline, civil precedent, and the trust clause in property deeds. Congregations and pastors can confidently appeal to these rights.

This is a memo on constitutional history for laity and pastors, and those who counsel with laity and pastors on their legal rights, who may be required to set forth arguments in cases requiring due process before judicatories, boards for examination for ordination, committees of investigation, and judicial councils (and even under extreme conditions of unremedied abuses, arguments in civil courts where questions of civil rights and due process may be contested). This is an opinion offered to the chancellors and legal advisors of conferences, who may not have had adequate access to the constitutional, legal, and historical documentation showing the unity and continuity of the doctrinal standards, and their relevance for the use of local church property. This is also an advisory opinion for bishops and their cabinets, who are charged with the duty of defending the doctrinal standards and implementing disciplinary standards.

If a church board or pastor is under pressure from denominational officials who do not themselves understand adequately their own fiduciary duty to defend classical Christian doctrine and discipline, the trustee must be prepared to state these arguments directly, and to quote accurately the precise texts of these long-standing legal and constitutional guarantees. This is what this exercise is for.

The courts facing disputed claims are being asked to decide whether the use and administration of church properties rightly belong to those who *follow* the doctrinal and disciplinary standards, or those who have regrettably *disavowed* these long-held standards without challenge. A reasonable assessment of conflicted views on the responsible uses of local church properties is required. This cannot occur adequately without understanding the history, continuity, cohesion, and juridical force of these doctrinal standards. These are next to be briefly reviewed.

18

Constitutional
Restrictions

Documenting the Continuous Historical Record: Property Deeds Always Assume Doctrinal Standards

The earliest American property deeds (1770–1784) followed in continuity with Wesley's "Model Deed" for meetinghouses of 1763. The sustained continuity and cohesion of this tradition can be demonstrated textually by six crucial documents:

- The *earliest recorded legal deeds* for use of Methodist church properties in America repeat verbatim the pivotal phrase in Wesley's "Model Deed": Preach "no other doctrine than is contained in the said John Wesley's Notes Upon the New Testament and his four volumes of Sermons," as is found in the deed of trust of the John Street Methodist Church in New York City, Nov. 2, 1770.
- Identical language is found in the deed for *St. George's meeting house* in Philadelphia (June 14, 1770, Bishop Thomas Neely, *Doctrinal Standards of Methodism*, New York: Revell, 1918, 139, hereafter DSM).
- *The Asbury Memorandum of 1773.* Francis Asbury wrote this memorandum on the first American Annual Conference (1773): "The following propositions were agreed to: (1) The old Methodist doctrine and

discipline shall be enforced and maintained amongst all our societies in America. (2) Any preacher who acts otherwise can not be retained amongst us as a fellow-laborer in the vineyard" (*Journal and Letters* 1:85). This showed that the doctrinal standards had not changed from Britain to America.

- *The Conference Minutes of 1780* legally formalized and confirmed the principle that "all the *deeds* shall be drawn in substance after that in the printed [then British] Minutes" (*Minutes of the Annual Conferences of the Methodist Episcopal Church for the Years 1773–1828*, New York: T. Mason and G. Lane, 1849, hereafter MAC, 1780, 12, italics added).

- Preachers were required in *the Subscription of 1781* to subscribe to this Minute: "after mature consideration, close observation and earnest prayer, to preach the old Methodist doctrine, and strictly enforce the discipline as contained in the Notes, Sermons, and Minutes published by Mr. Wesley" (MAC, 1781, 13, probably by signature).

- In *Wesley's letter of 1783 to the Conference*, he wrote "To the Preachers in America": "Let all of you be determined to abide by the Methodist doctrine and discipline, published in the four volumes of Sermons, and the Notes Upon the New Testament, together with the Large Minutes of the Conference" (*Letters of John Wesley*, 8 vols., London: Epworth, 1931, 7:191).

None of these six documents had their context in Britain. All were American, all before 1784. All of them specified the Sermons and Notes, and three of them specifically showed the relation of the Sermons and Notes to the making of Methodist deeds in America.

From these six documents and others John Tigert, in *A Constitutional History of American Episcopal Methodism*, 2nd ed. (Nashville: Smith and Lamar, 1904, hereafter CH, 113), the definitive study of Methodist doctrinal standards, concluded: "The American chapels and meetinghouses have been generally settled according to the form of the deed used in England since 1750" (Tigert, CH, 113). Bishop Ole Borgen agrees that "the earliest deeds of record in America followed Wesley's form of 1763," the model deed ("Standards of Doctrine in the United Methodist Church: Never Revoked, Altered or Changed?" Drew University lecture, Oct. 8, 1986, 2).

This shows beyond doubt that the standards of the Sermons and Notes were the central features of the earliest American Methodist property deeds. Hence there is no discontinuity or ambiguity whatever in this earliest American tradition, which takes the story up to:

The Founding Conference of 1784

For the Founding Conference, Baltimore, Christmas, 1784, Wesley's abbreviation of the Thirty-nine Anglican Articles was included among the already established doctrinal standards for American Methodists. *The Articles did not supplant, but complemented the Sermons and Notes.* There is no evidence to the contrary, despite active attempts to discover some. The reason the Articles were needed harks back to the fact that by the time of the revolution, the Anglican clergy had largely abandoned the colonies before the Revolutionary War. Wesley recognized the urgent need to free the Methodist preachers in America not only to preach the Word, but also to baptize and administer the Lord's Supper. Wesley found the Thirty-nine Anglican Articles inadequate in several passages, so he edited them down into Twenty-four Articles, to which another was added by the founding conference (as Article XXIII) on the sovereignty and independence of the United States of America, making Twenty-five Articles for the American Methodists. The Articles obviously were not trying to define doctrine that was original to American Methodists, but rather the opposite: to show the substantial continuity of Methodist teaching with the doctrine of the Church of England, despite the problematic phrases which were edited out. The Discipline of 1798 made it clear that these American Methodist Articles of Religion are the doctrines "maintained more or less, in part or whole, by every reformed church in the world" (Disc., 1798, Notes, Preface).

The "binding minute" of 1784 (Conference Minutes, MAC, 1784, Question 2) showed that there had been no change of doctrine in the transition to America, and that Methodists in America were still firmly bound to the connection with Mr. Wesley and his teaching. To be "in connection" precisely means to be in connection with Mr. Wesley and his teaching. Consistent with this motivation, Methodist preachers continued to "be active in dispensing Mr. Wesley's books" (John Tigert, CH, 27), a mandate repeated in all the Disciplines from 1784 to 1808. Wesley's sermons were thereafter regularly republished by the General Conference to make sure that these standards were not revised or issued without authorization (MAC, 1773, 5). Over sixty editions of *Wesley's Sermons on Several Occasions* were published in the years between 1784–1860! This is telling evidence that they were not, as some have imagined, neglected or set aside during this period between 1784 and 1808.

The Principle of Non-Abrogation

Throughout these developments the legal rule applied that "laws not repealed are laws in effect." This is the "principle of non-abrogation," agreed upon by virtually all key Methodist constitutional authorities (Curtiss, Wheatley, Tigert, Buckley, Harrison, Neely, Lewis, and Outler). There is no record of any abrogation of the basic form of the trust clause in Methodist deeds in America. If such an abrogation should have occurred, it surely would leave behind it a vast paper trail of controversy, and no such paper trail exists. Hence arguments from silence (that some documents do not specifically name the standard texts) are unconvincing.

Constructive Theological Reflection Affirmed by the Standards under the Limitation of the Standards

These standards have never pretended to be an end to all theological or exegetical debate. The 2004 Discipline strongly affirms that the present "theological task includes the *testing, renewal, elaboration and application of our doctrinal perspective.*" This encourages "serious reflection across the theological spectrum" (Disc., 2004, para. 104, Section Four, 75, italics added), but never apart from or contrary to the texts of the doctrinal standards themselves. While critical and constructive theological work is encouraged, however, the textually specified documents embodying the doctrinal standards have not changed, and constitutionally will remain in place.

The current Discipline affirms that "The United Methodist Church stands continually in need of doctrinal reinvigoration for the sake of authentic renewal, fruitful evangelism, and ecumenical dialogue" (Disc., 2004, para. 102, 59). Yet in the same paragraph it adds: "The process of creating new 'standards or rules of doctrine' thus continues to be restricted, requiring either that they be declared 'not contrary to' the present standards or that they go through the difficult process of constitutional amendment." (Disc., 2004, para. 102, 58–59, italics added). The trust clause protects these standards.

How Deeds Function in Relation to Doctrinal Standards

The purposes of the trust clause from its earliest inception have been quite clear, as stated by John Lawson: "(i) to secure that Methodist Trusts should everywhere be drawn up on a uniform and approved plan, and that the trustees be bound to administer them on behalf of the whole Methodist Church," yet conforming to varied local laws (Selections from John Wesley's Notes on the New Testament, ed. John Lawson, London: Epworth, 1955, Introduction, hereafter SWN). And "(ii) to secure legal power to exclude from Methodist pulpits any persons holding opinions alien to the genius of Methodism; (iii) to secure that if in any local Church a discontented section wishes to sever itself from the Methodist Church as a whole, and from Conference, it shall not have the power to take possession of the trust property" (SWN, ibid.). For two centuries the trust clause has exercised this steady service to connectional Methodism, as a rugged legal defense for the Wesleyan connectional system based on doctrinal standards, and a stumbling block to schism.

The Trust Clause Grants the Right to Property Use Only to Those Who Protect Doctrinal Standards

It is erroneously assumed by some that denominational officials, *whether faithful or unfaithful to the doctrinal standards,* have a right to direct the use of Methodist church property. The evidence proves the opposite. *It is only on the basis of faithfulness to the standards that one has a right to the use of the property.* One who abandons faithfulness to the standards has no right to the property. That is precisely what the deed says, and why it was written. Why else would these standards take the form of a deed, if not for legal purposes?

The crux of this argument: *the trust clause was not devised to protect the conferences as such, but the doctrinal standards. The trust clause guarantees the right to use property only to those who are guardians of its established doctrinal standards.*

The choice to inveigh against the doctrinal standards may under fair examination disqualify the abuser from the legitimate right to use the property with impunity. Those who are determined to preach against the trinity and incarnation and the authority of Scripture have dubious legitimate right to the property because these teachings are prominent in these standards. It is yet to be decided the extent to which these standards will be applied to a wide range of moral issues such as the rite of marriage, man and woman in the order of creation, idolatry, witchcraft, paganism, sexual abuse, and the value of life. There is no doubt that all these subjects are touched upon even if tangentially in various places in the Sermons, Notes, Articles, and Confession.

How the Trust Clause Affects Contemporary Church Property Usage

The trust clause entrusts the property to those who voluntarily follow Methodist doctrine and discipline. Lawson writes: "To have these considerable *legal powers in reserve* is a valuable and necessary factor in maintaining the life of our Church as an ordered connexion" (SWN, ibid., italics added). Those who preach Methodist doctrine have a right to use Methodist property.

Those who choose to dissent from or inveigh against Methodist doctrine have no such obvious legal right, prima facie, for they have chosen to work apart from the connection with Mr. Wesley and his teaching, and contrary to Methodist doctrine and discipline.

From the viewpoint of the civil courts, the issue cannot be directly about church doctrine but only about civil law. The courts will not enter the arena of doctrinal dispute, as they have repeatedly shown. Rather the issue can only be about fiduciary responsibility under civil law, about covenants made and covenants kept, about rights of access, which are questions of civil law. This is why the trust deeds are so important. The trust clause in the property deed transmission is a legal guarantee in a court of law. That is what deeds are for—legal protection.

This brings us, however, to the present irony: those who are *faithful* to the connection and its doctrines are now having to contend *against* those who imagine that they have the right to *disobey* these very teachings and do so in the name of connectionalism! This is why so many local congregations are now actively studying the history of property deeds. Many have expressed appreciation to learn that the trust clause embedded in every property deed in Methodism is not merely a sentimental piece of dated paper, but even today a binding legal instrument.

The Deed of Settlement (1796) Made Doctrinal Standards a Judicial Matter of Civil Law

The next steps in showing the continuity of the Articles, Sermons, and Notes for deed making are the legal bulwarks of protection for the doctrinal standards in America. They are found in the Deed of Settlement (1796), the Restrictive Rules (1808), and the Exception of 1832.

First, how did the *Deed of Settlement (1796)* make the Doctrinal Standards a judicable matter of civil law? *The Deed of Settlement* provided the standard post-Revolutionary model of the title deed for local churches in America (*Journal of the General Conference*, 1796–1836, see 1796 minutes, New York: Carleton and Phillips, 1855, hereafter JGC 1796, 9). This deed was a legal instrument that set aside properties for preaching in accord with and nothing contrary to Methodist doctrinal standards, standards firmly established prior to this time, and repeatedly reconfirmed.

By the Deed of Settlement *and all its successor deeds the local trustees were granted the right to mortgage, buy, and sell, but not to change doctrine.* No preacher could join the connection without agreeing to "abide by the Methodist doctrine and discipline published in the four volumes of Sermons and the Notes" (*Minutes of the Methodist Conference Annually Held in America from 1771 to 1794*, Philadelphia: Henry Tuckness, 1795, 1783; cf. Jesse Lee, *History of the*

Methodists, Baltimore: McGill and Clime, 1810). The Deed of Settlement provided a legal means by which American church properties in various states could conform to the various laws of the states, while reconfirming doctrinal unity with the previous connectional history of Methodism.

The Union of the Connection Was Defined by the Doctrinal Standards in the Deeds

There was a strong sense of *union* between British and American Methodist connections, despite the troubles of the Revolution. The very concept of "union" in the Methodist connection cannot be separated from doctrinal considerations. *The union was in order to preserve the doctrinal teaching, not vice versa.* The trust clause is provided *legally* to protect these local church properties from threatened abuses or offenses against established doctrinal standards.

When the various British Methodist traditions organically united in 1932 (Methodist New Connection, 1846; Bible Christians, 1863; United Methodist Free Churches, 1842–1864; and the Primitive Methodists, 1864), all of these church bodies were merged on the explicit doctrinal premise of "*the essential similarity of the trust deeds*" (*Notes on Wesley's Forty-four Sermons*, ed. John Lawson, London: Epworth, 1946, italics added). As a point of law, it was the doctrinally grounded trust deeds that legally held together the union, not the sentiment of union that legitimated the trust deed.

These three standards in American Methodism before The Plan of Union—Sermons, Notes, and Articles—(remembering that the Confession was added after the 1968 Union) thus became "the non-compressible core of 'our present existing and established standards of doctrine' and it is still in legal force to this day" (Albert Outler, "The Methodist Standards of Doctrine", Perkins School of Theology, 1958, iv, 6, mimeographed copy of syllabus addendum). Virtually all major Methodist constitutional historians (N. Bangs, N. Burwash, H. McTyeire, G. L. Curtiss, T. Neely, H. Wheeler, J. Tigert, and N. Harmon) agree on this point.

How Was the General Conference Strictly Prohibited from Changing the Doctrinal Standards by the First Restrictive Rule of 1808?

The central constitutional restriction on changing these standards was and remains The Restrictive Rules. The General Conference of 1808 devised and adopted the constitution of the Methodist Episcopal Church and its successor organizations. In the constitution it included what has come to be called "the First Restrictive Rule." Restrictive means that the Annual and General Conferences were placed under a restriction. The Rule put an absolute constraint on any future General Conference against establishing doctrinal standards contrary to those previously and presently established.

The *First Restrictive Rule* remains decisive for any judicial assessment of usage of local Methodist church property. It states: "*The General Conference shall not revoke, alter or change our Articles of Religion, nor establish any new standards or rules of doctrine contrary to our present existing and established standards of doctrine*" (JGC, 1808, 89 and all subsequent editions of the Discipline). Under this Rule, even if the General Conference unanimously wanted to change doctrinal standards, it could not do so constitutionally. That would require a constitutional amendment with a much more rigorous process of consent. The stringency of the Restrictive Rule intends to protect United Methodists from doctrinal tampering, and especially to protect Methodist properties from being wrongly used. It protects the title deeds from abrogation. Thereafter if the General Conference sought to modify the doctrinal standards, it would face the obstacle not only of the title deeds but the Restrictive Rule, which limits the power of the General Conference to act.

Distinguishing the Two Complementary Clauses of the First Restrictive Rule

In this restriction on legislation, there is *a twofold prohibition*, first *against any revocation, alteration or change in the Articles of Religion*, and second, *against any new standard or rule contrary to "present existing and established standards,"* that is, in reference to the same standards stated in the model deed (1763) and the deed of settlement (1796, see also JCD 243, 1966).

These two clauses confirm both ecumenical affirmations and Methodist distinctives, the two complementary dimensions of the doctrinal standards: The first clause addresses the teaching of the Articles, which were not intended to set forth distinctively Methodist teaching, but to indicate *what our doctrine shares with all Reformed Protestantism, and with all ecumenical Christianity generally*. The second clause deals with *the distinctives of Methodist teaching that shine forth in the Sermons and Notes (on themes like assurance, holiness of heart and life, and perfect love not treated in the Articles)*. This same distinction is sustained in recent Judicial Council Decisions (see JCD 486, 1979; Decisions 358 and 468 refer to the first part as "Landmark Documents," and the second part as "the present existing standards of doctrine"; these two questions "are different in nature and must be considered and answered separately").

Note that the defining phrase "shall not be revoked, altered, or changed," applies to the text of the Articles (and after 1968 the Confession), but not to the Sermons and Notes. For *there has never been any thought or active initiative for changing the text of Wesley's Sermons and Notes*, nor is one hardly imaginable. "The original distinction between the intended functions of the Articles on the one hand, and of the Sermons and Notes on the other, may be inferred from the double reference to them in the First Restrictive Rule (adopted in 1808 and unchanged ever since)" (Disc., 1984, 45). But there might at some point be proposed an attempt to change or amend the Articles or Confession.

The firm textual definition of this second part was consistently held to be the Sermons and Notes, but a definitive settlement of this question awaited the Plan of Union of 1968 and the Discipline of 1988 for its definitive confirmation and unambiguous textual definition. The General Conference of 1988 specified that the texts of "our present established standards of doctrine" include Wesley's Sermons and Notes. These are still listed as doctrinal standards in every Discipline (Disc., 2004, para.103, 71).[1]

How Is Continuous Binding Authority Established?

What protects the Articles, Sermons, and Notes under the First Restrictive Rule?

their inclusion in the constitution
their long history of consensual reception,
especially their inclusion in the trust clause for property deeds, and finally
the irrevocable Plan of Union as an instrument of civil law

If the binding authority of these "present existing and established standards" had been questioned in any decade, it surely would have been actively debated and there would have been some written residue of the debate, but there is no such residue. A motion explicitly stricken from the record (as in the case of the Ward motion in the 1808 minutes) cannot be used as an argument, since it is merely an argument from silence. Exactly what was meant by "our present and existing standards of doctrine" in 1808 was clear to all Methodist preachers and ordinands because it was simply the continuation of the steady textual tradition written into every trust clause. "The Articles did not annul anything in the old standards and there was no act of abrogation" (Bishop Thomas Neely, DSM 207). These standard documents have repeatedly been confirmed without any hint of a record of dissent from the earliest times. The argument against their consistent historical confirmation remains a weak one: an argument from silence.

When the Judicial Council was asked to allow "deletion by the General Conference of provisions of the Constitution no longer relevant because of passage of time," the Council reaffirmed: "No portion of the Constitution . . . may be amended or deleted by the General Conference without the required vote in the Annual Conference" (Judicial Council Decisions, hereafter JCD, 483, 1980). This is so difficult to obtain that it has never been challenged.

I have sometimes been asked what would ever cause me to leave the church that baptized and ordained me—surely there must be some limit. I always answer simply: "abrogation of the First Restrictive Rule." This is shorthand for "abrogation of doctrinal standards." Nathan Bangs, the preeminent nineteenth-century Methodist historian, showed why the First Restrictive Rule was written: "knowing the rage of man for novelty, and witnessing the destructive changes which have frequently laid waste the church by removing ancient land marks, and so modifying doctrines and usages as to suit the temper of the times, or to gratify either a corrupt taste or a perverse disposition, many had felt uneasy apprehensions for the safety and unity of the church and the stability of its doctrine" (*History of the M. E. Church*, 4 vols., New York: Carlton and Porter, 1859, 223–24). Hence the First Restrictive Rule has become a constitutional bulwark.

How the Exception of 1832 Made Any Amendments to the Trust Clause in Property Deeds Even More Formidable

After 1808 the First Restrictive Rule has remained continuously in effect, and indeed increased its force. This is clear from a decisive action in 1832. A resolute proviso was added that made the Restrictive Rule even more difficult to circumvent. This was a brilliant procedural defense to protect all Methodist pulpits and their property deeds legally from abuse or maladministration. It is somewhat analogous to the Bill of Rights.

What is *the Exception of 1832*? There the General Conference set forth a daunting method for amending the Restrictive Rule, so demanding as to be generally perceived to be virtually impossible. According to the Exception of 1832, the Restrictive Rule could be changed only by these supermajorities: "*the concurrent recommendation of three fourths of all the members of the several annual conferences who shall be present and vote on such a recommendation, then a majority of two thirds of the conference succeeding*" (JGC 1832, 378). Why such a double layer of safeguards? To protect the doctrinal standards.

This is the only method for changing the Restrictive Rule, and hence the trust clause, and hence the terms for legal property use. It is formidable and exacting. The provision for amending the Rule is a double process, as stated by Bishop Thomas Neely: "First it would be necessary to amend the provision for amendment by striking out the words 'excepting the first article.' This could be done by the . . . action of two thirds in the General Conference and the concurrence of three fourths in the Annual Conferences" (*A History of the Origin and Development of the Governing Conference in Methodism*, Cincinnati: Hunt and Eaton, 1892, 405).

This Exception still remains immovably fixed in the constitution that governs every deed of local church property. There has never been any serious attempt in Methodist history to abrogate or amend the First Restrictive Rule and very likely there will not be. The Restrictive Rules are the only portions of the constitution subject to such strict defense against amendment.

Hence no General Conference can amend the first and second Restrictive Rules on its own authority, without an insuperable "three-fourths majority of all the members of the annual conferences" (Disc., 2004, para. 57, 39). Any proposed amendment can occur only by this extremely demanding procedure that virtually insures its continuing effect.

This presents a formidable barrier, making the Rule virtually unamendable. Few today think the First Restrictive Rule can be changed. *It is the central fortress of the American Methodist constitutional system. But what is pertinent to this argument is that its doctrinal standards are guaranteed in every trust clause of every local church in all subsequent Disciplines.*

19

Pending Issues

The Interweaving of Property Administration with Doctrinal Accountability

It has been demonstrated that there is an intimate interweaving between the Restrictive Rules and the trust clause. The Restrictive Rules define and protect the inviolability of the texts of the doctrinal standards. The trust clause defines and protects the use of church property based on the doctrinal standards. These intermesh intrinsically. *These doctrinal standards are pertinent to the assessment of the work of any ordained minister or church leader, and to the proper use of church property, under the direct authority of the local church trust clause, as set forth in the Discipline.* Next it is necessary to specify:

Who Is Accountable?

The Discipline requires the *bishops* to take direct responsibility for "carrying into effect the rules, regulations, and responsibilities prescribed and enjoined by the General Conference and in accord with the provisions set forth in this Plan of Union" (Disc., 2000, para. 45, 35), which clearly specify these four doctrinal standards. If the Council of Bishops fails to carry into effect these responsibilities, the offending members of the Council could be liable to the charge of failure to provide episcopal supervision, for "The

Council of Bishops is charged with the oversight of the spiritual and temporal affairs of the whole church" (Disc., 2004, para. 427.3, 288).

These doctrinal texts are constitutional standards not amendable by General Conference, and that do not depend upon approval from any Annual Conference or denominational executive or church leader or pastor because *all levels of United Methodist leadership* are strictly accountable to them.

No candidate for ordained *ministry* can ignore them, or be approved without answering the questions on willingness to preach United Methodist doctrine and implement United Methodist Discipline (Disc., 2004, para. 330.4d.8–10.225, 214). If ordained ministers do not know or cannot in good conscience consent to the doctrinal standards they once voluntarily agreed to teach, then they may be subject to chargeable offenses, as well as vocational disingenuousness.

The Fourth Restrictive Rule (Disc., 2004, para. 20, 27), which provides the *right to fair trial* for both clergy and laity, does so under the assumption of accountability to the doctrinal standards protected by the First and Second Restrictive Rules. No judiciary or local church or person has the right to deny due process to those seeking to obey church law.

The General Conference Decision of 1988 on Doctrinal Standards

The clarity and firmness of the Plan of Union was one of the major reasons why the Committee on Our Theological Task in 1988 resisted an interpretation of the doctrinal standards that would privilege the Articles as more decisive. The argument for this approach (based upon a presumed motion that was subsequently *stricken* from the minutes of the 1808 General Conference) elicited a two-year debate that ended in 1988. That debate ended with a firm action of the General Conference. The idea of deleting the Sermons and Notes from constitutional protection was defeated. However stressful the debate was, it had one salutary effect: it made it necessary for the General Conference to make entirely unambiguous the protected status of the Sermons and Notes as "our doctrinal standards."

Hence all Disciplines after 1988 confirm the textual definition of "Our Doctrinal Standards." The headings of the current Discipline clearly list the texts of Our Doctrinal Standards and General Rules (Disc., 2004, para.103, 59–74). They are the outcome of the 1988 decision. In order to avoid any confusion, they are listed by document title as follows: The Articles of Religion of the Methodist Church, The Confession of Faith of the Evangelical United Brethren, The Standard Sermons of Wesley, The Explanatory Notes Upon the New Testament, and The General Rules of the Methodist Church. Together they define the standards.

All are important. The General Rules assert "the connection between doctrine and ethics" (Disc., 2004, para. 101, 49). They are sometimes treated under doctrinal standards, but more specifically as a bridge between doctrine and ethics. They too are protected by a Restrictive Rule, Article V (Disc., 2004, para. 21, 27). They "convey the expectation of discipline within the experience of individuals and the life of the Church. Such discipline assumes accountability to the community of faith by those who claim that community's support" (ibid.). Thus it is a constitutional requirement that the doctrinal standards are expected to be understood by and remain obligatory for any church official.

Free Inquiry within Doctrinal Guidelines

The Discipline rightly protects "free inquiry *within* the boundaries defined by" our doctrinal tradition and standards, assuming that "*Scripture is the primary source and criterion for Christian doctrine*" (Disc., 2004, para. 104, 78, italics added). "Our standards affirm the Bible as the source of all that is 'necessary' and 'sufficient' unto salvation (Articles of Religion) and 'is to be received' through the Holy Spirit as the true rule and guide for faith and practice' (Confession of Faith)" (Disc., 2004, para. 104, 78).

For laypersons there is no formal ascription to these standards, but they are binding upon all "who assume accountability" to the connection, and especially all who have been duly ordained to fulfill the teaching office. Our doctrinal standards do not demand of laity "unqualified assent on pain of excommunication," but the questions for ordination and the possible charges against elders place the ordained clergy under rigorous voluntary requirements. The standards are to be viewed as model sermons, exegetical notes, and explicit condensed confessions, as guidelines "for the sake of authentic renewal" (Disc., 2004, para.102, 59). But this does not give license to "'theological indifferentism'—the notion that there are no essential doctrines" (Disc., 1980, para. 69, 73). Other doctrinal summaries or theological interpretations may be licitly argued, but "*without displacing those we already have*" (Disc., 1980, para. 67, 50, italics added).

The Next Stages for Church Law and Civil Law

These historical facts and constitutional guarantees provide a new opportunity for regrounding the mainline Protestant tradition in its doctrinal heritage: Scripture, ancient ecumenical teaching (and in the case of United Methodists, the Wesleyan standards), tempered by reason and Spirit-filled experience.

The rediscovery and appropriation of the trust clause provides a promising opportunity for those faithful to the United Methodist connection to reconfigure their struggle for theological integrity with greater confidence, since these are legal guarantees. Laity can now examine the Discipline under which their own local church title deed functions, and understand how it interweaves intrinsically with their property deed and the established doctrinal standards.

It has only been due to the neglect of this constitutional history that some have assumed that the church is virtually irreformable or that it is hazardous to be Wesleyan, scriptural, or evangelical.

The Persistent Misstatement of the Trust Clause

The trust clause has sometimes been wrongly interpreted as an *obstacle to the faithful* who seek to protect their own church property from takeover or abuse. Some evangelicals have developed a mistaken habit of assuming that the trust clause was a stumbling block for them. It is the opposite. It protects the faithful from domination by the unfaithful. Laypersons have imagined that if they disagreed with the Conference leadership, they would be faced with the dire alternative of surrendering the local church property itself to an entity that itself is arguably unaccountable to the Discipline. In most cases where property has been surrendered, the local church has not known its constitutional rights under church and civil law. Their legal counsel has often not understood the history of deeds and its documentation.

Now the tables are turning. The reconsideration of these constitutional guarantees reflected in the trust clause places our property dilemmas in an entirely different light: now the trust clause can be rightly understood to be a legal instrument to call the judicatory itself to account under its own constitution, based on a continuing unchanging tradition of both historical and contemporary documents that have juridical and binding import.

The very trust clause that has sometimes been abused so as to intimidate faithful local churches and threaten to wrest their very property from them may now be seen itself as a powerful argument in their defense. But all this assumes that they are well informed, are rigorously faithful to doctrinal and disciplinary standards, and have not sought to withdraw from the church.

The most ill-advised decision that can be made by the local church is too quickly to declare itself independent of the church and its discipline, the very instruments that seek to protect it from abuse. Attorneys for congregations need to be advised of this constitutional history, which is still in effect, and embedded in their own property deeds.

Are Painful and Expensive Court Challenges Ahead for Those Who Defy Church Law?

It is reasonable to ask about the potential cost of court challenges that would seek accountability to established doctrinal standards. These challenges, it is said, would temporarily divert monies away from mission to doctrinal defense. Insofar as this is so, such challenges need to be strictly limited, and focused on constitutional issues. But far more important is that *the abusive causes leading to the need for property challenges must be corrected in order to avoid incurring these costs.*

The diversion of church funds into civil litigation and attorney fees must be kept to an absolute minimum, and never opted for impulsively or impetuously. Any test of church or civil law should be selected with great prudence and wisdom, and never as an expression of outrage. The intent is less to change church law than to call church officials to take their own church law and discipline seriously.

There is available a very simple remedy for all parties, whether conservative or liberal: teach according to the established doctrinal standards. That would instantly clear up most difficulties. It is those who insist on teaching *contrary* to our doctrinal and disciplinary standards who are most responsible for initiating divisive actions and expensive legal contests. But when the very teaching center of the church is at stake, the faithful will most certainly be expected to defend it.

These doctrinal standards have been in effect and textually reconfirmed and specifically incorporated into the legal deeds for church properties for the entire history of Methodism, well over 200 years, and never abrogated. Any who challenge this tradition must do so on the basis of law and fact. The faithful must be willing to defend their own local investment in church property by reasonable argument.

This issue is now being debated. In some conferences of the beleaguered connection there will be open contests on specific points of administrative law, made necessary not by the recalcitrance of the faithful, but by those who wish to circumvent or avoid the historic trust clause pertaining to the use of church property.

Are These Legally Binding Standards Testable in a Court of Law?

But many may doubt that these historic doctrinal standards are legally binding standards in a court of civil law. Are they not merely church law with no standing before the civil courts?

The civil courts have no jurisdiction whatever entering into doctrinal disputes or determining church law as such. They have a consistent record of not entering this privileged territory, commendably.

But they do have jurisdiction and valid interest in certain *spheres of distinctively civil action* (as distinguished from church law, doctrine, or polity). Here is a short list of ten of these arenas where civil court judgments do not infringe on the right to freedom of religion, but rather protect that right:

- abuses of constitutional rights under the U.S. Constitution and Bill of Rights (such as limiting freedom of worship, speech, press, or assembly),
- taking of property without just compensation,
- the due performance of contracts,
- the fair examination of evidences of fraud or malfeasance,
- abuses of due process under civil law,
- actions against public policy or actions disruptive of public order that offend public decency (such as the disruption of communities, the embitterment of long-standing peaceful communities of worship, or the preemptive exercise of questionable authority),
- the legal guarantee that organizations be allowed to operate under their own legal and constitutional constraints,
- the rights of laity who have paid for church property to use church property in accord with church discipline, and especially,
- the fair use of property under the trust clause in legal deeds.

The above points of law are all issues of *civil* law, hence referable to civil courts if need be. These are not rights granted by the church constitution, but by the United States Constitution and state constitutions. There is little doubt that the trust clause in property deeds will have directive, judicial, and legally binding authority enforceable under civil law in these civil justice arenas. It is along the lines of these civil issues that actions are almost certainly going to occur.

Remaining Questions

What does all this mean? When the use of property is disputed in cases of church officials inveighing against church doctrine, any member of the United Methodist Church has the right to ask the judicatory or conference to show cause why they have not offended against or acted unaccountably under the Articles, Confession, Notes, and Sermons. That is not an unreasonable request.

Among specific questions ahead: What is to be done about those who presume to remain in the connection but refuse to obey its rules? What are the rights of those faithful to the connection under the civil law to use their local church property? At what points could current controversies on doctrinal standards (such as the Trinity, creation, incarnation, the unique lordship of Jesus Christ, atonement, resurrection, and the Great Commission, as found in the Articles, Confession, Sermons, and Notes) erupt into fair-use-of-property issues? And on what legitimate grounds do those faithful to the connection stand in the attempt to guarantee the terms of use of church property according to the church's constitution as embedded in the trust clause?

The Understandable Reticence of the Judicial Council to Deal with Doctrinal Questions

The church courts have a long record of being rightly wary of engaging in any adjudication of any theological issues. They know that their native and proper role and competency is basically in matters of contested specific points of church law, constitutional interpretation, and administrative issues. The conferences with their investigatory procedures have been viewed as the proper place to adjudicate most doctrinal issues. That is correct, provided the Conference itself is accountable to its own constitution and hence to the doctrine of the church. But what if it is not?

The church judiciary has wisely declined to become an arbiter of doctrine. But also it has rightly made judgments when necessary on how the doctrinal standards are to be administered under church law and historic precedents. The church judiciary has not hesitated on some occasions to enter the doctrinal arena in cases where constitutional and disciplinary questions intertwine with doctrinal issues (see Judicial Council Decisions 86, 142, 243, 358, 847, and 871).

There are at least four examples of this: (a) The Judicial Council has declared a strict interpretation of the First Restrictive Rule, by concluding that "The phrase 'is the creation of God and,' though generally accepted as true, would be changing or altering the plain and simple language of Articles XIII. and is therefore in violation of the First Restrictive Rule" (JCD 86, 1952). (b) While the Council has preferred to act not on "a matter of theological interpretation rather than of judicial decision," the Council has not hesitated to confirm constitutional protection not only of the Confession and Articles but also "the Wesleyan standards" (as in JCD 243, 1966). (c) Although "The Judicial Council, historically . . . has refused jurisdiction over

Questions which demand of it theological interpretations" (JCD 358, 1972, also 468, 1979), nonetheless the Council ruled that it did have jurisdiction on the authorization of the General Conference to adopt the Report of the Theological Study Commission. (d) In a Decision handed down May 7, 1948 (see Decision 59) the Judicial Council held that it not be "set up as an interpreter of doctrine but as an interpreter of law from the strictly legal standpoint" (JCD 86, 1952). Yet precisely in doing so, it acted to disallow any addition to the doctrinal standards. So church law is by precedent firmly committed to sustaining, and not changing, the doctrinal standards. If doctrinal standards are legally and textually established (as argued here) as the primary criteria for judging the proper use of church property, it seems inevitable that the Judicial Council will be called upon to enter this arena in contested cases. If Conference Committees of Investigation, for example, refuse to investigate blatant violations, and if church leaders take a hands-off posture toward continued abuses and willful disobedience to the church's doctrine and discipline, and if they refuse to call their fellow church leaders to account on outrageous acts of doctrinal defiance, the laity will seek some remedy.

It is unacceptable to say that there simply is no remedy. It is not just that the church's trust in judicial fairness will be impaired—that has already occurred. Rather it is the case that some remedy *will* be found to ongoing injustices. The faithful worshiping community is in the long run *determined* to find a way of correcting abuses, to better manifest the holiness of the body of Christ. It may seem at times that the church and its laity may be left temporarily without remedy, but history proves that this is always only temporarily. The Holy Spirit has plenty of time to mend the church.

If an ordained elder teaches or acts contrary to a point of doctrine specifically defined in the doctrinal standards, such as the Trinity or the sufficiency of the Holy Scriptures for salvation, then he or she can be charged with disseminating doctrine contrary to the church. The conference or judicatory that protects such a person cannot be considered blameless.

If a church leader publicly disavows a central point of classic doctrinal teaching, one that is consensually unquestionable, such as the incarnation or resurrection, this can under established church law be contested. If the church judiciary has no remedy except to pass the buck and refer it to other judicatories or conferences or committees of investigation or denominational entities who are unwilling to act on it on pain of embarrassing their fellow church leaders, then those faithful to the connection eventually will seek a remedy through legislative change. Such stalling has been rife in some cases of defiance of church discipline.

Most would agree, however, that the *legislative* remedies are much more painful and difficult than the more simple and direct route of appealing to the *conscience* of the church leaders and judiciary to do the right thing—their already sworn and consecrated duty. Church leaders and elders and conferences are bound by their own voluntary commitments to uphold doctrinal standards. Failure to do so may be contested. There is good reason for those faithful to the connection to guard and hold their property, as a parallel duty to guarding and holding the faith.

But Should Christians Ever Even Be in Court?

Those faithful to the connection have a moral duty seldom if ever to go to civil court, although they have a case in point with Paul's appeal to Caesar. It is far better to resolve all matters without the civil authorities being requested to resolve internal abuses. But *if* those faithful to the connection cannot solve constitutional issues in accord with their doctrinal standards, and no remedies are provided, especially in the case of ordained church leaders and investigative committees covering up one for another contrary to church law, *then* in self-defense they can and at times will appeal to due process under law to ensure those rights.

When those faithful to the connection and its doctrines have been expelled from their own church property, when the keys to the church locks have been abruptly changed without notice or due process, the laity may find it necessary to ask the courts to guarantee their legal rights to follow the established doctrine of their own local church under the provisions of its trust clause.

Such abuses and challenges should never have happened, and should never have been pressed so far by schismatic denominational ideologues in defiance of established church law. But the fact is that those most faithful to the connection have at times been threatened to be expelled from their local church property by judicatories and officials willing to act unconstitutionally. When this happens they are able justly to appeal to their rights under civil law, just as Paul appealed to Caesar. Paul's appeal was a civil action under a civil magistrate (Acts 25:11).

The motive for making this complicated history more accessible is this: it may help advise laypersons or pastors or counselors to pastors, or any who wish to understand their legal rights to use their local United Methodist church property according to established church doctrine and polity. Those who are faithful to the connection have good reason to face those courts with confidence.

The Keys to Church Property

The local board of trustees along with the pastor as administrative officer are in charge of the keys to church property. If an appeal is deemed necessary to ask for civil protection of the church property under the conditions of the title deeds tradition, then the pastor and trustees should be thoroughly prepared with historical arguments to make their case. Under conditions of controversy the presumption must be that the keys belong in the hands of the local board until denied by a court of church law or civil law. In the intervening period the board or pastor may see fit to order a change of keys. There is no presumption in United Methodist polity that the conference has a right to seize property arbitrarily without due process, without investigation, and without fair inquiry.

These are not theoretical questions. In a number of contested cases in California, Iowa, Washington, Alaska, and other places, some of these appeals have been required. Thankfully only a few have come before civil courts. Most would agree that it is better to settle such disputes on biblical grounds (Matt. 18:15–17) under due processes ordered by church law and without any civil appeal. But when church law is in question, there may be no recourse but the civil courts.

The Biblical Constraints on Believers in Court

Faithful Christians are right to remember the biblical mandate not to bring into court other believers who seek to be ordered according to apostolic teaching (1 Cor. 5:9–6:8). The question remains, however, as to whether an apostatizing church official can rightly be viewed as a "believer." One who rejects the Triune God and the resurrection of Jesus cannot, according to our established doctrinal standards, rightly be called a practicing believer. There would have been no reason for Wesley to write a model deed with doctrinal standards as its centerpiece if there were absolutely no possible reasons for civil protection.

The pertinent texts are 1 Corinthians 5 and 6, where Paul has instructed the Corinthian church "not to associate with sexually immoral persons" (5:9). Paul's words are sharp: "Do not even eat with such a one. For what have I to do with judging those outside? Is it not those who are inside that you are to judge? God will judge those outside. Drive out the wicked person from among you" (5:12–13 NRSV). *Those inside* refers to those who proclaim Christ crucified, who receive the true wisdom of God, who do not cause divisions in the church, who follow the apostolic teaching, and who do not defile the church by sexual immorality. *Those outside* refers to those who have chosen not to be accountable to apostolic teaching. Let God be their judge. Within this context, within the community of the faithful, Paul instructed the Corinthians not to take a grievance "to court before the unrighteous, instead of taking it before the saints" (6:1). "If you have *ordinary cases*, then, do you appoint as judges those who have no standing in the church?" (6:4, italics added).

In reference to *believing Christians* who have no taint of apostasy or defiance of discipline, Paul makes it clear that: "In fact, to have lawsuits at all with one another [as believing Christians] is already a defeat for you" (6:7). "Do you not know that wrongdoers will not inherit the kingdom of God?" (6:9a). "Fornicators, idolaters, adulterers, male prostitutes, sodomites, thieves, the greedy, drunkards, revilers, robbers—none of these will inherit the kingdom of God" (6:9–10). The point: if one gets so far as to go "to court against a believer" (one who is seeking to be accountable to the Lord) the litigious one has already been thereby defeated. It is better to be wronged.

The argument of 1 Corinthians 5 and 6 pertains primarily to believers (not nonbelievers) contesting "ordinary" (not extraordinary) cases (6:4). But where unbelievers pretend to be believers, in *extraordinary cases*, they must be gently admonished first, according to Jesus, and by due process counseled toward repentance, remembering that God will bring to judgment both the righteous and the wicked (Matt. 18:15–17).

In matters of dispute over fraud or truth-telling or contractual accountability or due process under civil law, then disputants may rightly "come into court and the judges decide between them" (Deut. 25:1). But it is always wiser to "Come to terms quickly with your accuser *while you are going with him to court*" (Matt. 5:25 ESV, italics added). We are not to go to court at all unless all church due processes and canon law measures have been actively pursued, exhausted, and no remedies found, and the faithful laity are still without any resolution consistent with Christian teaching.

Maintaining Civil Discourse

Amid any controverted question it is crucial to the unity of the body of Christ to maintain civil discourse, willingness to repent, gentle admonition, and charity toward all.

Contested questions should be rationally argued on the basis of accurate historic textual evidence and constitutionally licit grounds. They should be argued charitably, and without undue passion, yet with determination to continue in a guardianship role for classic Christian teaching.

The rules of fair process call for the presumption of innocence, a right to be heard, due notice, right of counsel, full disclosure, and access to records. Due process seeks just resolution of differences in the hope that God's work of justice may be realized in the body of Christ (Disc., 2000, para. 2701).

On Cover-ups: When Church Leaders Protect Each Other from Investigation

The crisis of pedophilia in the Catholic Church surely should have taught us something about the public accountability of church leaders. Here the church, having failed to solve a problem internally, had to face civil action that was much more painful than if it had been solved internally.

An eruption may be ahead that may require local congregations to call to accountability church leaders who have repeatedly left unadmonished pastors who openly inveigh against established doctrine and discipline, or who cover up for others' misdeeds. If someone repeatedly and blatantly offends against good church order, and the offense is then hidden from view by a church official responsible for due administration of discipline, then that church leader may be liable to being charged with "failure to perform the work of ministry." Within the Methodist system, the leader may be charged with "disobedience to the Order and Discipline of the United Methodist Church," or "dissemination of doctrines contrary to the established standards of doctrine of the United Methodist Church" (Disc., 2004, para. 2702, 119–20). The church leader has the solemn duty to follow and enforce church law. Among explicit duties, the bishop is consecrated first of all to "guard the faith, order, liturgy, doctrine, and discipline of the Church against all that is contrary to God's Word" (Order for the Consecration of Bishops).

But what if the process of appeal is itself blocked by those very judicatory officers who are ordained and voluntarily pledged to protect these doctrines and disciplines? What if a church leader charged with protecting church law stands in the way of a local church committed to classic doctrinal and disciplinary standards? When all church due processes are exhausted, it may require a remedy under civil law, but that appeal must be made with due awareness of church constitutional history and deeds of conveyance.

If an unfaithful judicatory or official should attempt to shut down a faithful local church or change its locks or intrude upon its right to teach the Scriptures or classic Christian doctrine, then be assured that the trust clause protects the local church against such intrusions. If due processes within church law cannot find remedies, they must be sought under broader rights protected by civil law.

The Wide Range of Moral Questions Explicitly Addressed in the Discipline

There is good reason to search for a distinction between moral questions (such as sexuality issues) as distinguished from obvious points of doctrine such as Trinity, incarnation, atonement, the lordship of Christ, and the resurrection. In these cases where no central doctrine is repudiated, but moral accountability is involved or discipline is neglected or abused, appeal may be made first to Scripture and then to the clear moral requirements of the Book of Discipline under the guidance of The General Rules.

In relation to the moral responsibilities of the clergy, these texts sufficiently cover such questions as the stated duties of pastors (Disc., 2004, para. 324–327), immorality in the pastoral office (2702a), the concealment or obscuration or cover-up of incompetence or immorality in the pastoral office (2701–2714), fraud (806), dissemination of doctrines contrary to the established standards of doctrine (2702f), failure to perform the work of the ministry (2702d), performing prohibited ceremonies for same sex unions (341), ordination candidacy for homosexual persons (304.3, 306.4f, footnote 2), self-avowed practicing homosexuals (304.3, and note 1), and performance evaluations of pastors (331).

In relation to the moral responsibilities of all who have official responsibilities with the church, these texts clearly cover such questions as abuses in bequests and/or in accountability to donor intent (1504.17), abuse of open financial record-keeping and public disclosure requirements (806), restrictions on closed meetings of official agencies (721), racial discrimination (604.1), pedophilia and child sexual abuse (2702 h, i; 1118.1; Book of Resolutions 2000, p. 180), prohibition of funds to promote the acceptance of homosexuality (806.9), fidelity in marriage and celibacy in singleness (311.4.f and note 2), and many other issues. The Book of Discipline has already provided in most cases adequate remedies.

We are not here attempting to set forth any new arguments on moral questions, least of all on polity or sexuality issues. The Book of Discipline has already repeatedly and adequately defined these. They are long established as church law. The contest is no longer about what church law is. That is already defined by the Discipline, which some officials, purporting connectionalism, now seek to ignore or contravene or disguise.

When Clergy Protect Clergy

The dilemma of discipline sometimes runs aground, however, in cases where church officials protect other church officials from fair-minded investigation.

The Order of Consecration of Bishops and the Discipline's paragraphs on the duties of the bishop clearly require the presiding bishop to maintain the doctrinal standards (Disc., 2004, para. 404, 1). If clergy protect clergy from investigation and trial, leaving the laity with no remedy against wayward clergy who are not being disciplined by their colleagues, then the faithful in the connection must go back to the most basic understanding of what is permissible according to their own local church trust clause. The laity may find it necessary to take the lead here, where pastors are working under more rigorous and explicit disciplinary constraints, hazards, and obligations than laity. If church leaders ignore, delay, or circumvent efforts at due process, or if they collude to protect each other from investigation or trial, then the issue may become one of failure to perform the work of ministry, or disobedience to the Discipline, or refusal to protect the laity from abuses or practices specifically declared unconstitutional. The faithful laity will in due time find a way of seeking a fair remedy over against unfaithful abusers of connectionalism who are disrespectful of doctrinal standards, and who thereby cause schism and divisions.

The Appeal to the Trust Clause of Property Deeds

The Judicial Council does not make church law; rather it interprets it. Administration of church law is defined by the church constitution and by the due legislative entity acting under that constitution, not by the courts.

All remedies must first be sought through ordinary church law, but when those remedies fail, the only remaining remedy may be the appeal to the title deeds under which local church buildings and properties are legally protected and duly constituted. Any remedy should be sought under strict disciplinary procedures and with due process, and only under extreme conditions in civil actions, if needed—never unnecessarily, but only if no other judicable remedies are available within church law. The courts have no jurisdiction except in cases of flagrant repeated abuses of *civil* liberties, or in enforcing the *contracts* legally binding, or when title *deeds* that govern the use of local church property are ignored, or in cases where some of the civil guarantees require resolution (such as the constitutional right to freedom of assembly or speech or religion, or the taking of property without just compensation, due performance of contracts, fraud, malfeasance, or due process).

If faithful congregations are deprived of or threatened to be expelled from their church property, as they have been in some instances, they need not be afraid to ask that the civil rights of those faithful to the connection be protected. It is a *civil* right to receive due process under law concerning fair use of title deeds. The faithful have a civil right to have the constituting rules of order that have prevailed for over two centuries respected by their own clergy, Conferences, and judicatories.

Answering the Three Most Common Objections

There are three common objections to this line of argument, familiar to any who have entered the threshold of this debate. They are:

"But we are not a doctrinal church." The most common objection to taking doctrinal standards seriously is the historically uninformed view that the church has no doctrine, or no textually defined church teaching. If the church lacks doctrine, why does it have the doctrinal standards written into its Constitution? Why does its Discipline guarantee them to be rigorously unchangeable? Why are clergy required to understand and consent to them and preach them in good conscience? Why would there be a provision for chargeable offenses when they are inveighed against?

We do in fact have doctrinal standards that are embedded in our daily use of church property. These doctrinal standards have enjoyed respect from the courts and laity for over two centuries of consent and continuity, with no abrogation. It is a specious assumption that any mainline church is without doctrinal constraints, or can define its own doctrine arbitrarily, apart from its constitution and history.

"But we encourage theology based on experience." In fact the Discipline instead calls the worshiping community to "interpret our *experience in terms of Scripture*" (Disc., 2004, para. 104, italics added). Indeed "We interpret experience *in the light of scriptural norms*" (ibid. 82, italics added). Experiential theology is viewed as standing under the guidance of Mr. Wesley and his writings: "We follow Wesley's practice of examining experience, both individual and corporate, *for confirmations of the realities of God's grace attested in Scripture*" (Disc., 2004, para. 104, italics added).

Finally it is sometimes objected that: "*We are not a confessional church.*" The argument that we are entirely nonconfessional is evasive. We actually do have a constitutionally recognized Confession—the Confession of Faith (Disc., 2004, para. 103). If we are not a confessional church, why do we have a Confession? And why would we protect that Confession with an extraordinary bulwark of constitutional guarantees that cannot be revoked, altered, or changed (para. 17)?

Confessing Christians are not cranks, not historically unsophisticated, and not divisive. They will not be intimidated. And they are going to stay within the church, with all its faults, and uphold church teaching. They understand that they can no longer keep silent, and will not be harassed or chased out of the church that baptized them and taught them to respect the integrity of due process.

Conclusion

Spine

Believing Christians require spine if they are to revive mainline churches that lack discipline. Many orthodox Christians in unorthodox church bodies indeed are demonstrating that they do have spine in these difficult times.

Spine refers to those willing to stand up and be counted even against the odds, and amid tragic choices. Confessors are always countercultural. They are persistent and rugged. Some are unwavering, intrepid, and indefatigable. They view their strength as coming not from themselves but from the source and ground of their faith.

To those who desperately try to buttress the troubled status quo, the faithful often appear rambunctious and assertive. In some circles they will be described as headstrong, obstinate, tenacious, or adamant. If these epithets result from telling the truth, they are to be received as a badge of honor.

The faithful do not go away. They do not leave the church. They keep coming. They are determined to attest the faith even where strong social and institutional pressures stand against them.

The opposite of spine is flabbiness or slackness. Where spine should be there is jelly—soft, gelatinous, semi-liquid. The chief virtues in some precincts of the mainline are flexibility, tolerance, and vacillation. They lack muscle tone. Something is *spineless* if it has no backbone. Confessing Christians were not raised in Sunday school to be spineless.

To survive, vertebrates must have backbone, a center that unites the musculature and neural systems together. The bony spinal column holds the central nervous system intact. The ridge of a mountain has a spine that remains resistant even after softer minerals are worn away. Without a spine neither the body nor the book holds together.

The metaphor that characterizes confessing Christians is *spine*—determination, nerve, and persistence. They have decided to remain in their churches to transform them. They are not intimidated. Confessing Christians within the mainline have courage to stay in and speak out unapologetically for classic Christian teaching.

Contrasted with spine is *spin*. To spin is to twist. The Latin root means to snare or hang. Spine is firm and straight, spin is flexible and warped. The catchwords of spin are elasticity, softness, and evasion. The virtues of elasticity are the central concern of the egalitarian spinners. They are dogmatic in being opposed to any dogma, any centered teaching, and any assertion of any clear truth.

Today many Christian believers are called upon to have spine within a mainline church tangled in spin. The story we have told is about believers with spine.

Appendix

A Response to a Distinguished Critic

In "A Brief Response to Dr. Thomas C. Oden's Recent Paper, 'The Trust Clause Governing the Use of Property in the United Methodist Church,'" Bishop Jack M. Tuell has graciously offered a number of criticisms and suggestions. He is also a lawyer and a respected constitutional historian, having thoughtfully scrutinized the arguments that appear in part 6 on property usage.

Bishop Tuell, my esteemed colleague and friend of twenty years, has argued that in this denomination "the locus of theological interpretation" is the Conference. He goes much further to say that the Conference is the "ultimate arbitrator of doctrinal matters." Does that mean that the Conference can arbitrarily act contrary to the doctrinal standards and constitution? Rather in my view it seems clear that the Conference is bound by the constitution to be the place where doctrinal standards are acknowledged and implemented, but it is not authorized to interpret church law contrary to the Discipline and its Constitution.

He is right to say that "the determination of whether doctrinal standards are being violated must be lodged with some appropriate body in the Church." He argues that this body is exclusively the Conference. I agree that such questions are normally to be referred to the Annual Conference, but the Annual Conference is not authorized to act contrary to church law, constitutions, and Discipline. Then the decision may fall to the Judicial Council. If a series of judicatories act contrary to the legal provision of the property deed, it could conceivably find its way into a civil action.

It is also a part of the task of the General Conference to seek discernment in theological questions, but only within its strict constitutional limits (the doctrinal standards). The General Conference could not, for example, legis-

263

late to change a single word in the Articles of Religion, except through the unlikely route of amending the constitution itself by supermajorities in both the General Conference and all the members of the Annual Conferences.

Although the General Conference has resolved issues between the Articles of Religion and the Confession of Faith by declaring them consistent with each other as historic doctrinal standards, and consistent with the doctrinal standards, the General Conference would not have any legitimate power to change these standards. Thus the power of the Conference is not to determine doctrine contrary to the constitution, but to bring the church to discipline under the constitution.

Bishop Tuell is quite correct to say that specific wording of the trust clause is not precisely the same as in the Wesley's Model Deed, but incorrect to assert that the doctrinal standards after 1796 differ substantively from the Model Deed. I do not contend that the precise wording of the trust clause "as it was in Wesley's 'model deed' is still in effect." In fact I quote variable forms of wording for the same unchanging standards. Different words can point to the same standards.

My worthy colleague holds that the argument is "without foundation" that the language and terms of deeds in the eighteenth century are "still operative." It is not the language as such that is operative, but the standards to which each successive layer of language of constitutional interpretation has affirmed. These standards remain in effect, as is clear from all Disciplines from 1968 to the present.

Bishop Tuell is technically correct to say to his fellow bishops that "the 1796 General Conference put the first form of the trust clause in the Discipline." But it would be more precise to say that the American trust clause was a continuation without any change of doctrinal standards from the earlier deeds both in Britain and America, as has been documented. The Americans did not invent the doctrinal standards. On many instances, as cited, the language of the American General Conferences appeals to the direct pattern of the earlier deeds. If my friend is arguing that there is a substantive difference in the standards protected by the model deed and by the American deeds, I think that is a difficult case to argue. That would require textual proof that he does not have. He appears to assume that the language "preach and expound God's holy word" is different from or supersedes the substantive standards protected by the trust clause. If that were so, what would be the sense of repeatedly citing the Sermons and Notes as doctrinal standards in subsequent official American documents and decisions (all the way down to the Plan of Union)?

My honorable friend presents an argument from silence that lacks persuasive power when he asserts that there was a "deliberate omission" of the particular language of the model deed in 1796, and that this omission was "re-iterated" in 1812, and therefore the implication is that what is omitted is no longer valid. Does the omission of a term constitute an argument for its positive assertion, even if it is asserted twice? He argues that my reasoning "poses a false dichotomy between the 'Conference' and 'the doctrinal standards.'" He has somehow failed to notice that at the center of my argument is the conviction that the Annual Conference is accountable to the General Conference, which is accountable to the constitution, hence the doctrinal standards. Never have I written or even imagined that "the Conference is merely an administrative unit unconcerned and uninvolved with matters of doctrine and discipline." Rather the Conference is intimately involved in both doctrine and discipline when it is functioning well. But when it is opposing church law and discipline, one can say only by a stretch of language that it is legitimated.

My friend argues that the decision of 1796, which he apparently thinks supersedes the Wesleyan standards, does not have any relevance for real estate. He maintains that "when dealing with a matter in the civic arena such as real estate, it was far better not to hook title to real estate to a specified interpretation of theology, but rather to hook it to a recognized church body whose task included theological interpretation." If it has no relevance for real estate, why was it designed from the outset as a doctrinal constraint on the usage of real estate? There is no evidence that the decision of 1796 supersedes the Wesleyan standards. The specific purpose of the model deed, and the deeds of trust in America, pertains to the rules governing the use of property in Methodist properties. Why else would one write doctrinal standards into a property deed? Why else would those standards become central to the constitution through its very first Amendment?

Although he claims that I presume "a dichotomy between the 'Conference' and the 'doctrinal standards,'" it is precisely that dichotomy that I want to see overcome and restored to its constitutional balance. It is true, as he says, that "while an Annual Conference action to discontinue a church may involve theological issues, it often involves other issues of church order and discipline." But the salient issue is whether the Annual Conference has the power to discontinue a church that is indeed scrupulously following the Discipline, especially when the Annual Conference itself may be defying church law.

Bishop Tuell quotes Thomas Coke and Henry Moore as implying that they thought Wesley was opposing orthodoxy, or that it was "at least a very slender part of religion." The only "orthodoxy" Wesley was opposing was inactive, dead faith, not the orthodoxy of the undivided ancient church, which he strongly avowed and which his own doctrinal standards repeatedly affirm. Bishop Tuell concludes that "the attempt to make orthodoxy the heart of the trust clause seems to fail the test of proportionality." There is nothing in my argument that makes some alternative or speculative idea of orthodoxy the heart of the trust clause. Rather it is clear from textual evidence that the heart of the trust clause is the protection of specific doctrinal standards, not an abstract notion of some sort of "orthodoxy" apart from or contrary to the doctrinal standards.

Finally, my honorable critic and friend argues that supermajorities of both the General Conference and members of the Annual Conferences "could change" the doctrinal standards. He knows that this is a purely theoretical fantasy. It can be tested only by attempting to do it. Such an attempt could only be accomplished first by eliminating the Exception of 1832, and then by seeking these supermajorities. I respectfully challenge anyone, including my dear friend, to attempt to do that, and see how far that goes.

Notes

Introduction

1. Michael S. Hamilton and Jennifer KcKinney, "Turning the Mainline Around," *Christianity Today* 47, no. 8, August 2003, 34–40. The turnaround metaphor has been used for two decades in the renewing and confessing movements. I am especially grateful to these authors for the insight their article offered and for the stimulus they provided for the cover art.

Chapter 1: The Emergence of Confessing Christians in the Mainline

1. A fuller statement of the rationale for the views expressed in chapter 1 will be found in my previous studies: *Agenda for Theology* (Harper & Row, 1979), *After Modernity, What?* (Zondervan, 1990), *Systematic Theology*, 3 vols. (HarperSanFrancisco, 1984–90) and *Requiem* (Abingdon, 1995), from which some portions of this chapter have been adapted.

Chapter 4: How Confessing Christians Are Changing Their Churches

1. The Book of Worship, United Methodist Church.

Chapter 5: Be Steadfast

1. Among the organizations and movements whose leaders comprise the Association for Church Renewal (alphabetically) are the American Anglican Council, seeking "to transform the Episcopal Church from within." American Baptist Evangelicals, whose "mission is to serve the renewal of American Baptist churches by building partnerships to serve, connect, nurture, and grow healthy congregations." Biblical Witness Fellowship, "a confessing church movement in the United Church of Christ," publishing *The Witness*. Community of Concern of the United Church of Canada, publishing *Concern*, and with Church Alive of the United Church of Canada, and the National Alliance of Covenanting Congregations, cosponsoring *Fellowship Magazine*. The Confessing Movement Within the United Methodist Church, publishing *We Confess*, and seeking to retrieve the church's "classical doctrinal identity, and to live it out as disciples of Jesus Christ." Disciples Heritage Fellowship, publishing *Disciple Renewal*, and "working for change and reform in the Christian Church (Disciples of Christ)." Episcopalians United. Evangelical Fellowship of Canada, publishing *Faith Today*, and Focus Renewal Ministries. Good News,

A Forum for Scriptural Christianity Within the United Methodist Church. The Institute of Religion and Democracy, publishing *Faith and Freedom*. Mission Renewal Network, publishing *The Mission Herald*, "serving Christ in the Evangelical, Reformed and Congregational Christian Heritage." RENEW Network, publishing the *Renew Newsletter*. And several Presbyterian renewal groups including The Confessing Churches Movement, the Presbyterian Coalition, Presbyterian Renewal, Presbyterians for Faith, Family, and Ministry, Presbyterian Layman, and Presbyterians Pro-Life.

Chapter 6: Redefining Ecumenism

1. For further development of some themes of this chapter see my *The Rebirth of Orthodoxy* (HarperSanFrancisco, 2003).

Chapter 7: The Deepening Tide of Confession

1. 308 E. Main St., Wilmore, KY 40390, 606-858-4661, jim@goodnewsmag.org, www .acrchurches.org.

2. 1110 Vermont Ave. NW, Suite 1189, Washington, DC 20005, 202-696-8430.

3. 4125 W. Newport Ave., Chicago, IL 60641, 877-375-7373, www.touchstonemag.com.

4. 1716 Spruce St., Philadelphia, PA 19103, 215-546-3696.

5. 422 Santa Fe Circle, Chanhassen, MN 55317-9792, phone 612-546-5122, fax 612-546-8818.

6. 422 Sante Fe Circle, Chanhassen, MN 55317.

7. P.O. Box 7146, Penndel, PA 19047, 215-752-9655, TransCong@aol.com.

8. Regeneration.bob@juno.com.

9. kairos_news@yahoogroups.com.

10. 800-465-7186, publishing *Concern*, Box 79013 Garth Postal Outlet, Hamilton, ON L9C 7N6, 905-318-9244, 800-465-8186, www.unityofconcern.org.

11. Lakeshore Rd., W., RR 2, Port Colbourne, ON L3K 5V4, 905-835-2884.

12. Box 237, Barrie, ON L4M 3T2, 800-678-2607, 416-767-0300, felmag@on.aibn.com, www.fellowshipmagazine.org.

13. 489 East Osborn Rd., North Vancouver, BC V7N 1M4, 604-987-9876, blckbrn24@ hotmail.com.

14. MIP Box 3745, Markham, ON L3R 0Y4, 905-479-4742, ft@efc-canada.com.

15. P.O. Box 102, Candia, NH 03034, 800-494-9172, areformer@aol.com.

16. *The Mission Herald*, PO Box 102, Candia, NH 03034, 800-494-9172.

17. P.O. Box 495, De Forest, WI 53532-0495.

18. This description was originally drafted by Dr. Gabriel Fackre, Andover-Newton Theological Seminary, Newton, Massachusetts.

19. ACMC, P.O. Box ACMC, Wheaton, IL 60189-8000.

20. P.O. Box 330, Sassamansville, PA, 19472, 610-754-6446, frmucc@aol.com.

21. P.O. Box 327, Delhi, NY 13753-0327, dkralpb@aol.com.

22. 11633 Wren St. NW, Minneapolis, MN 55433-2955.

23. 11633 Wren St. NW, Minneapolis, MN 55433, 763-754-4860, gcnusa@aol.com, www .gcnusa.com.

24. 10855 Irma Dr., Suite B, Northglenn, CO 80233, 303-252-7902, 877-223-8264, www .abeonline.org.

Chapter 8: Core Movements of Confessing Christianity

1. 1110 Vermont Ave., NW, Suite 1180, Washington, DC 20005, 800-914-2000, info@ameri cananglican.org, www.americananglican.org.

2. P.O. Box 797425, Dallas, TX 75379, 800-553-3645, eunited@worldnet.att.net, www.epis copalian.org/eu.

3. St. John's Church, 3738 Butler Road, Glyndon, MD 21071.

4. Trinity Episcopal School for Ministry, 311 Eleventh St., Ambridge, PA 15003.

5. 405 Frederick Ave., Sewickley, PA 15143, 800-707-NOEL, NOELife@aol.com, www .episcopalian.org/NOEL.

6. *The Presbyterian Layman*, April 2001, 1.

7. Washington, DC 20005, www.ird-renew.org.

8. P.O. Box 2210 Lenoir, NC 28645, 828-758-8716, ptw@abts.net, www.layman.org.

9. 8134 New La Grange Road, Suite 227, P.O. Box 22069, Louisville, KY 40222-0069.

10. P.O. Box 11130, Burke, VA 22009, 703-569-9474, PresProLife@compuserve.com.

11. www.presbycoalition.org

12. For further information, see www.newwineconvo.com.

13. 308 E. Main St., Wilmore, KY 40390, 606-858-4661, jim@goodnewsmag.org, www .goodnewsmag.org.

14. P.O. Box 889, Cornelia, GA 30531, 706-778-4812, renewl@hemc.net.

15. 7995 E. 21st St., Indianapolis, IN 46219, 317-256-9729, www.confessingumc.org, www .confessingumc@iquest.net.

16. 512 Florence St., Dothan, AL 36391, 334-794-8543, tumaslw@sprynet.com, www.life watch.org.

17. Bristol303@aol.com, www.bristolhouseltd.com, 800-451-7323.

18. Info@msum.org, www.themissionsociety.org, 800-478-8963.

19. Ed Robb Evangelistic Association, 2904 Victory Drive, PO Box 1945, Marshall, TX 75671, publishers of *Challenge to Evangelism Today*, www.edrobb.com, 903-938-8305.

20. PO Box 186, Marshallville, GA 31057, JosJournal@Prodigy.com.

21. PO Box 2864, Fayetteville, NC 28302.

22. 551 Lakeshore Drive, P.O. Box 985, Lake Junaluska, NC 28745, www.evangelize.org.

23. 1110 Vermont Ave. NW, Suite 1189, Washington, DC 20005, 202-696-8430, mtooley@ ird-renew.org, davejeanie@muscanet.com.

Chapter 9: Truth-Driven Unity

1. I am deeply indebted to David Mills, former Anglican theologian, now Catholic, editor of *Touchstone*, for providing me with sharp categories I have considered before but never seen presented more intelligently or systematically. In his essay "Necessary Doctrines: Why Dogma is Needed and Why Substitutes Fail," he has stated a new form of the classic argument on how the unity of the church is grounded in the truth of its doctrine. Everything hinges on the seriousness with which it takes its guardianship role in relation to the revealed truth.

Part 4: Core Teachings of Confessing Christians

1. To preserve the literal integrity of the original text of these leading confessions and teaching texts we have not standardized capitalization and have retained the headings and numbering systems in the extracts themselves.

Chapter 10: On the Crisis of Integrity

1. This is a faith statement of church Alive, subsequently redrafted in 2004.

Chapter 14: The Biblical Teaching of Confession

1. Didache, *Ante-Nicene Fathers* (Mahwah, NJ: Paulist, 1946–), 7:378.
2. Letter to Corinth, 57.
3. Ibid., 51.
4. Mandates 3.3.
5. Didache 14:1, *Ante-Nicene Fathers*, 7:379.
6. Cyprian, ANF 5:445.
7. Leo the Great, *Letters*, 28, FC34:103.

Chapter 15: The Confessing Movement

1. Earlier a Lutheran pastor, then later a Roman Catholic priest.
2. Carlisle, Cumbria: Paternoster, 2001.

Chapter 16: How the United Church of Canada Lost Its Confessional Identity

1. Concern, XI.6, Oct. 2000, 3.
2. Thirty-seventh General Council, August 19, 2000.
3. Concern, XI.6, Oct. 2000, 3.
4. See page 174.
5. Pages 195–96.
6. T. C. Oden, "The Classic Christian Exegesis on Romans 1:22–28," in *Staying the Course*, ed. Maxie D. Dunnam and H. Newton Maloney (Nashville: Abingdon, 2003).
7. *Christianity Today*, November 11, 1996, 37, italics added.

Chapter 18: Constitutional Restrictions

1. Referring to the first clause, there are several Judicial Council decisions, JCD 358, 1972; JCD 947, 1998; JCD 871, 1999, that speak of the Articles, Confession, and Rules, not to "be revoked, altered, or changed." But the earlier Judicial Council ruling 358, 1972, had clearly divided the documents covered under the Restrictive Rules into these two parts, first, Articles, Confession, and Rules, and second "any new standards or rules of doctrine contrary to our present existing standards of doctrine," JCD 358, 1972. When this ruling was made in 1972, the Judicial Council elected not to rule on whether the 1968 Report of the Theological Study Commission on Doctrine violates the Restrictive Rules. Subsequently the General Conference of 1988 did act to make this clear in all subsequent Disciplines.

Thomas C. Oden (Ph.D., Yale University) is a widely respected theologian and leading figure in the emerging post-denominational ecumenical scene. Uniquely positioned as one of the executive editors of *Christianity Today*, he is the author or editor of many books, including *The Rebirth of Orthodoxy, One Faith*, and *After Modernity—What?* He is the Henry Anson Buttz Professor of Theology and Ethics Emeritus at Drew University. In addition, Oden has served as board chairman of The Institute on Religion and Democracy and is the general editor of the acclaimed Ancient Christian Commentary on Scripture series.